KEITH RUMJAHN

Complete guide to basketball defense

First edition

ISBN: 978-988-77649-1-5

This book was professionally typeset on Reedsy.
Find out more at reedsy.com

Contents

1

Foreword

Nowadays it can seem like there are so many defensive systems to choose from when coaching basketball. Just up to a high-school level we are already seeing teams run man to man, zone defense, pressure defense, scramble defense and the pack line defense.

Picking a defense to run isn't as easy as simply copying what the best teams are doing. However, there are so many options out there that the choice can seem overwhelming at times. When I was coaching, I wished that somebody handed me a blueprint that let me know exactly what to run with the team I had. Choosing a defensive system should depend on critical decisions about how you wish to defend. Every system has weaknesses and you must choose what you are willing to give up in order to get an advantage. For example:

- Do you want your players to crash the offensive boards?
- What happens when you miss/make a shot?
- Where do you want to pick up the ball handler on a fast

break?

- Do you force middle or force baseline?
- Do you give up threes or penetration?
- Will you force your opponent to go left?

All of these decisions make up core principles that you need to decide on to choose the right defensive system for you and your team. My old high-school coach ran a denial man to man defensive system where we denied the passing lane and forced baseline. When I became a coach, pack line defense became popular and it was the opposite of what I learned from my coach: help defense from one pass away and forcing middle.

I watched a lot of videos on YouTube to try and understand more about these defense strategies, but I found that a lot of these videos only showed drills or focused on how to run the defense in a very narrow set of specific situations. This was great, but nobody explained to me the underlying reasons for why your team should be doing this. As a result, when players came to me with questions I didn't always have the best answers. It was not until much later that I realized that defensive systems are based on principles that you choose as a coach.

Having a set of core defensive principles is all about knowing what your team is giving up, just as much as what your team is gaining. And if your players don't have a true grasp of the principles behind their defense, you can't expect them to make the best decisions in the game.

One example: the shot goes up and my starting point guard runs in from above the free-throw line to crash the glass. He manages to secure a putback and save the play, but I bench him at the next time out. Why?

Some coaches might reward or praise their point guard for his hustle, but if I was running a defense where we send our guards back after every shot attempt, he just blew his assignment. Basketball is a game of probability: 10% of the time he might get the rebound and score, but the other 90% is an easy fast break bucket for the opponent that my team was not prepared for.

Principles Beat Plays Over the Long Run

In this book I hope to provide a framework for coaches to understand the principles behind some popular modern defensive systems and how you can build one that suits you. Similar to my other publication *The Complete Guide to Motion Offense*, this book will be focused on team concepts and not on individual skills for defense. We will not be covering how to close out and other individual defensive skills, as there are already many great resources for that available.

We will cover many defenses but mainly focus on man to man defense principles because this book is intended for coaching youth players and man to man is undoubtedly the best defense for player development. In this book, we will provide a detailed breakdown of the pack line, man to man, one full-court press, and one zone defense. There are too many defenses to cover in one book, but if you understand the principle behind them you will be able to easily pick up on other defensive schemes.

2

Choosing Your Defensive System

Now let's get into the principles of defense. The different areas of this can be broken down into the following:

- Transition (fast break) defense
- Full-court defense
- Half-court defense
- Help, rotations, and pick-and-roll defense

Transition Principles

Defense happens the moment your team makes or misses a shot. At this point you have two options:

1. Pressure the ball handler immediately
2. Protect the basket immediately

Applying pressure for the full length of the basketball court is very effective, especially at youth basketball levels. With a full-court press you can choose to apply a lot of pressure or just stay in front of the ball handler. However, if you do the latter you risk giving up an easy basket on a fast break. On the other hand, you can choose to ask all your players to sprint back to prevent an easy basket or a numbers advantage. These are your fundamental transition defense principles.

You also need to decide on your offensive boards principles. Do you want everyone to crash the boards? Or do you only allow your power forward and center to do it? If you choose to fight for offensive rebounds, you risk losing a few easy transition baskets every game, but you can more than make up for that if you have the right players.

Full-court Principles

Next is choosing if you want to press full-court. The argument for a full-court press is because statistically it works better at youth levels. Why let the ball carrier casually walk up the court? By pressing you get to:

- Use up the clock
- Any turnover is easier to convert into points

However, the disadvantage of a full-court press is that if beaten it can lead to easy points because your defense won't be set up.

A full-court press also requires a lot of energy and concentration from your team. If you have a deep team then this won't be a problem, but if you rely on one or two star players you risk them being too tired on the offensive end.

Half-court Principles

If you decide not to do a full-court press then you will need to choose your half-court system. You need to ask yourself the following:

- Do you want to give up three point shots and protect the lane by sagging?
- Or do you want to deny the ball and try to force turnovers?

If you go pack line, or any other pack the paint defense, you are sagging. If you go for denial, you are pressuring the ball and denying one pass away.

We need to think about a few defensive priorities. In order of importance, here they are:

The Basket: Even though the modern game has evolved to be very three-point dependent, the fact is that the closer you are to the basket the higher the shot percentage is. So the decision is whether you want to take away 'points in the paint' and lose out on the threes or vice versa. If you are coaching at the youth level, it is unlikely that the opponent team will have many good shooters so packing the paint can become a more viable option.

The Ball: How do you want to defend the ball handler? Do you force the ball sideline, baseline, or play the ball handler chest-to-chest? The fundamental question here is about how much pressure you can afford to put on the ball handler or whether you are better off having your team stay in front of the offense at all costs. For example, where you choose to force the ball determines how you play pick-and-roll:

- If you play pick-and-roll and force the ball down, you need to drop your big and force the ball baseline.
- If you play pick-and-roll and you blitz, then you need to force the ball to the middle.

Some of the decision-making is also personnel driven:

- If you have posts that don't move very well, you're probably better off forcing the ball down to the sideline. This allows the post to stay closer to the basket and the pick-and-roll will be pushed down.
- If your posts are active, athletic, and can get out and blitz the ball, then you can push the ball middle. This allows the post to get out away from the basket to put more pressure on the dribbler on pick-and-roll with the knowledge that they can scramble and recover later.

The Players: How will your players matchup? How will you deal with a superstar opponent? For example, if the other team has a star ball handler, you can assign a guard to pick them up full court to wear them out.

Here are some more questions to stimulate your thinking:

- What personnel do you have? Are your players great defenders that can force turnovers? Or will they get beaten one-on-one and need help?
- How will you defend the players that don't have the ball? Will you try to deny them it but potentially risk getting

beaten with cuts? Or will you give them some space that may make them feel less pressured on offense?

Space: If you choose to defend space more than a player you are looking at choosing a zone. In this book, we will cover the one-one-three zone but a pack line defense is also similar to a zone in that you can use it to defend space too.

Help, Rotation, and Pick-and-Roll Defense Principles

Now that you've determined the major principles we can finish off with some help defense details. How will you defend screens and how will you help defense rotate? 'Help' refers to how the defenders who are not guarding the ball help the defender who is guarding the ball.

Rotations refer to how all defenders rotate once the initial help on the ball has occurred. In some cases that means the player who began by defending the ball no longer does and must rotate to a new assignment, but more often it refers to the players helping out the defender on the ball by either threatening to pressure the ball handler or their man.

You don't want your players in no man's land guarding no one at all, so it's important to ask yourself what you want your rotations to do on defense – pressure the ball handler or their man?

The usual order of priority in considering how to help and rotate is to help on the ball and then rotate to each of the closest passes from the ball. The easiest pass the offense can make when a team helps and rotates should also be the furthest pass. In doing so, this is also the easiest pass for the defense to recover as the ball will spend more time in the air (and can therefore get picked off).

However, some defenses (such as the pack-line defense) knowingly help one pass away (but recover quickly) to enable the defenders to pack the paint and deny any easy layups or drive and kick opportunities. This is why principles are important –defensive principles let your team know exactly where the offense will be sending their next pass.

There are nine different ways to defend a screen (we'll break them down in more depth later) and you'll need to decide which ones you will use.

Summary

As the great coach Bob Knight says: "The key is not the will to win. Everybody has that. It is the will to prepare that is important."

A great defense doesn't necessarily have to 'destroy' an offense, but rather it forces the offense into situations that the defense is prepared for. And as I mentioned above, basketball is a numbers game. If your coaching puts your team in more situations that they are prepared to deal than the offense with over the course of a game, your chances of winning go up dramatically.

So in summary, at each stage of defense you have to ask yourself tough questions and force yourself to define your team's defensive principles:

- Transition defense principles – pressure the ball handler

or protect the basket? Offensive rebounds or stopping fast breaks?

- Full-court principles – turnovers and easy baskets or a set defense every time? 'Load management' or non-stop effort?
- Half-court principles – protect the paint or force turnovers? Pressure the ball or stay in front of your man? Will you make team-to-team adjustments or stick to your principles 100%? Will you defend space or players?
- Help, rotation, and pick-and-roll defense principles – will your help and rotations pressure the ball handler or their man?

In the following chapters, we will go through:

- Two types of man-to-man defense: pack line and denial
- Havoc full-court press
- One-one-three zone defense
- Transition defense

I hope that by understanding the principles behind each system, it can help you decide on what suits you best. The best defenses are about making tough decisions on what you are willing to sacrifice in return for better results in winning areas. I hope you will be able to do exactly that by the end of this book.

3

Pack Line Defense

The Pack-line defense is a half-court defensive system that literally packs the middle of the paint to make it difficult to score inside. Developed by legendary coach Dick Bennett, he used it in the 1990s with great success to lead his underdog Green Bay and Wisconsin teams to success against much more talented NCAA powerhouses. Today in the NCAA we see the pack line employed by his son Tony Bennett where he's perfected it while coaching at Virginia with accolades including being regarded as the best defensive coach by his peers in 2015.

The pack line is an imaginary line that is two feet within the three point line. It forces opponents to take perimeter shots and is especially effective against offenses based on dribble penetrations or low post play. The reality of the school and even some college teams is that they're not filled with knockdown shooters – this defense is good enough to stop one-two key sharpshooters with the huge boost of protecting your paint.

Advantages of Pack-line Defense

1. Force outside shots and reduce shots inside paint
2. Make it difficult to score low post
3. Effective against dribble penetration

Disadvantages of Pack-line Defense

1. Can be exploited by elite outside shooting
2. Requires great closeouts
3. Requires great team work

coachbase
10 PACK LINE DEFENSE PRINCIPLES
Reduce high percentage shots in the paint with this defense.
1 CHOKE THE LOW POST
Immediately double team the low post if the ball gets there.
2 NO PASS FROM TOP
Don't allow a direct pass to low post from the top. It'll create easy 1 on 1 scoring chances.
3 NO BASELINE DRIVES
Force the offense into the pack and away from the low post.
4 SPRINT TO HELP
Sprint to the help position. You should already be in position when help is needed.
5 CLOSEOUT HANDS HIGH
No rhythm shots or passes. Keep both hands high to discourage passing and shooting.
6 MOVE ON FLIGHT OF BALL
The moment the ball leaves passer, all 5 players must move to new position.
7 NO STRAIGHT LINES
Unacceptable to allow offense direct drive to rim. No help can be offered in this scenario.
8 KEEP OUT OF POST BOX
Use your arm to keep the offense out of the post box.
9 PRESSURE THE BALL
The defender on the ball can leave pack area and MUST apply pressure at all times.
10 KEEP 2 FEET INSIDE PACK AREA
Non ball defenders must stay within pack area at all times and in the gap.
DOWNLOAD COACHBASE APP
Get drills to practice these inside our practice planner app
WWW.COACHBASE.COM

1. Post defense

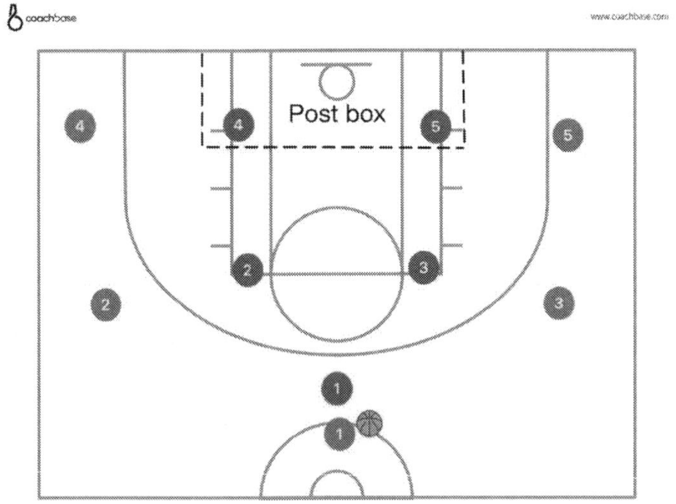

Post box

The pack line's system revolves around how it guards the post. As such, this defense is perfect for small teams having trouble guarding it. First, you don't want the post player to receive the ball inside the post box.

Low-post Defense Key Points:

- Keep players out of post box
- Use the arm bar to push your man out
- Three-quarters high deny when ball is above free throw
- Full deny below free throw

You must use your arm to push the player outside of the post box. A clenched fist arm bar can be used to push his man out of the post box. Second, you want to deny the ball high and force the post to receive the ball closer to the baseline. Post defender should be positioned three-quarters on the high side when the ball is above the free-throw line and move to complete front if the ball is below the free-throw line.

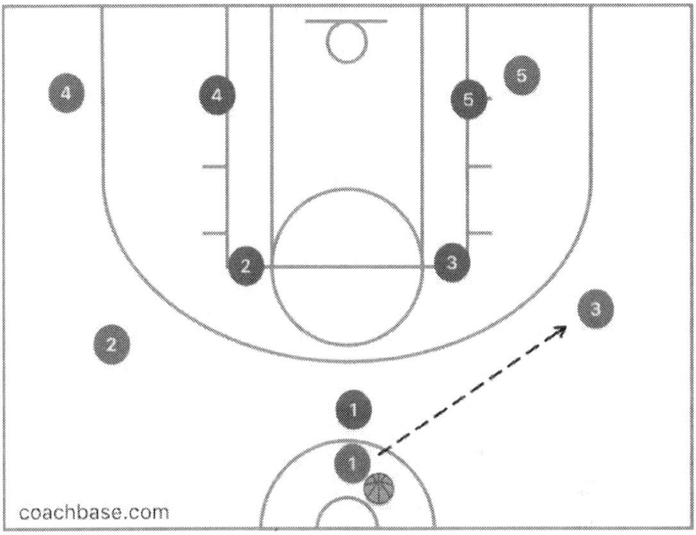

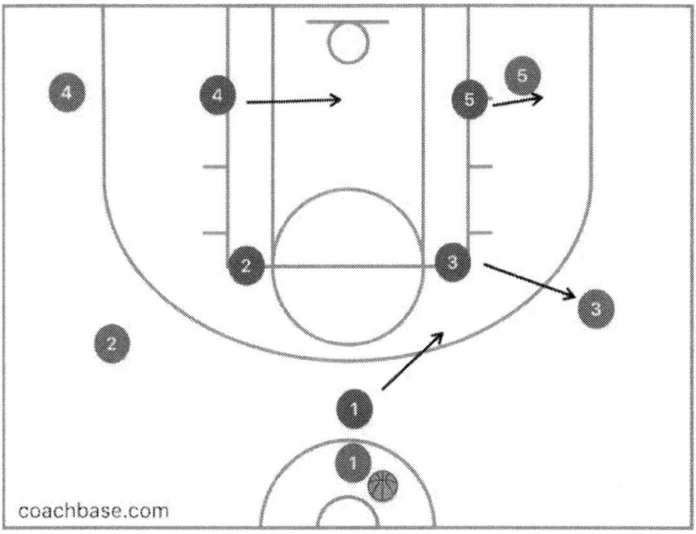
4
4
5
5
2
3
3
2
1
1
coachbase.com

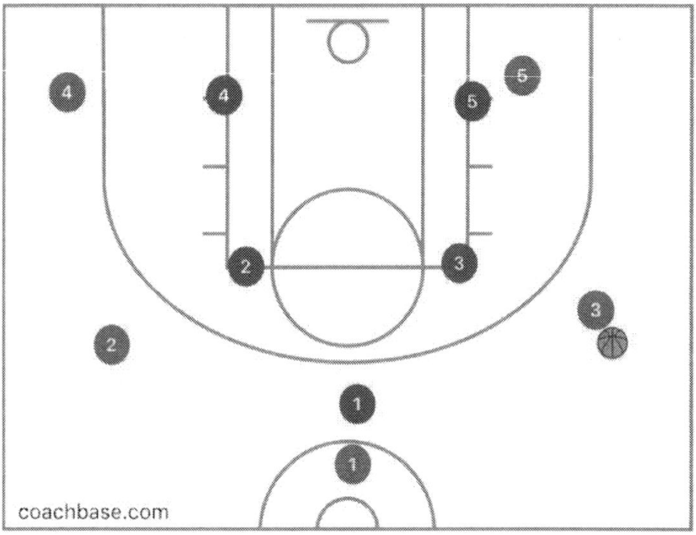
4
4
5
5
2
3
3
2
1
1
coachbase.com

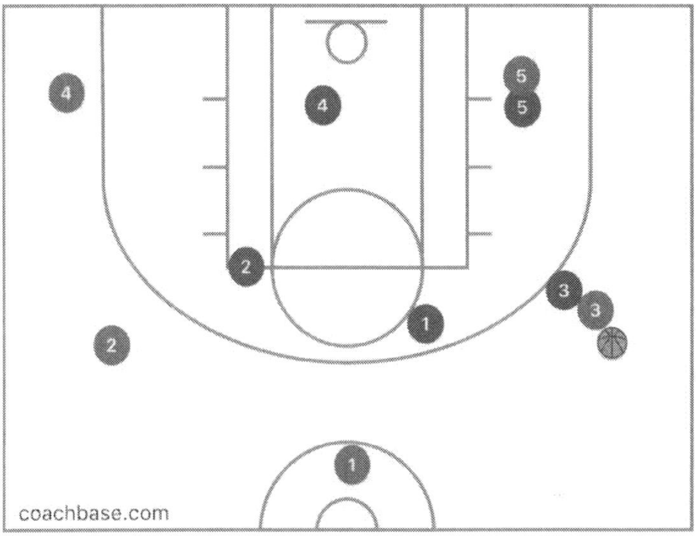

Three-quarters High Defense on Low Post

That is also why in the pack line you always force the offense middle and not give up the baseline. If they dribbler attacks baseline they can pass to the low post easily.

You don't want the post player to receive the ball near the middle of the basket so you cannot let the ball come from the top directly.

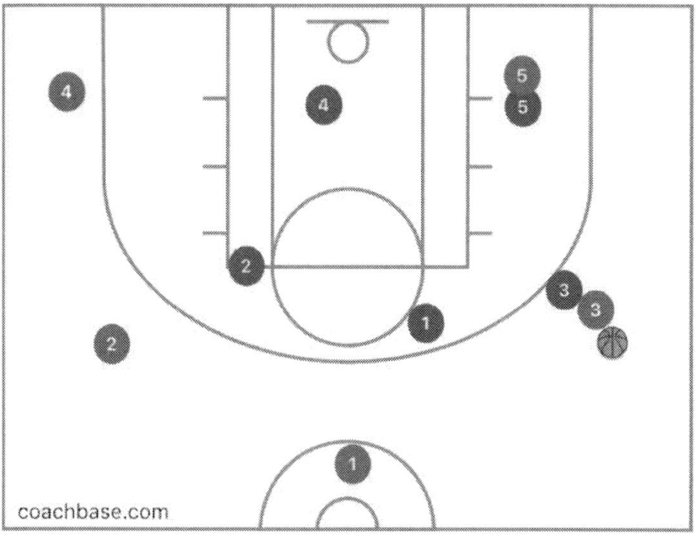
coachbase.com

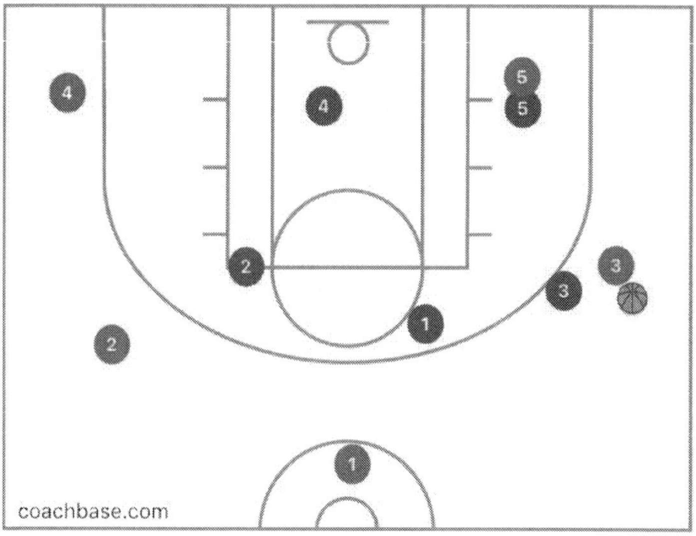
coachbase.com

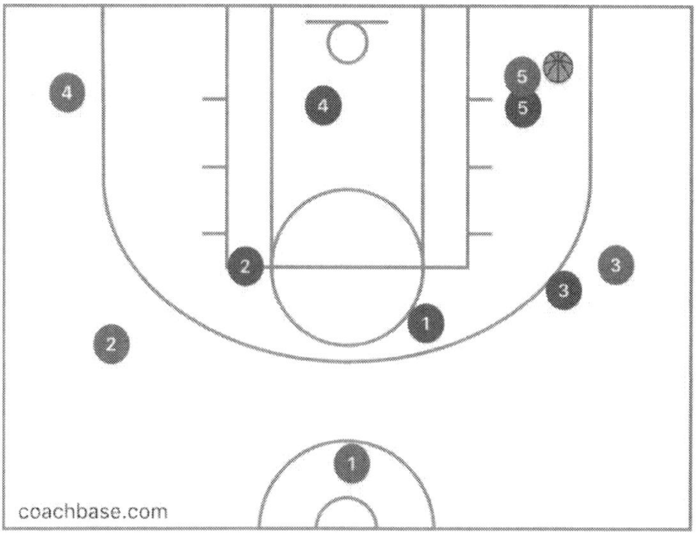
coachbase.com

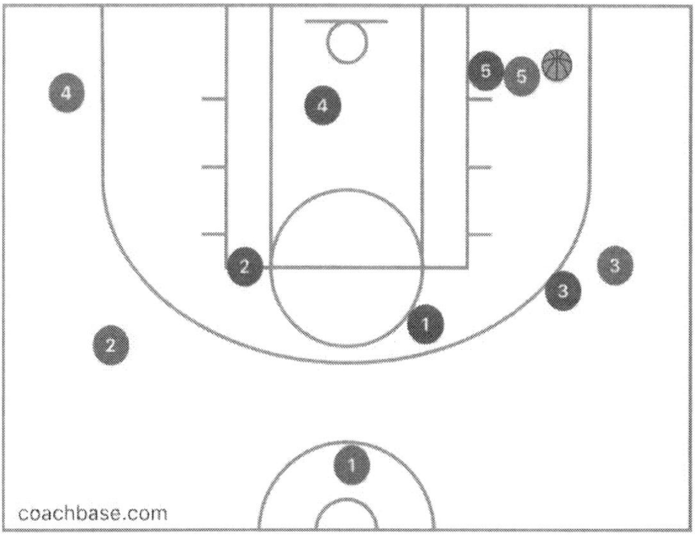
coachbase.com

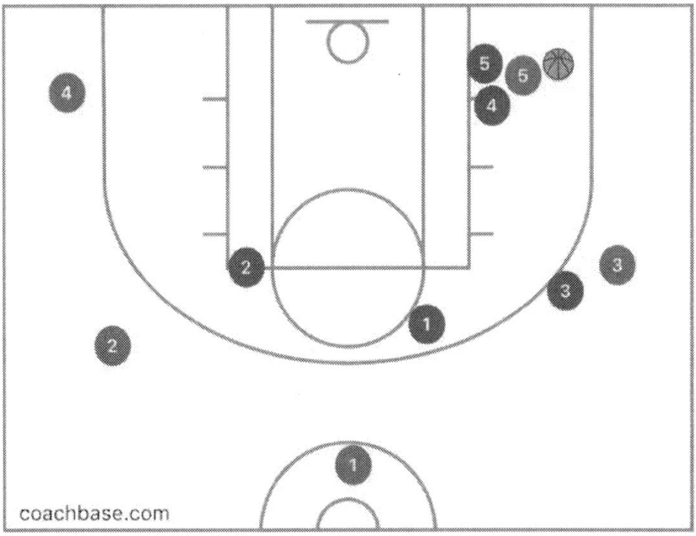

Choking Low Post

If the post receives the ball, you must 'choke' (double team) them immediately. The help defenders must immediately back off and wall up.

2. On-ball Defense

The defender on the ball handler must apply ball pressure. The on-ball defender doesn't need to stay inside the pack area, their job is to pressure the ball handler, meaning they need to get close. The only rule here is that the defender cannot be beat in a straight line, if they do then there's no help available.

3. Off-ball Defense Positioning

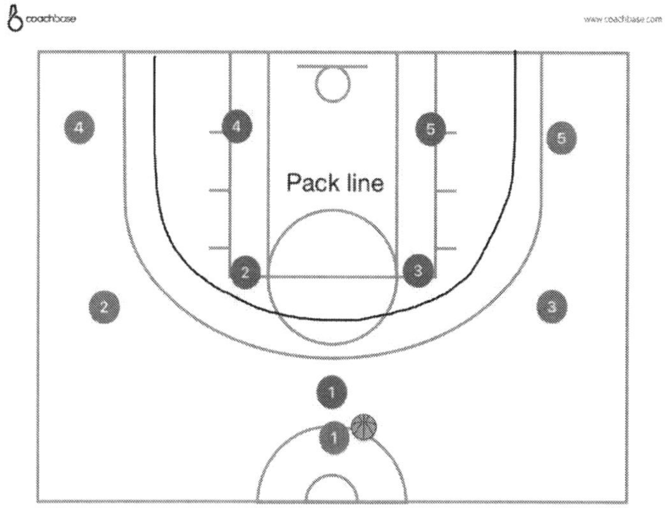

Pack line – the player guarding the man with the ball is to provide intense ball-pressure well beyond the three-point line while the other four help defenders are to all be within an imaginary 16-foot arc.

Positioning key points

- Must be inside pack area
- Should be around halfway between ball and your man
- Already be in help position
- Always be in a low defensive stance – no standing tall

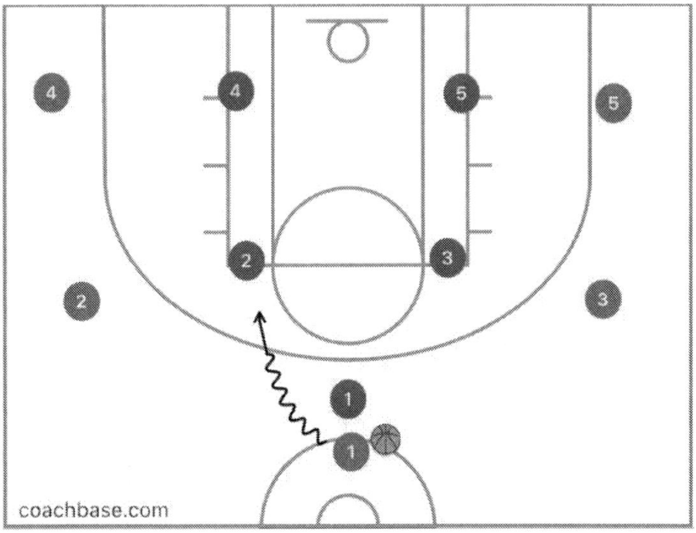
coachbase.com

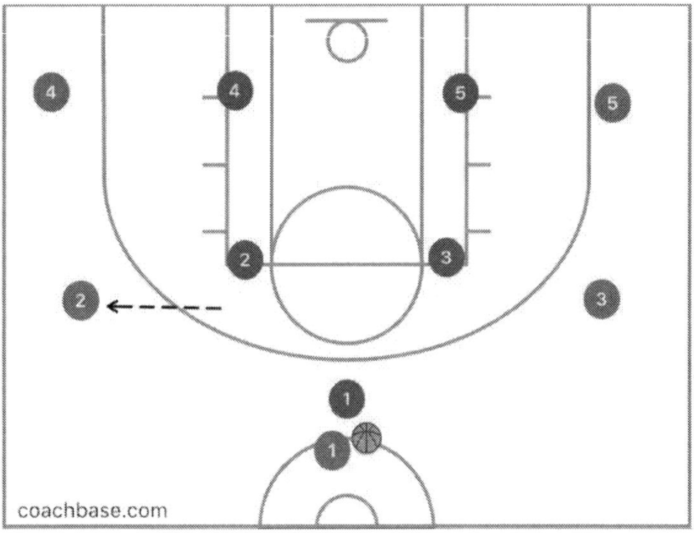
coachbase.com

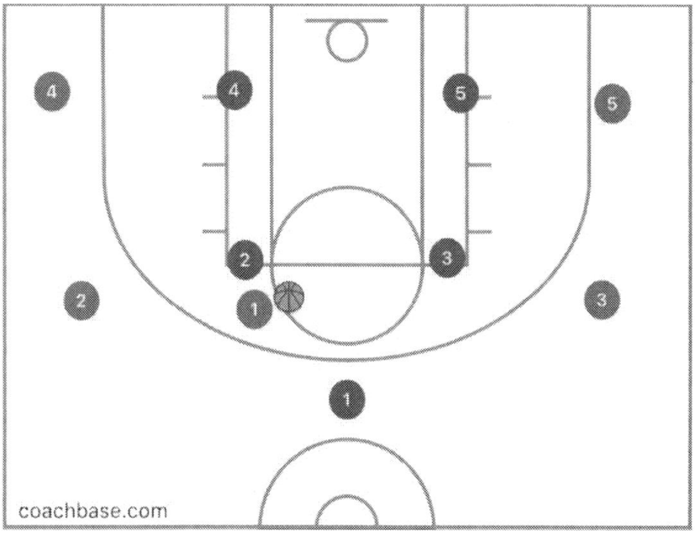
coachbase.com

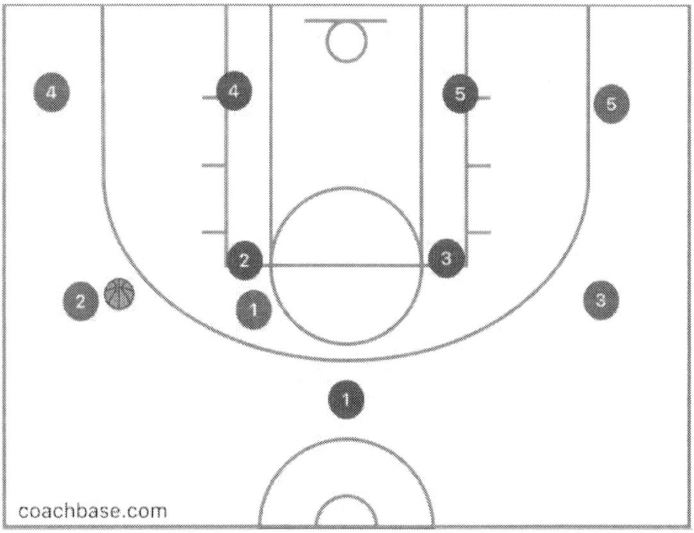
coachbase.com

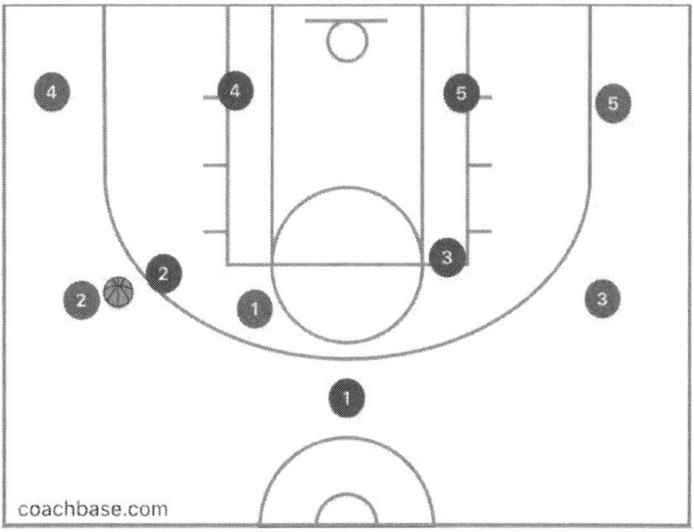

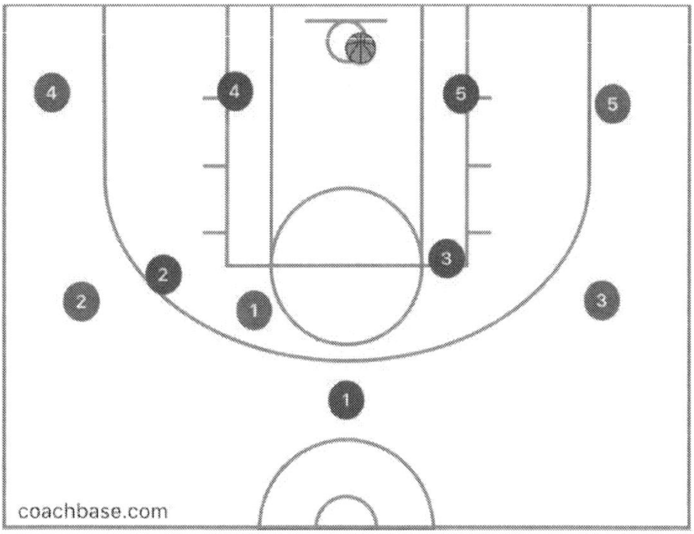

Any player that is going to get all the way to the rim is going to have to beat his man and a help defender before finishing over a shot-blocker around the basket. Unlike most defenses, the help is coming from the strong side. This creates lots of closeout opportunities and is one of the weaknesses of the system, so it's paramount your players closeout well.

Closeout key points

- Move on flight of the ball
- short choppy steps
- high hands and then settle into your stance
- must not allow shots in rhythm
- Level off the dribbler by getting him to go east-west
- Take away the north-south direct drive
- Bother the shooter (hands in face, etc.)

Three Types of Closeouts

- Pure shooter (Kyle Korver) – close out close
- Dribble penetrator (Rajon Rondo) – keep distance in close-out
- Both (Kobe) – one arm's distance

4. Communication

Since this defense relies so much on team work, it is paramount your players communicate. Vocal communication is essential, so shout these words out while defending:

A. Ball – this call means I have the player

B. Gap – this call means my player does not have the ball but I am in your dribble gap

C. Help – this call means my players does not have the ball

but I am on the opposite half of the court than the ball is

Transition defense

"Always take a guy out if he loafs back during a game." – Dick Bennett

The first rule is to get all five players below the ball: all players must sprint back. This is non-negotiable. Then someone must apply ball pressure to the ball handler. The other players should also load to the ball, meaning if your player has not crossed the half-court line then stay high and help apply ball pressure on the ball handler.

Screens and cutters

"If you touch the guy at all times, you will not get screened." – Dick Bennett

Defenders of the screener should be in help position (in the direction of the cutter) but must stay attached to their defender at all times. Bennett doesn't like switching because he feels that the more you allow switching, the more it will handicap your team late in the season. Switching only works for teams that are experienced and have roughly equally talented players. When a cutter cuts, make sure your players tap the player and stay in contact throughout the pack area.

Conclusion

If you want to force outside shots and if your team is short, this might be a good defensive system. It will require a lot of teamwork but has been proven to work.

4

Drills for Pack-line Defense

In the pack-line defense, it's critical that players position themselves in the right spots and closeout correctly. Here's a comprehensive list of drills you can incorporate into your practice if you plan on running the pack-line defense.

One-on-One Closeouts

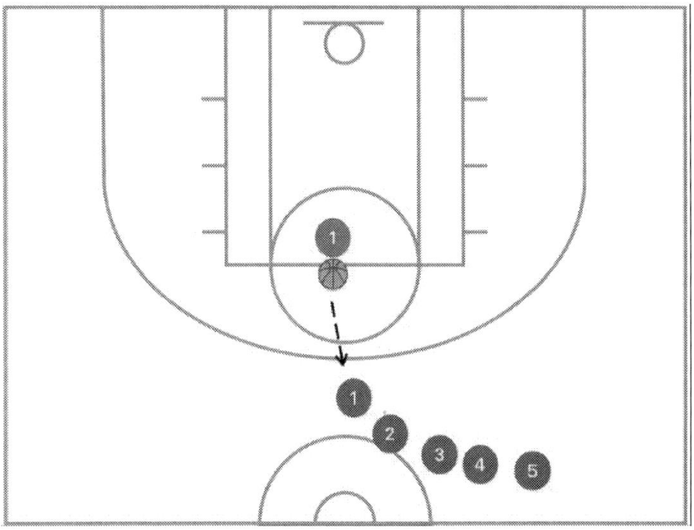
1
1
2
3
4
5

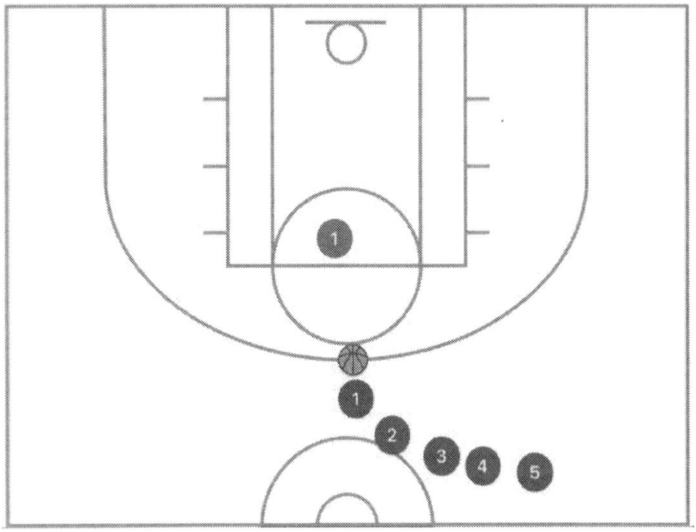
1
1
2
3
4
5

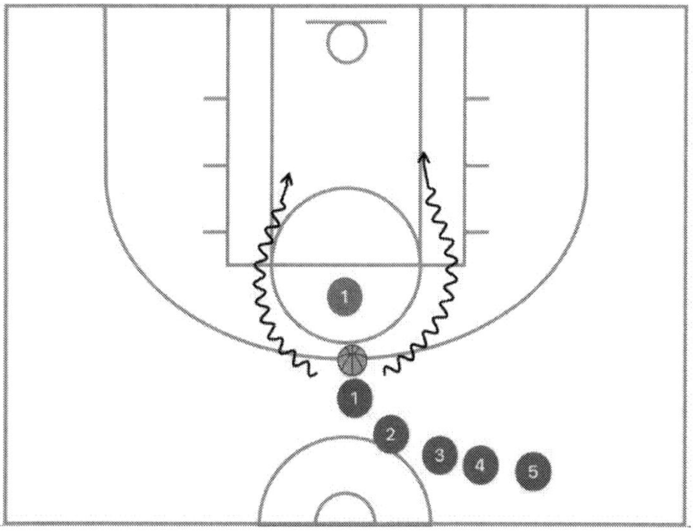
1
1
2
3
4
5

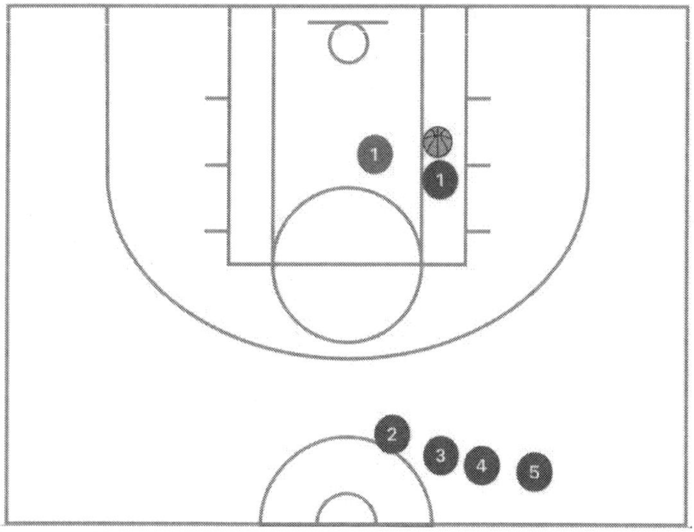
1
1
2
3
4
5

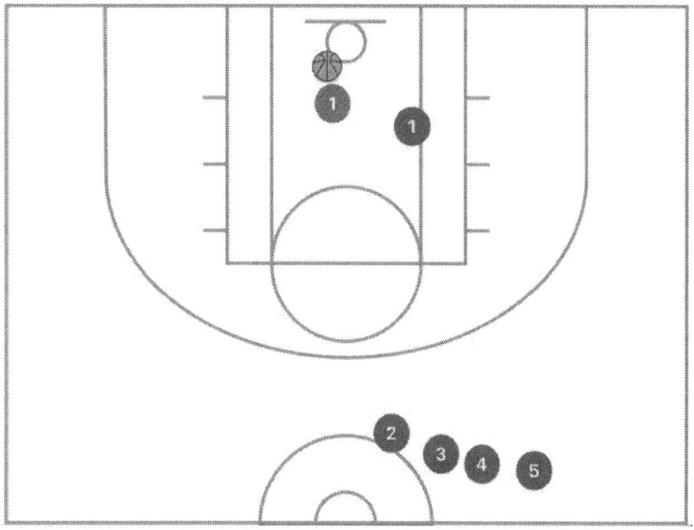

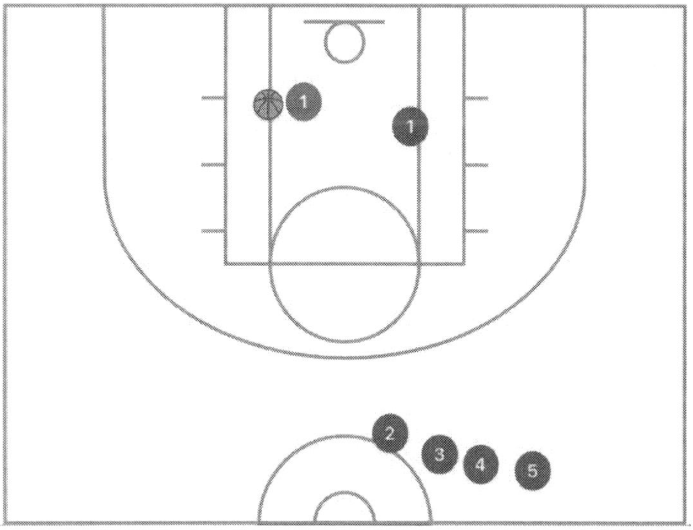

Instructions:

- Defensive player tosses ball to offensive player in line from above the three-point line
- Offensive player gets a maximum of two dribbles to score
- Play until defensive player gets a stop and secures the rebound
- If offense scores, defense stays and plays next player inline.

Focus

Focus on proper closeouts.

- Two high hands
- Elbows bent
- Low stance
- Short/choppy steps
- Stay square
- Yell "SHOT" early

Vegas Closeouts

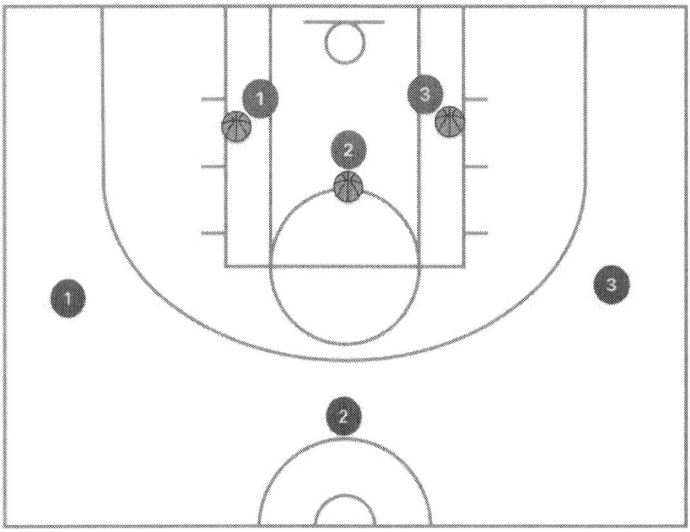
1
3
2
1
3
2

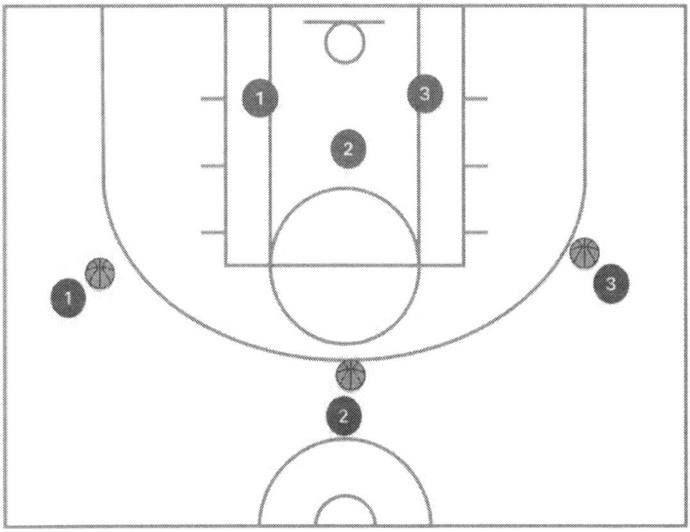
1
3
2
1
3
2

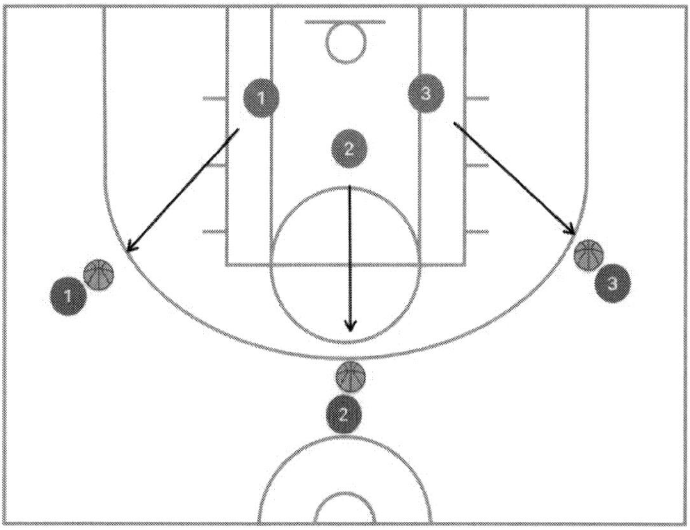

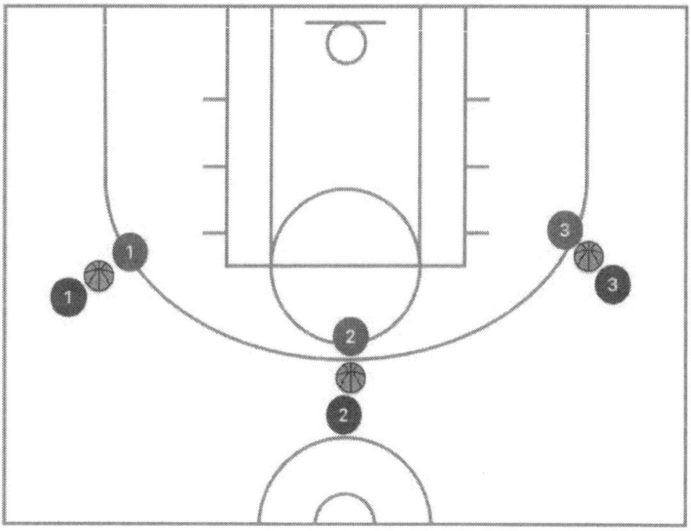

Instructions:

- Three defensive players start below the basket with a ball each
- Toss the ball to an offensive player and closeout
- Practice three types of closeouts: short, long, and medium distance
- Rotate after each closeout

Focus

Practice closing out on different types of players.

- Player one 'Rondo' – can't shoot. Closeout further away
- Player two 'Korver' – pure shooter. Not much of a penetrator. Closeout closer
- Player three 'Kobe' – can shoot and penetrate. One arm's length away

Blackhawk

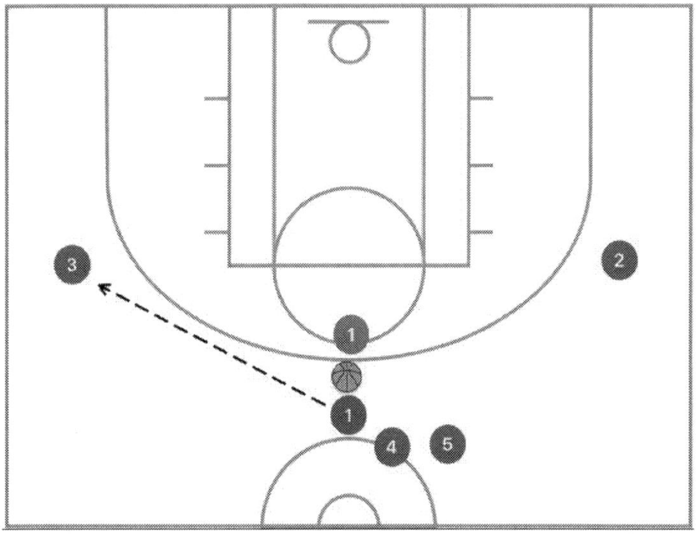
3
2
1
1
4
5

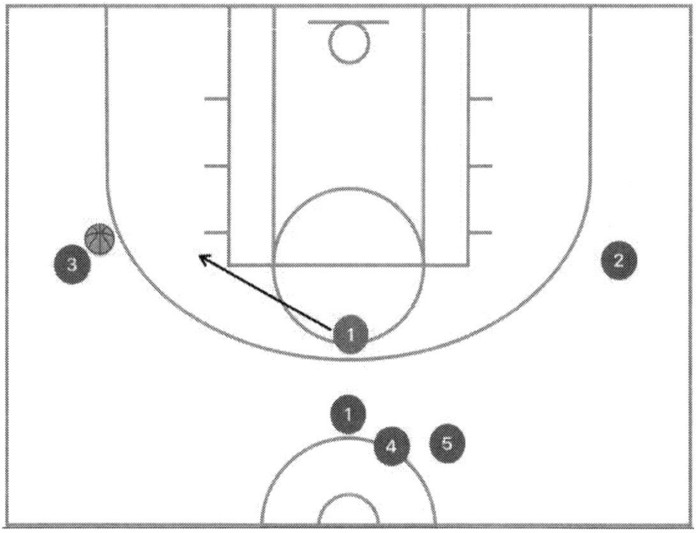
3
2
1
1
4
5

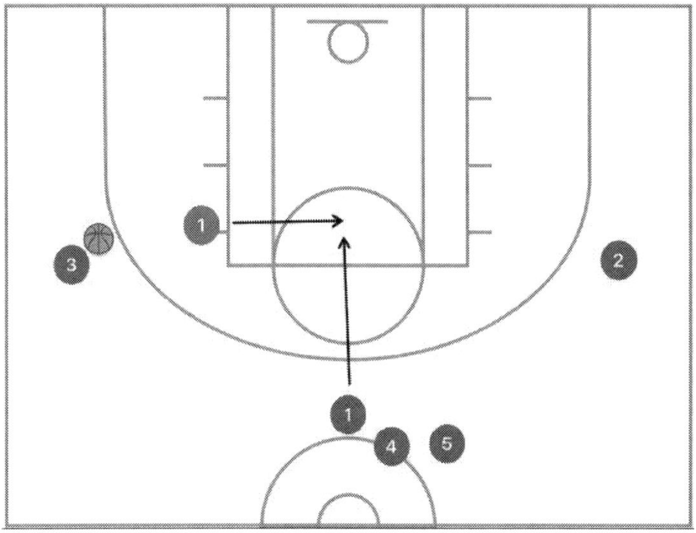
1
3
2
1
4
5

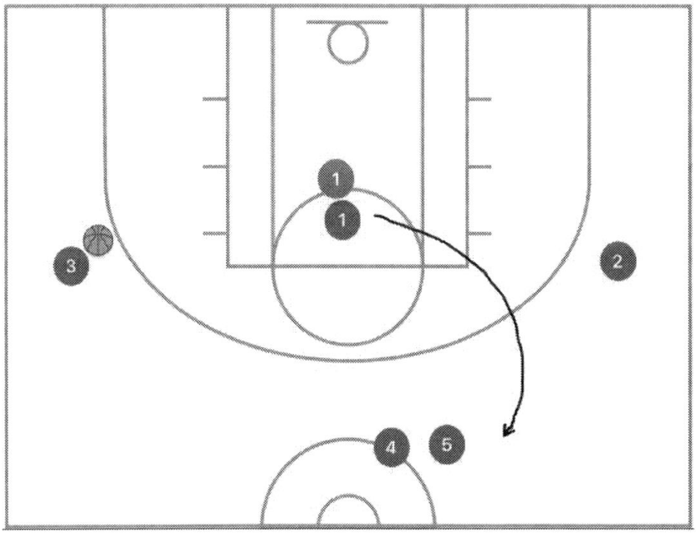
1
1
3
2
4
5

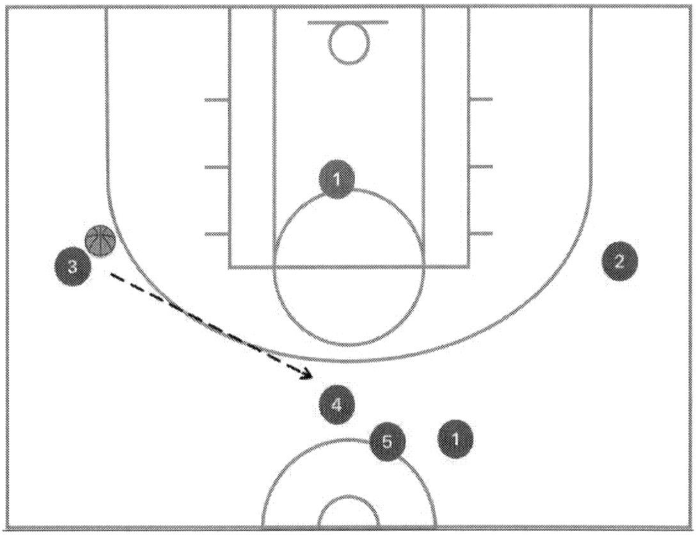
1
3
2
4
5
1

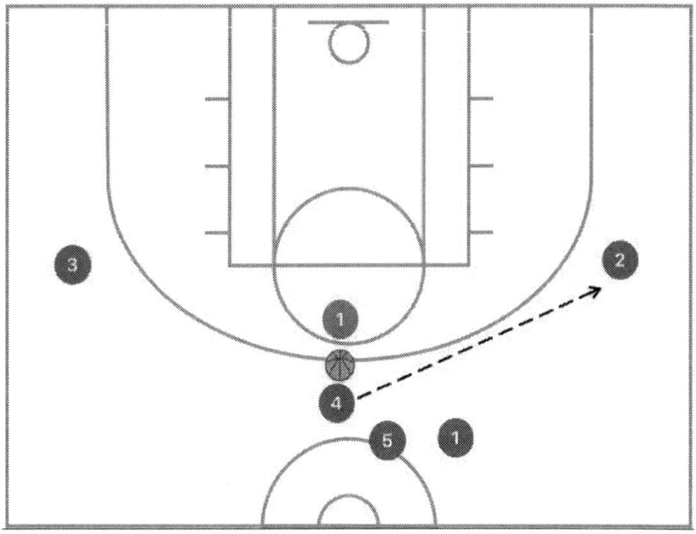
3
2
1
4
5
1

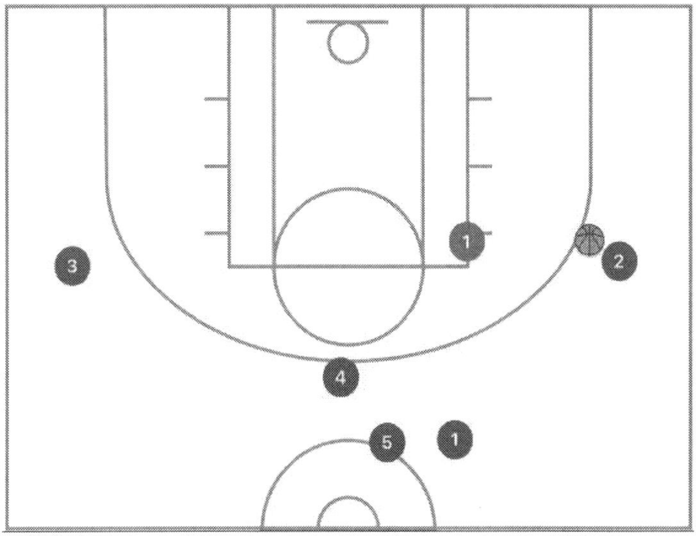
1
2
3
4
5
1

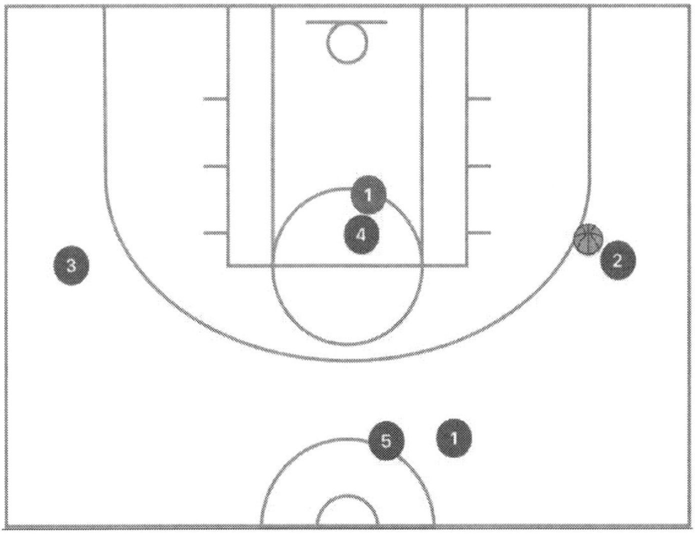
1
4
3
2
5
1

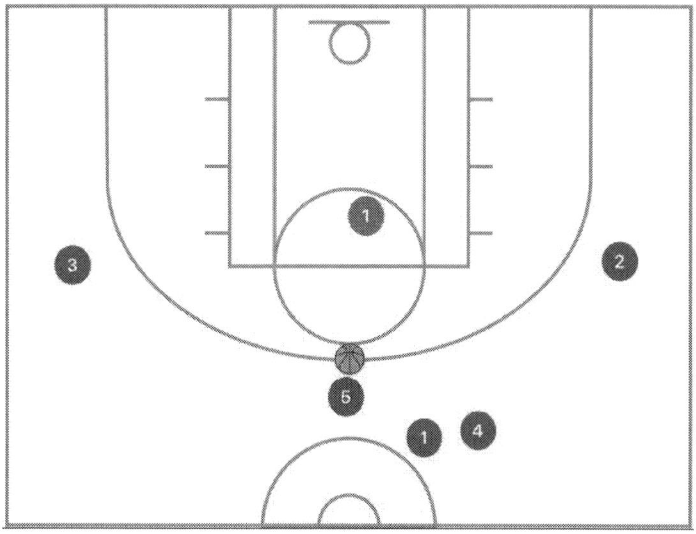
1
3
2
5
1
4

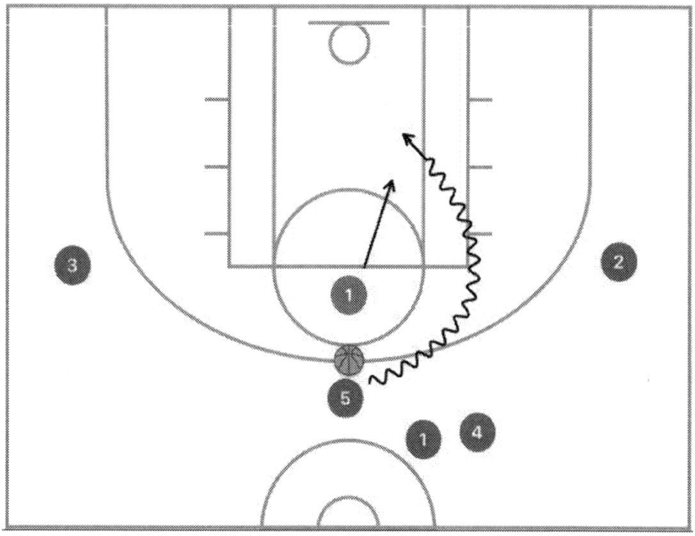
3
2
1
5
1
4

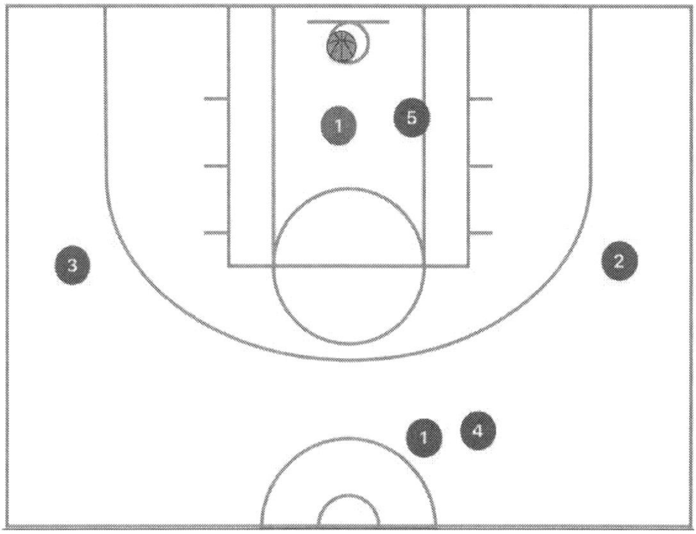

Focus

This is a drill that incorporates closing out, ball pressure, jumping to help position, fronting cutters, and closing out from help position. Closing out from a help position is one of the toughest fundamental skills required to master defensively.

Instructions

- Defender one throws ball to first offensive player (one) in line and closes out
- Offensive player one can pass to either wing
- Defender must 'jump and swipe' to get to the appropriate help position
- Offensive player one basket cuts
- Defender must use arm bar and 'bump cutter' to the logo (below the FT line)

- Wing will pass to next offensive player in line (two) and the defender must close out again – this time from a help position
- After two or three passes from wing to top to wing back to top, the coach will yell "LIVE"
- Two players play one-on-one off the close out
- Offense has two–three dribble max to score
- Defender must get a stop to complete the drill – if offense scores, offense restarts the drill

Coaching Points

- Make sure the defender keeps proper fundamentals during the dummy period of the drill

Two-on-One Positioning

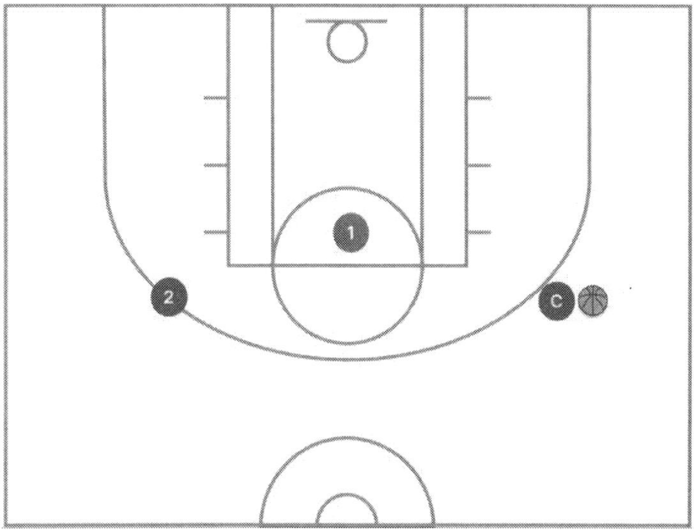
1
2
C

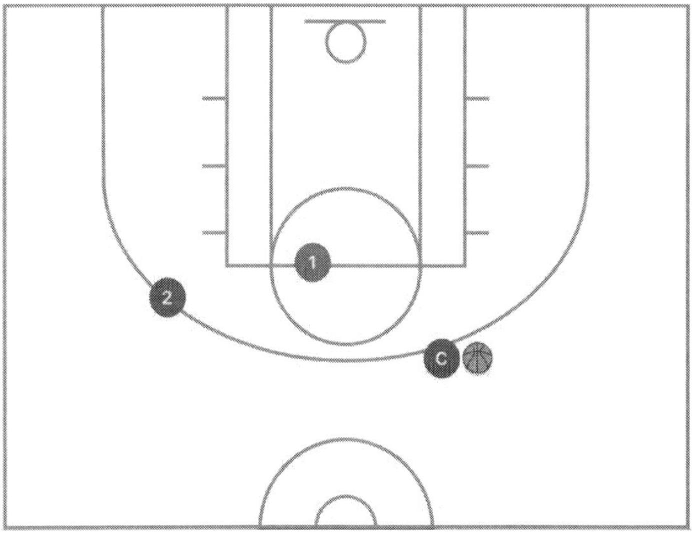
1
2
C

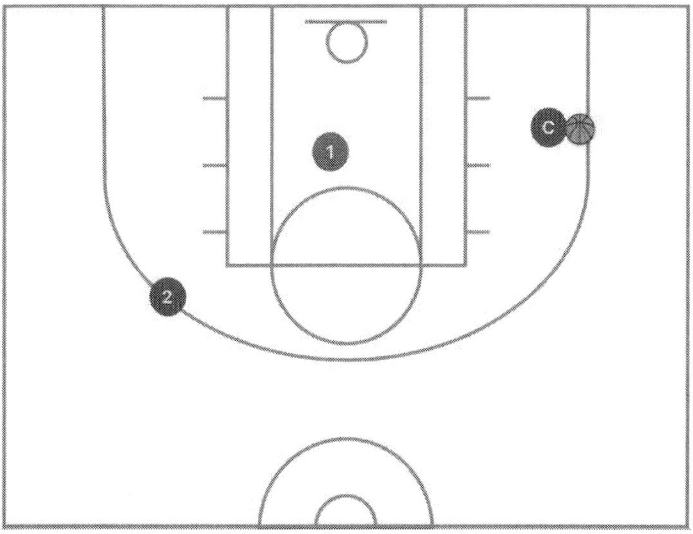
C
1
2

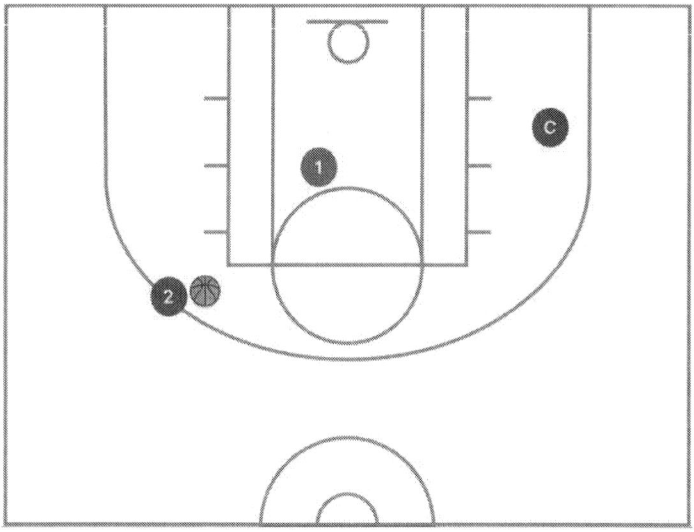
C
1
2

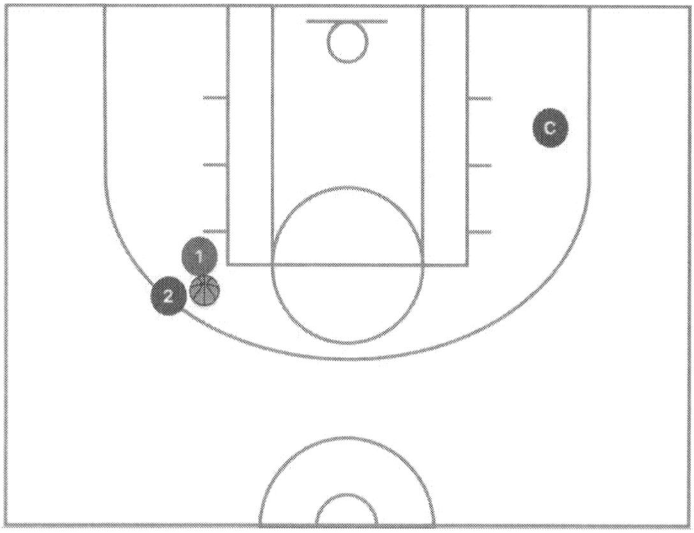

Instructions

- Coach starts with the ball, defender is matched up with one
- Coach can pass to one, dribble him out, cut him through, etc., forcing defender 1 to play on and off the ball
- The drill lasts for a prescribed amount of time and no one looks to score – instead, just focus on constant offensive movement

Coaching Points

Make sure x one plays with proper fundamentals throughout the drill:

- Close outs from ball to help and help to ball
- Jump and swipe
- Bump cutter

- Protect against baseline and straight-line drives
- Intense ball pressure

One-on-One Wall Up

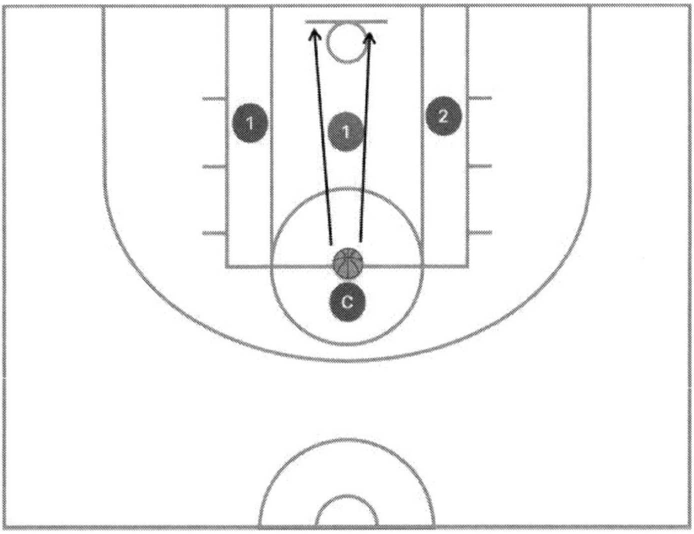

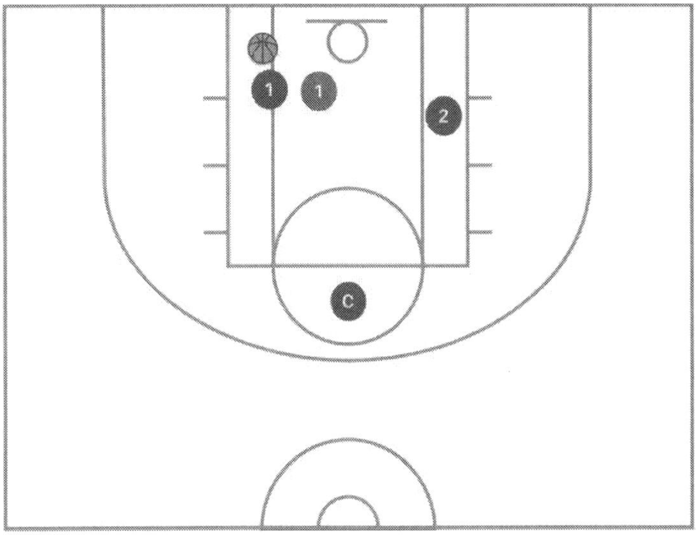
1
1
2
C

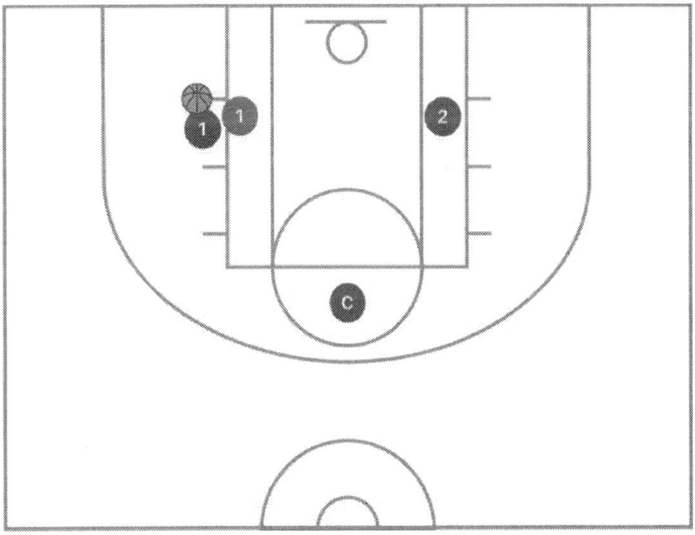
1
1
2
C

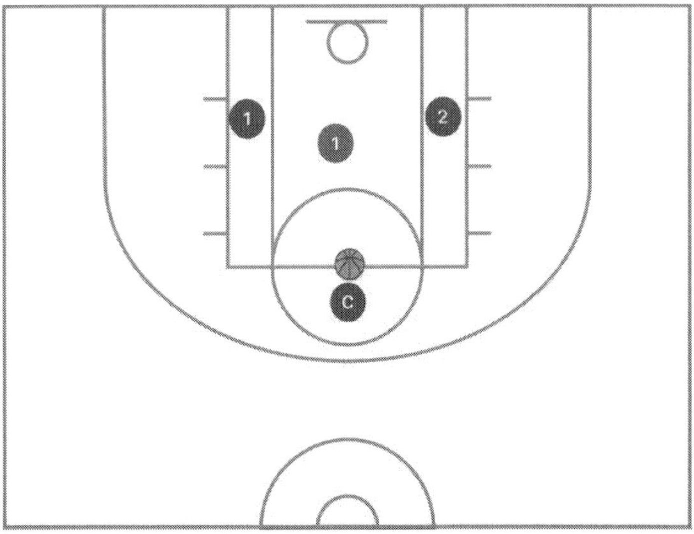
1
1
2
C

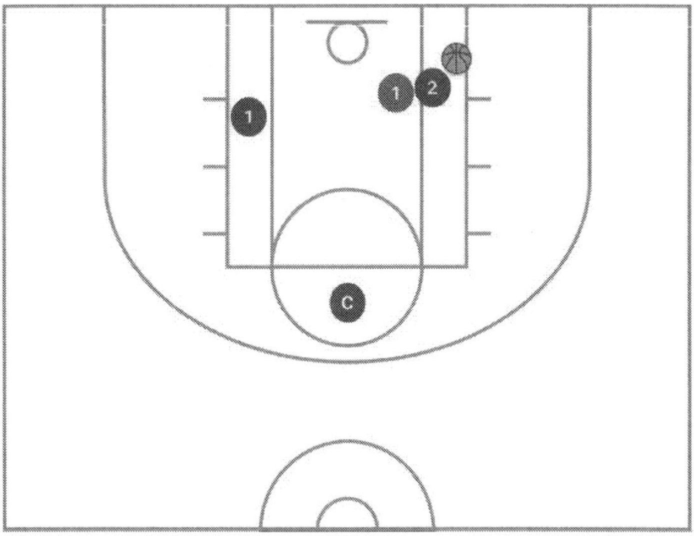
1
1
2
C

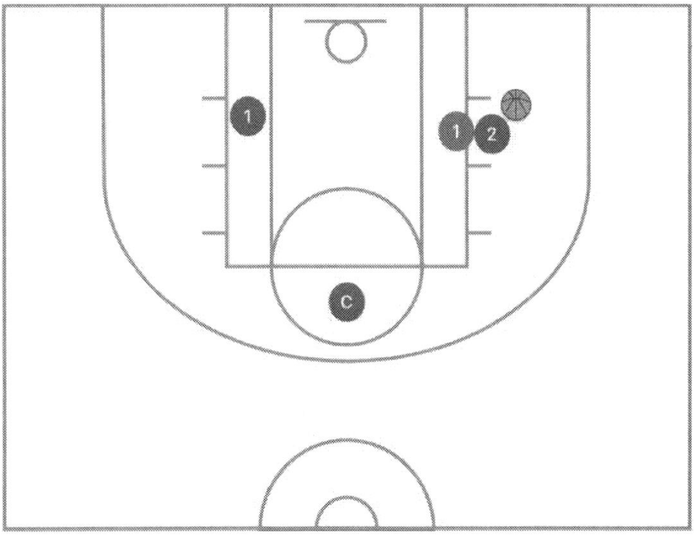

Focus

Drill works on 'walling up' against shot attempts from offensive rebounds. Both hands up and use the lower body to push the offensive player out.

Instructions

- Coach will lob the ball up off of the backboard to offensive player one
- Offense will offensive rebound the ball, defender one will 'wall up' and try to push one out of the post box with the hips
- 'Show the ref your hands'
- Do not jump!
- The player does not try to shoot, rather just battle for shooting position inside the post box

- After a few pivots, one will pass the ball back to Coach who will then repeat the drill on the opposite side with player two
- Run this drill for a prescribed number of reps
- Optional conclusion to drill: defender one has to finish the drill by taking a charge from either one or two lowering their shoulder

Coaching Point

So many offensive players will throw up bad lay-up attempts either because their feet are not set or because their positioning is poor in relation to the basket.

Three-Out One-In Guarded

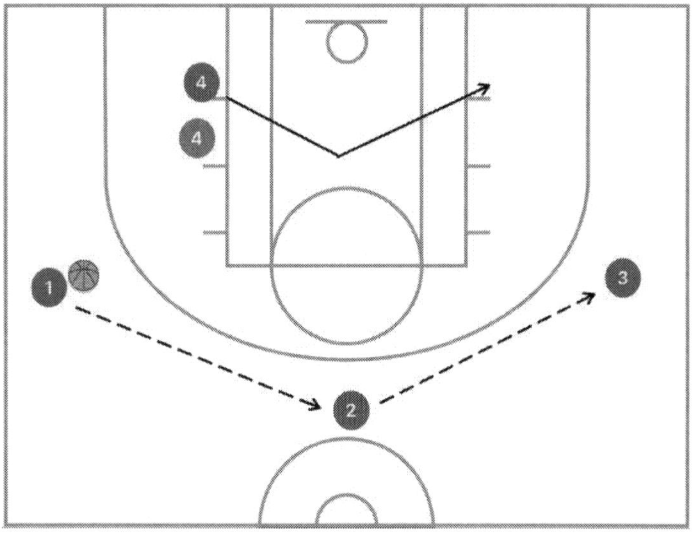

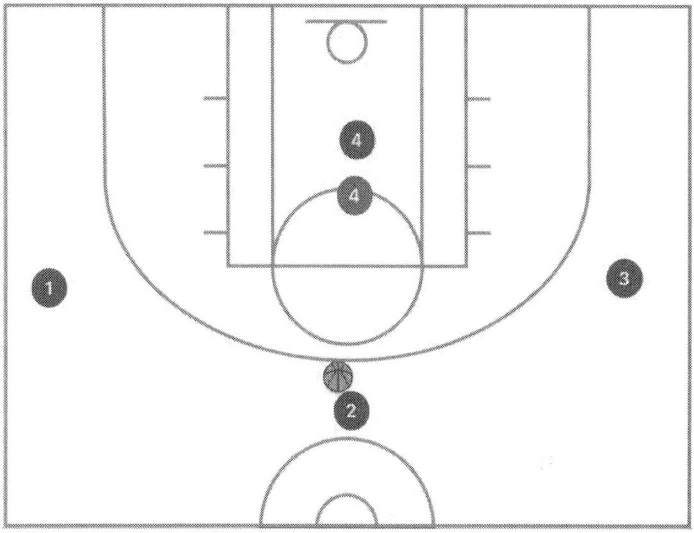

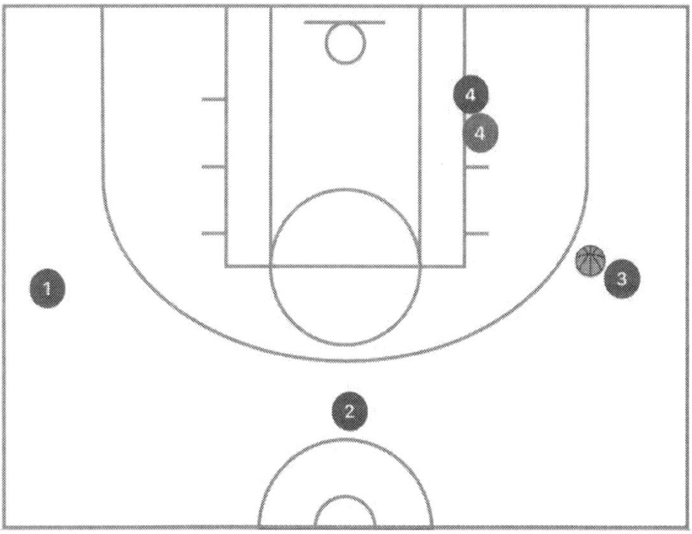

Focus

In the pack-line system, you want to keep the ball outside of the post box area and deny the pass from the top at all costs. This drill focuses on ball denial in the low post.

Instructions

- Drill begins with ball on the wing
- Offensive post tries to get position inside the box, post defender plays three-quarters on the high side and uses arm bar to force a catch outside the box
- On a pass from wing to top, post defender plays 'on the line, up the line' as offensive post tries to leg whip and seal, post defender can't play too high and give up lob
- On a pass from the top to opposite wing, the post defender hits offensive post with an arm bar and 'peels' to resume three-quarters high-side positioning outside the post box

Two-on-Two Top to Wing

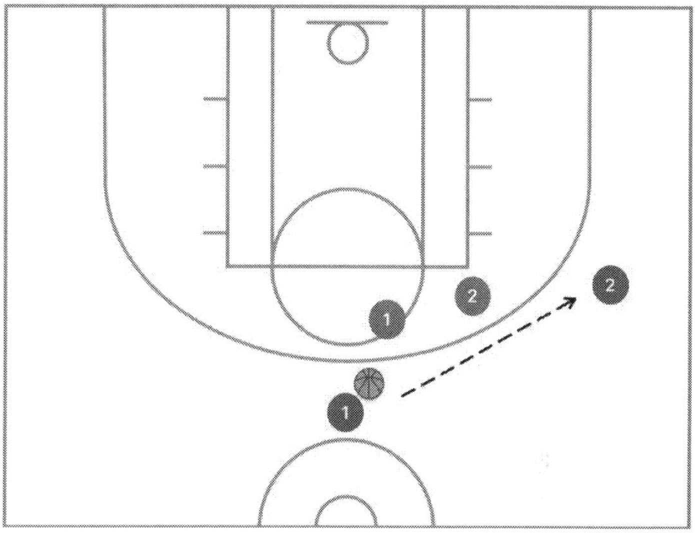
2
2
1
1

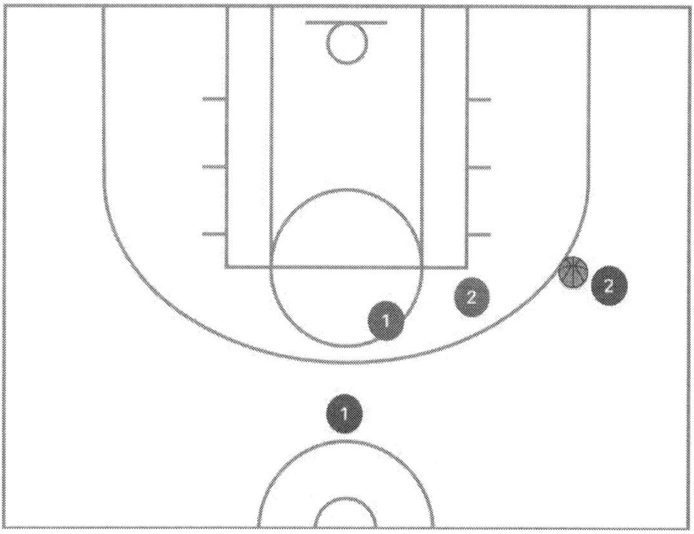
2
2
1
1

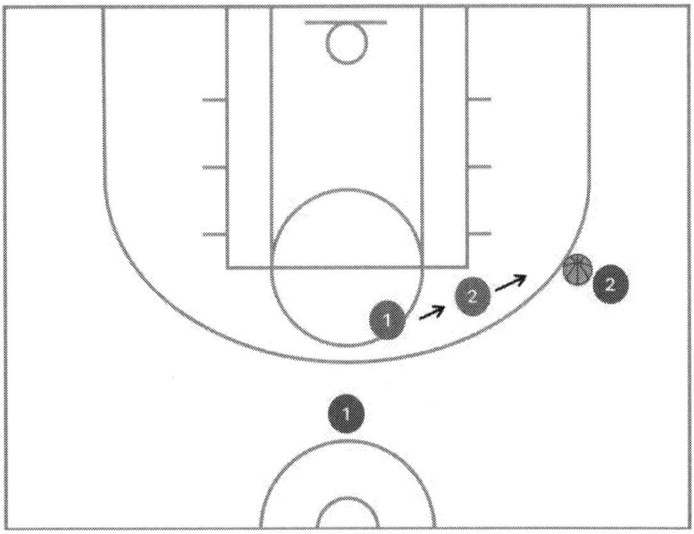
1
2
2
1

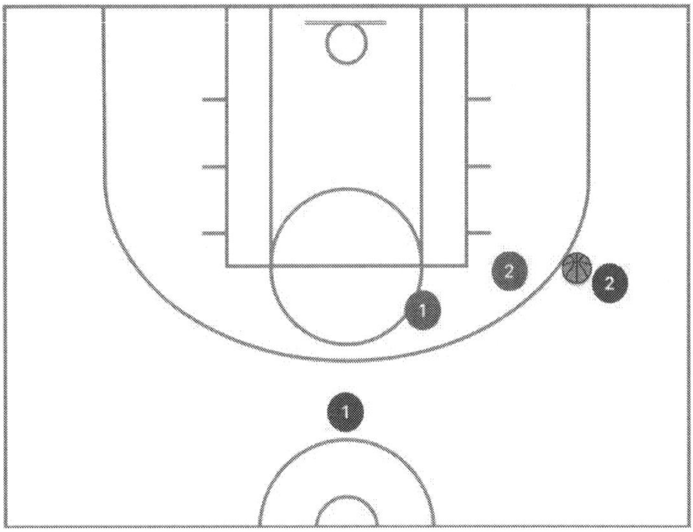
2
2
1
1

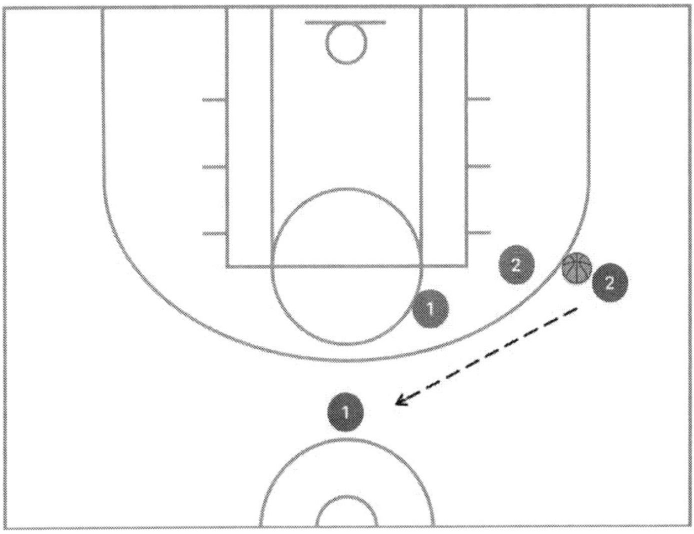

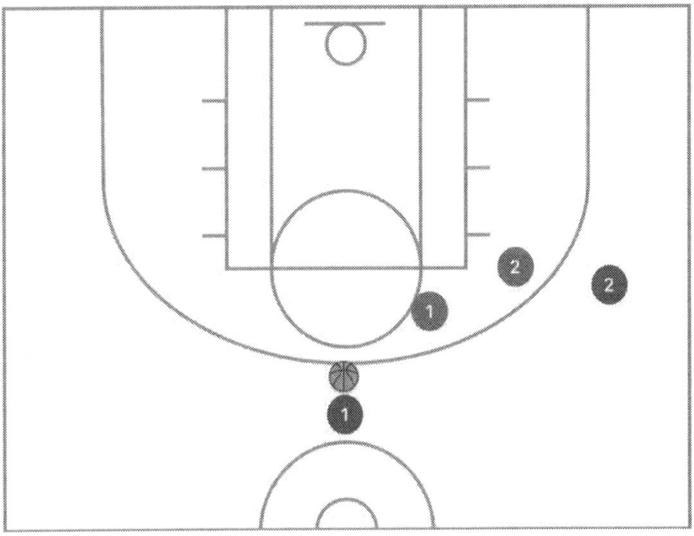

Focus

Proper help positioning and closing out.

Instructions

- Start by applying ball pressure (within arm's length) with the defender in the gap (already in help position inside pack-line area)
- Offensive players pass between each other
- Defense must shift as the ball is being passed

Coaching Points

- Stay in low defensive stance
- Move on the flight of the ball, not after
- Apply ball pressure
- Be in help position

Two-on-Two Wing to Corner

Similar to two-on-two top to wing but instead wing to corner.

Three-on-Three Positioning

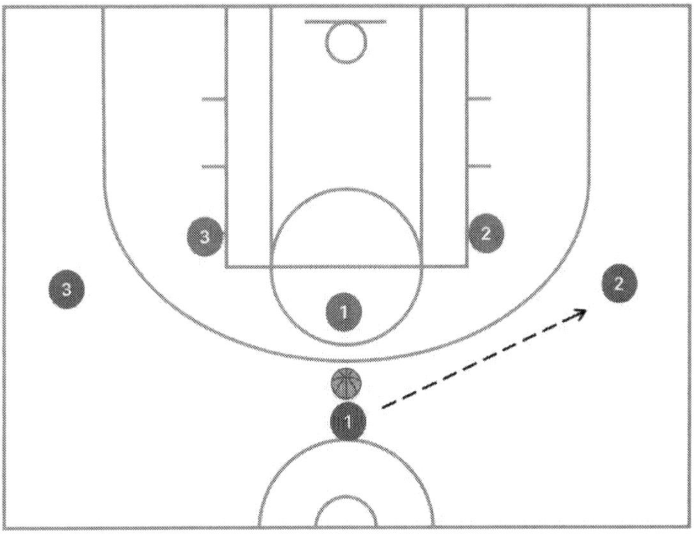
3
2
3
1
2
1

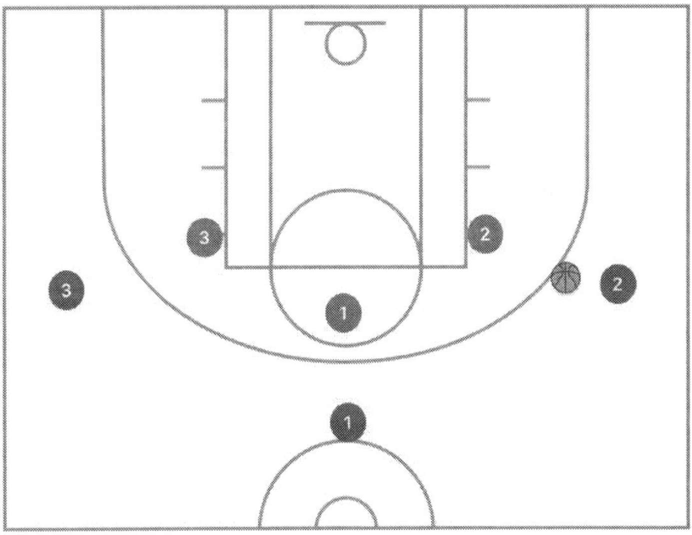
3
2
3
1
2
1

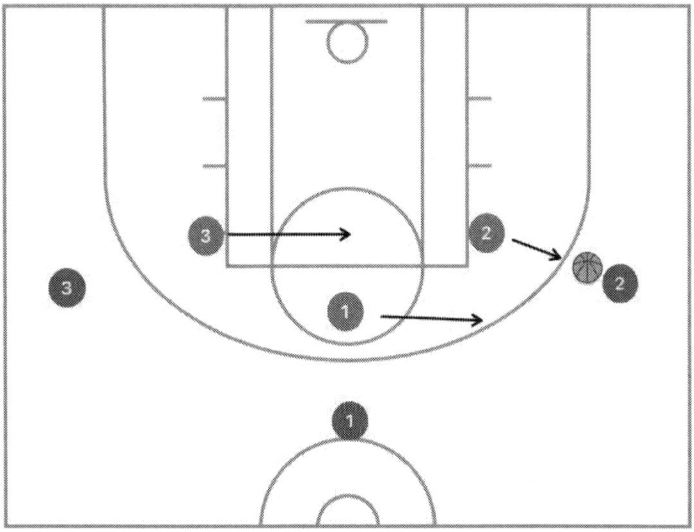
3
2
3
2
1
1

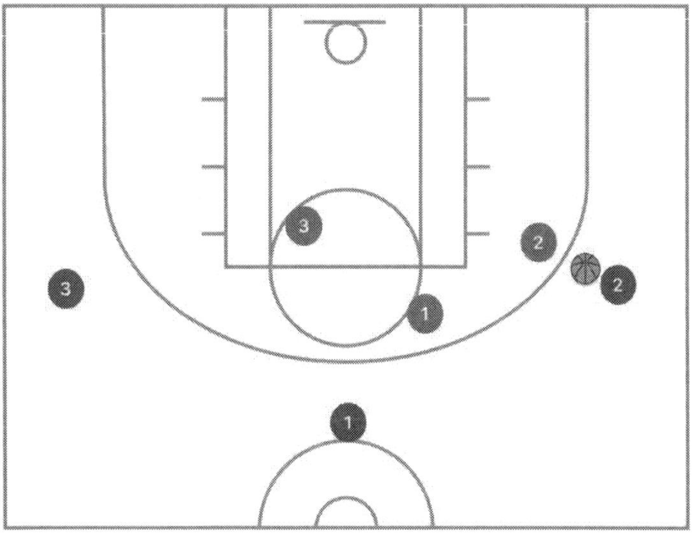
3
2
3
2
1
1

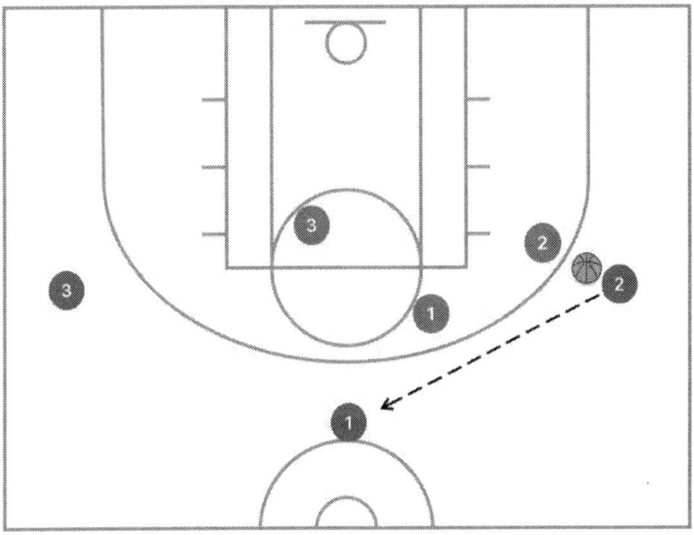
3
2
3
2
1
1

3
2
3
2
1
1

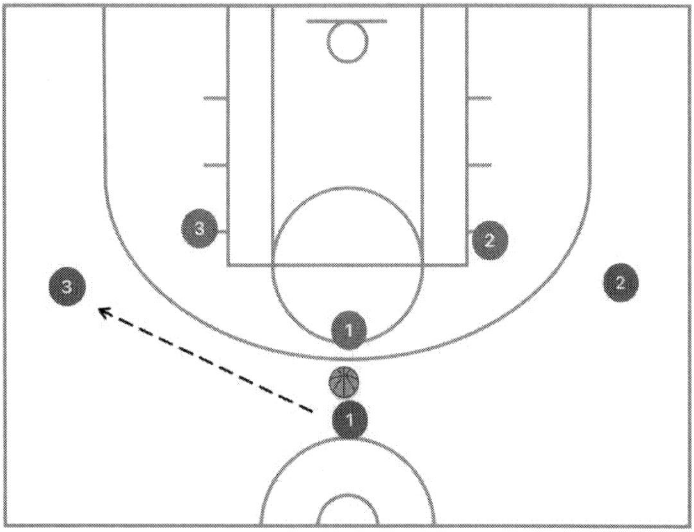
3
3
2
2
1
1

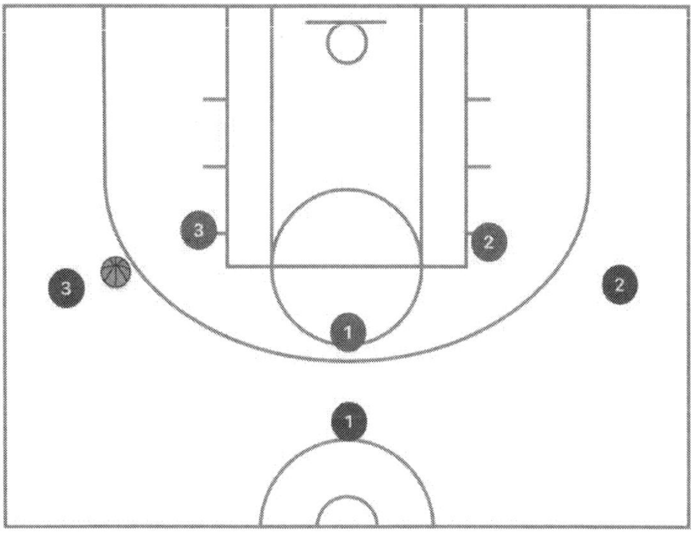
3
3
2
2
1
1

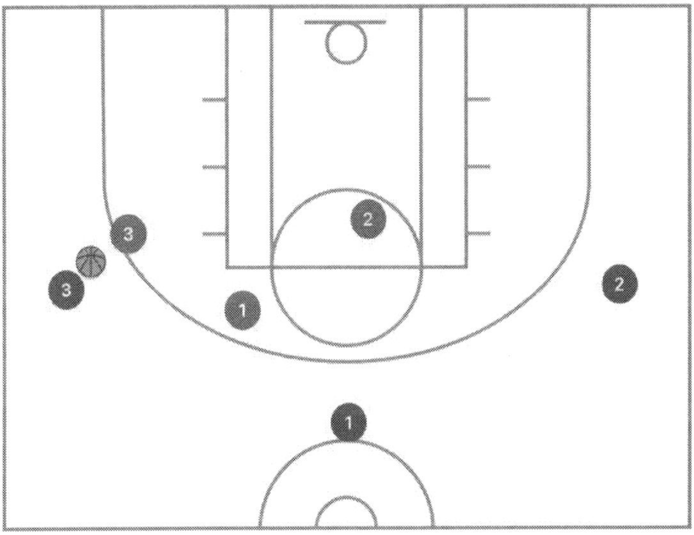

Focus

Positioning, closing out, and ball pressure.

Instructions

- The offensive players pass to each other
- Defenders must apply ball pressure to the offense with the ball
- Off-ball defenders must move into help positions within the pack line on the flight of ball

Three-on-Three Identity Game

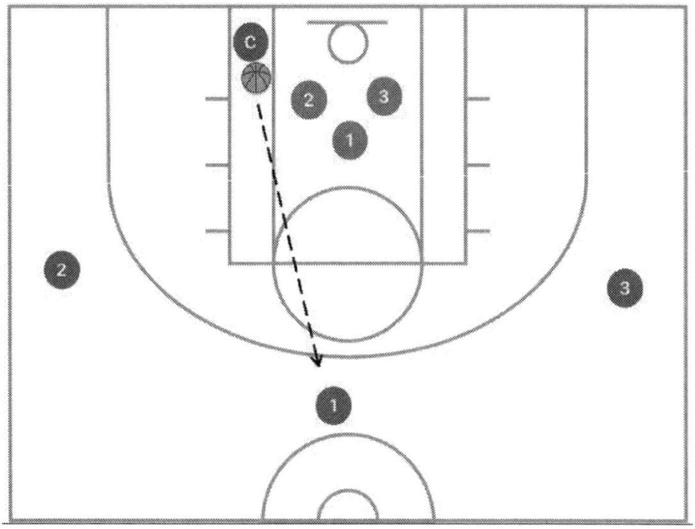

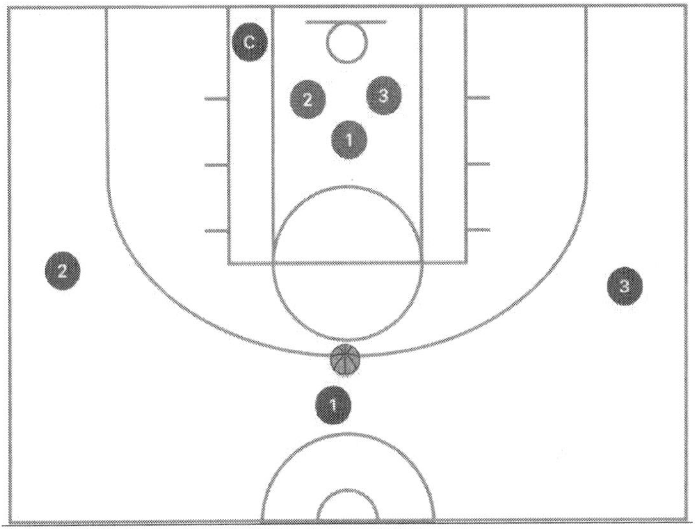
C
2
3
1
2
3
1

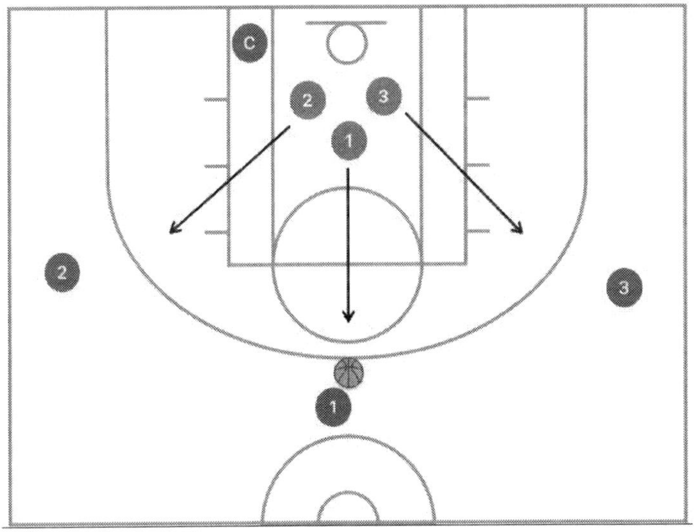
C
2
3
1
2
3
1

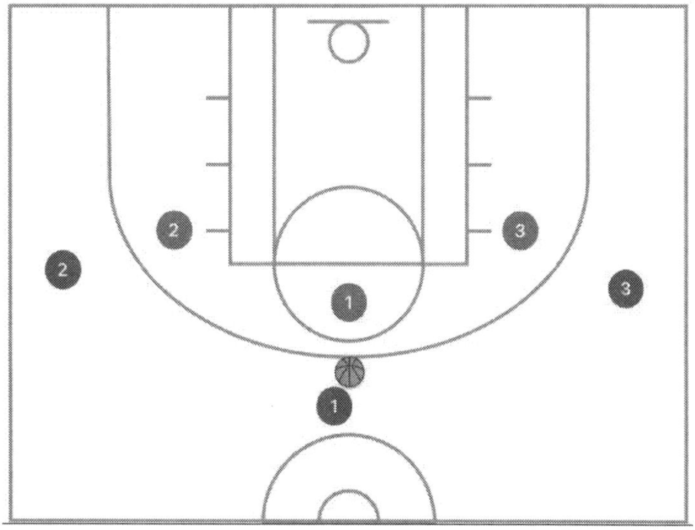

Focus

Tie in all the concepts of pack line into a small-sided game. Focus is to closeout properly and positioning, being in the help position early and staying within the pack line.

Instructions

- Coach is under basket and passes ball to one of the three offensive players
- Offense has 20 seconds to score
- Offense can do whatever they want to score, except ball screens
- Three dribble max per touch

Tips

- Early season practice: four-five possessions for each team
- In-season practice: two-three possessions for each team

Scoring

- Three point shot = +3
- Two point shot = +2
- Turnover = -1 for offense
- Foul = -1 for defense (still same possession)
- Off. Rebound = +2
- If the ball ever goes inside of the post box (not including an offensive rebound) this equals +2 (still same possession)

Four-on-Four Stationary Drill

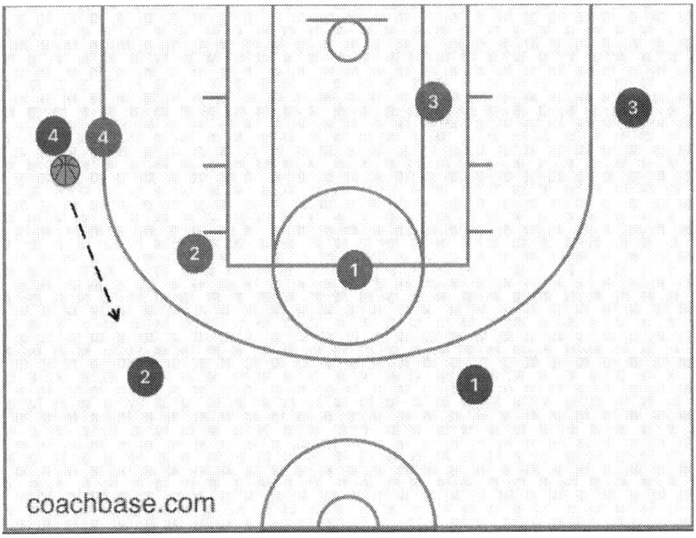

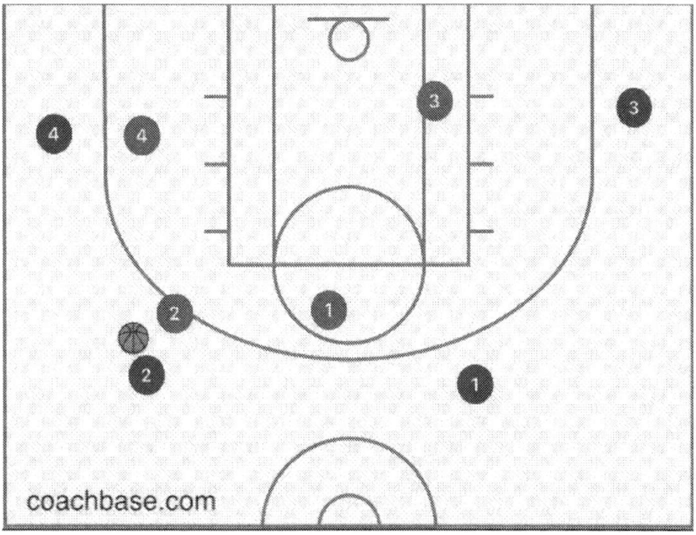
coachbase.com

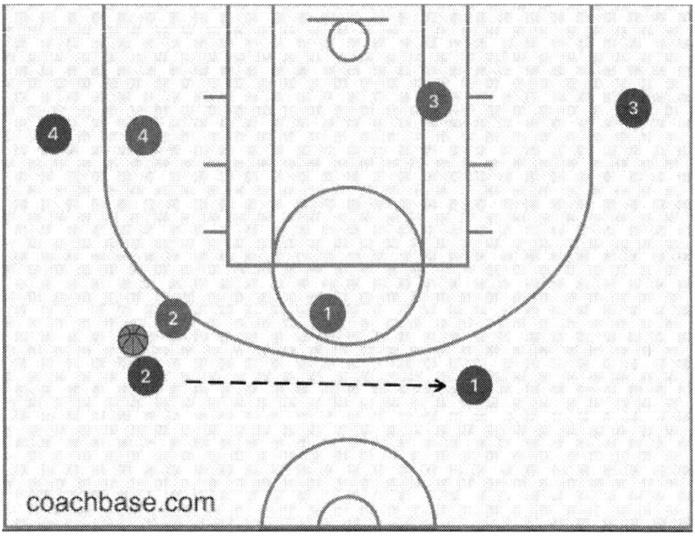
coachbase.com

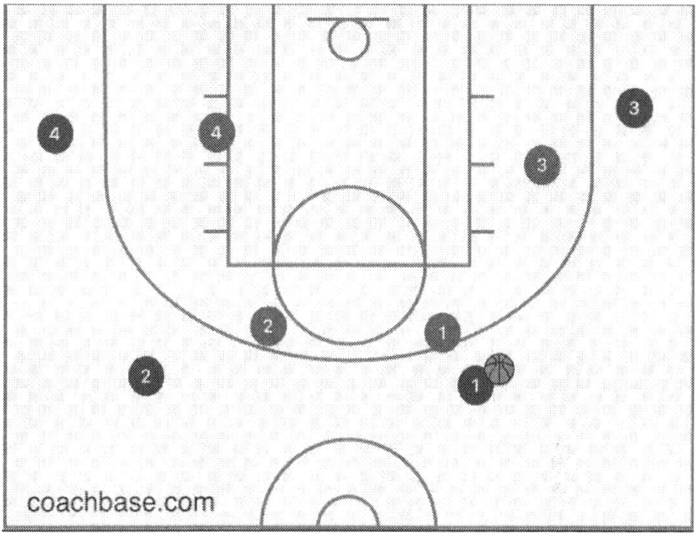
4
4
3
3
2
1
2
1
coachbase.com

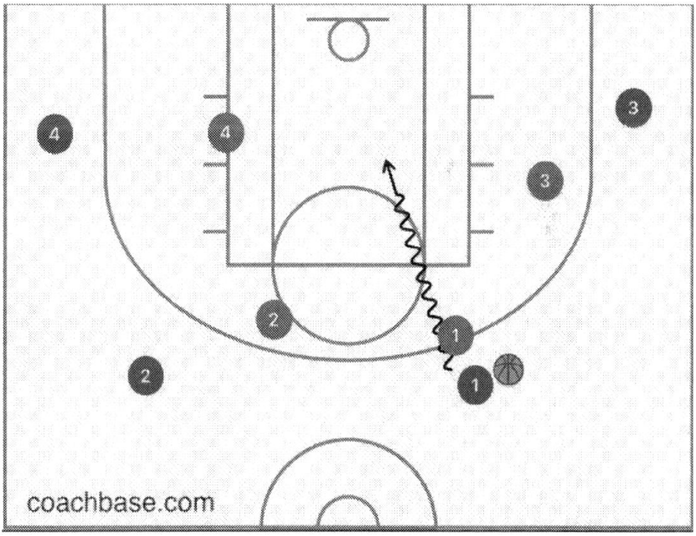
4
4
3
3
2
1
2
1
coachbase.com

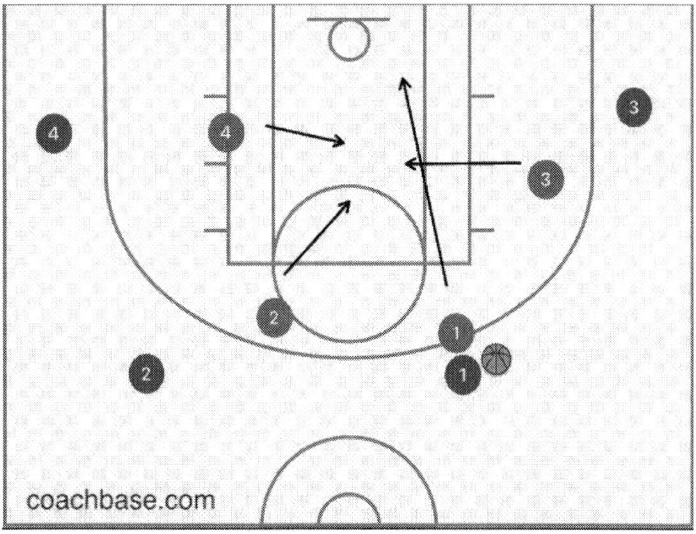
4
4
3
3
2
1
1
2
coachbase.com

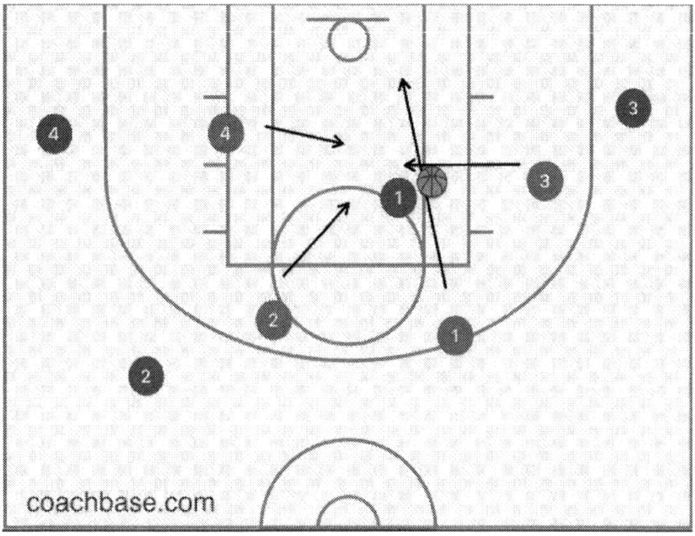
4
4
3
3
1
2
1
2
coachbase.com

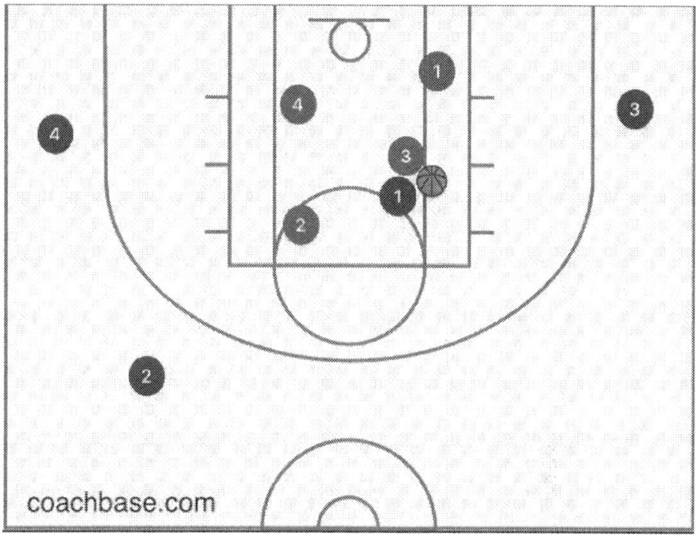

Shell drill to start. Pass the ball until coach yells "CHANGE." Offense drives to basket, on-ball defender must let offense pass and guard a new man. New defender must stop the ball while the other three must get into paint and communicate to find an open man.

Three-on-Three Get Back Drill

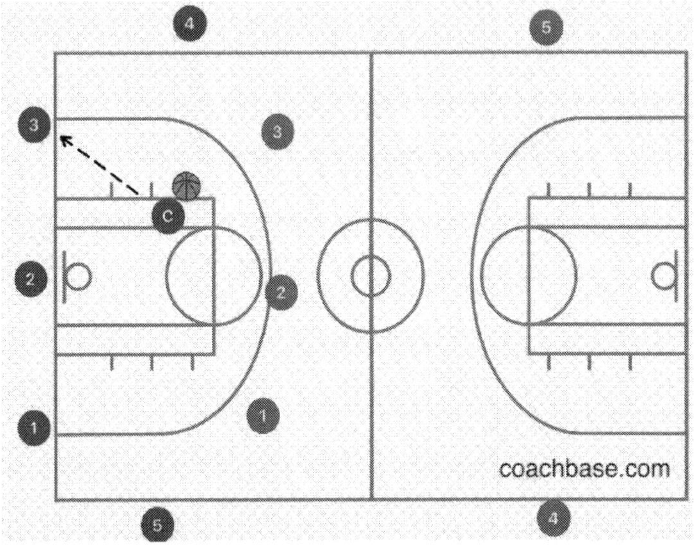
4
5
3
3
C
2
2
1
1
coachbase.com
5
4

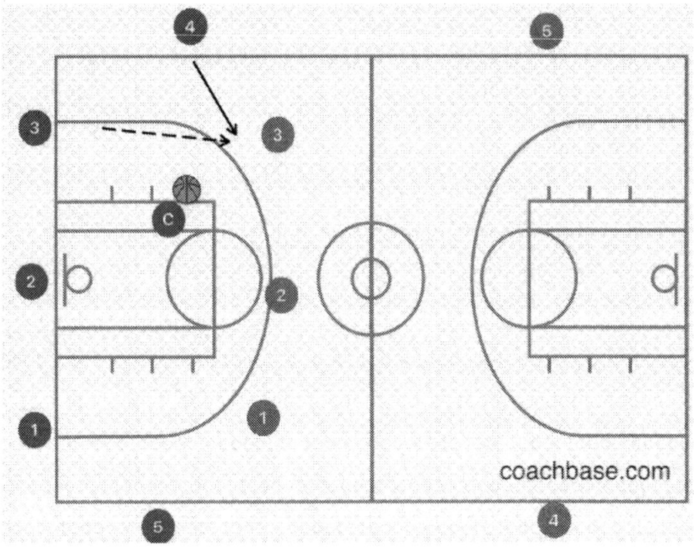
4
5
3
3
C
2
2
1
1
coachbase.com
5
4

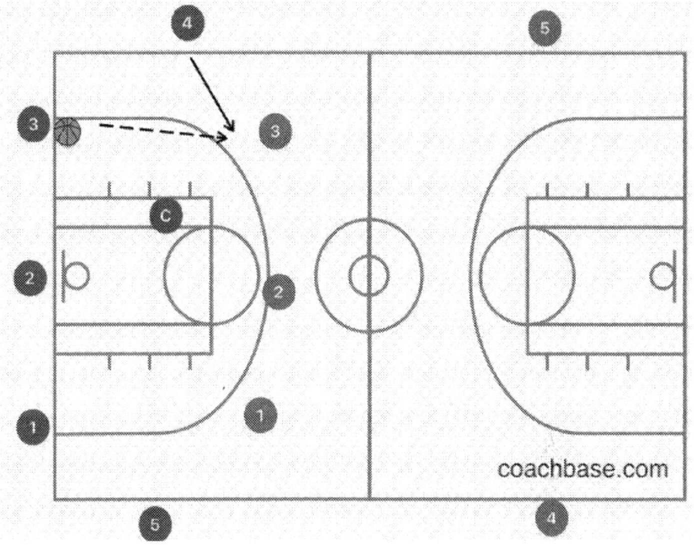
4
5
3
3
C
2
2
1
1
coachbase.com
5
4

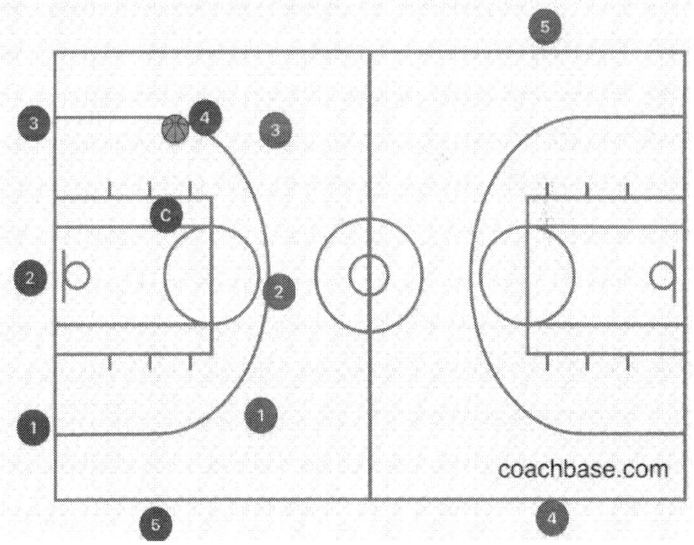
5
3
4
3
C
2
2
1
1
coachbase.com
5
4

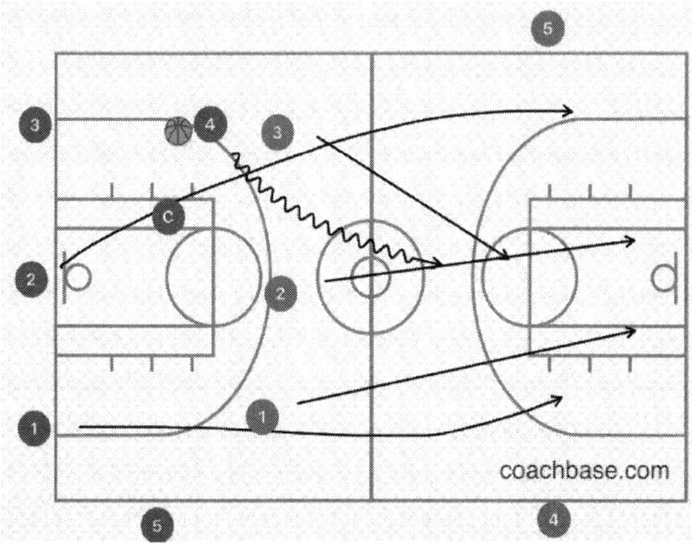
5
3
4
3
C
2
2
1
1
coachbase.com
5
4

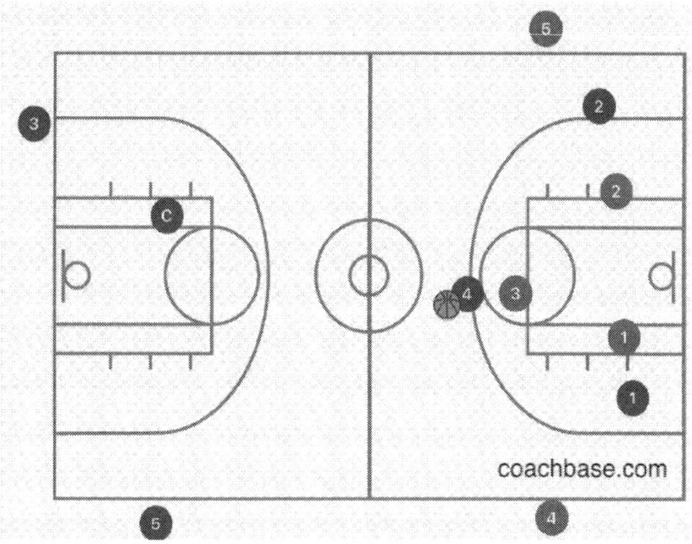
5
3
2
C
2
4
3
1
1
coachbase.com
5
4

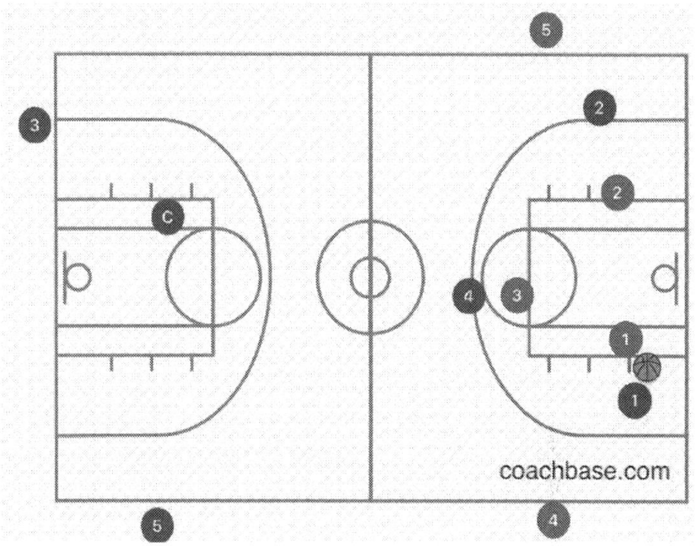

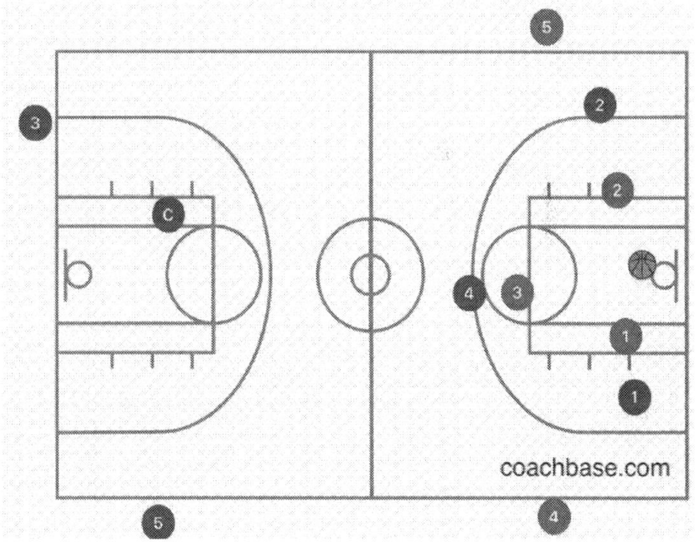

- Coach starts by throwing a pass to any of the three on the baseline

- Player who catches the ball outlets the ball to the player on the sideline
- Offense tries to score
- Defense must sprint, get to paint, and stop the ball

3/0 with 1/1 Inside

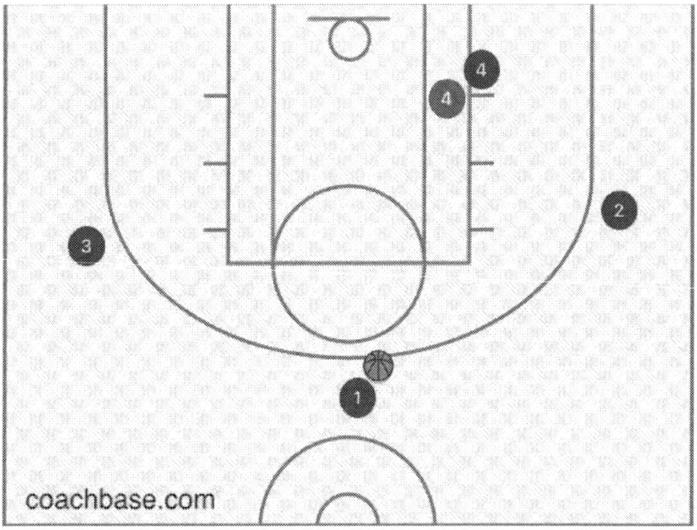

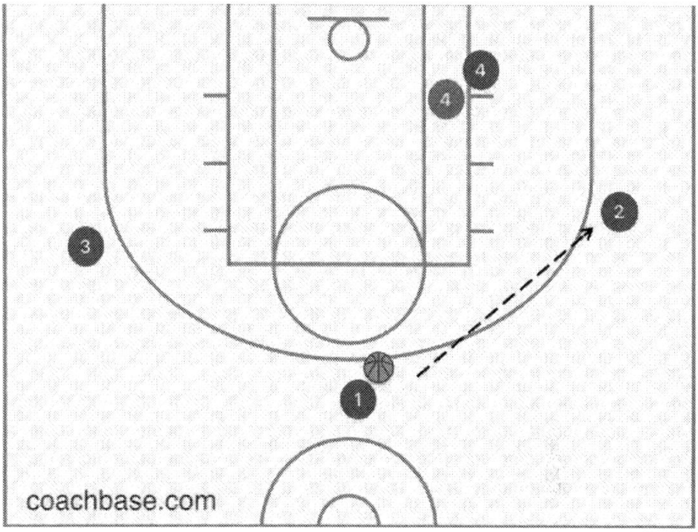
4
4
2
3
1
coachbase.com

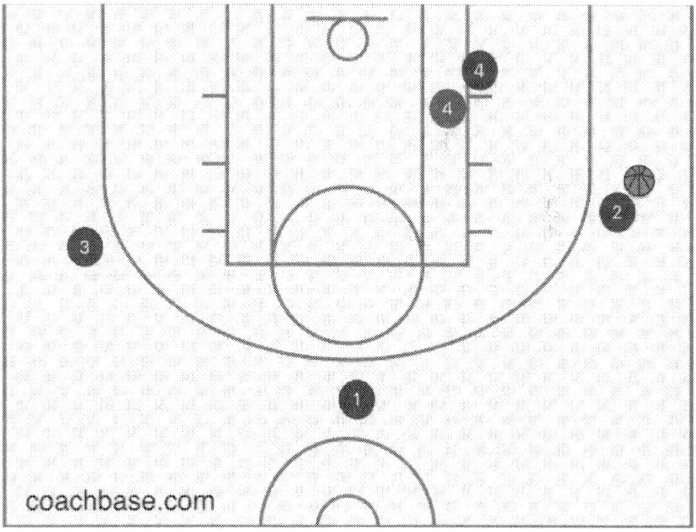
4
4
2
3
1
coachbase.com

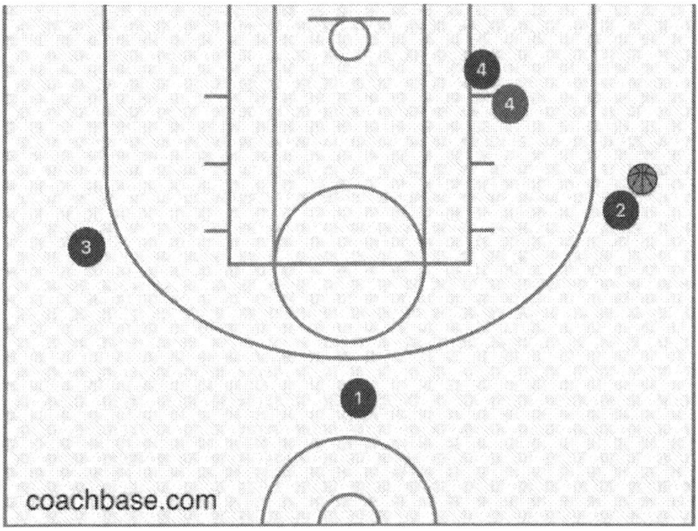
4
4
2
3
1
coachbase.com

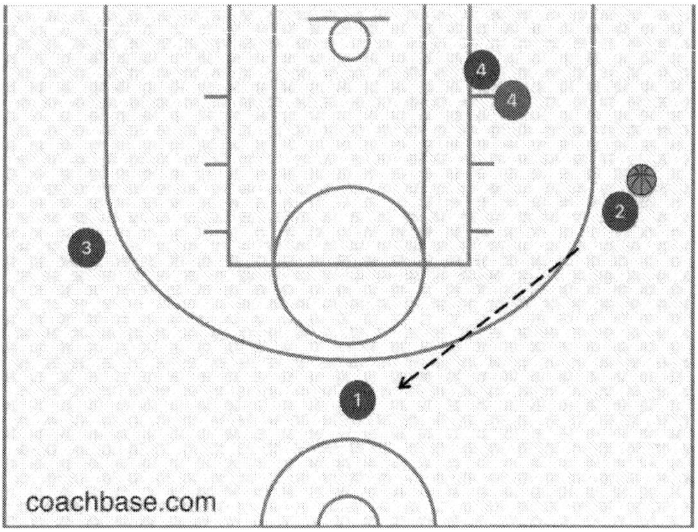
4
4
2
3
1
coachbase.com

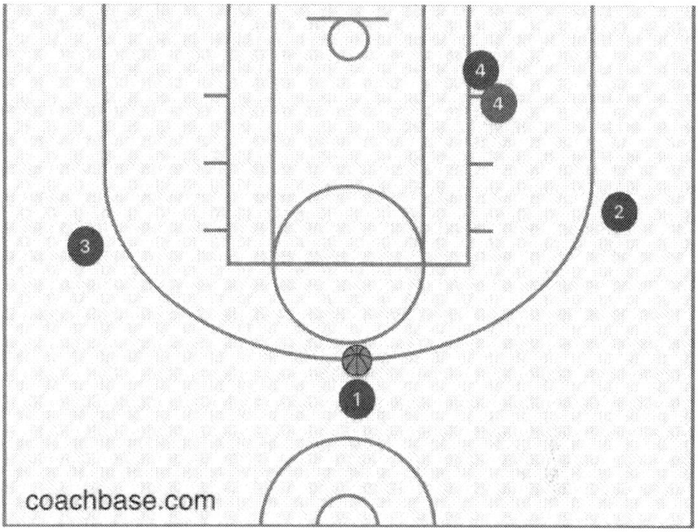

Ball is passed around the perimeter. May skip the ball. Post defender is working on positioning. Offensive post follows the ball.

Low-post Defense Key Points

- Keep players out of post box
- Use the arm bar to push your man out
- Three-quarters high deny when ball is above free throw
- Full deny below free throw

Three-on-Three with One-on-One Inside

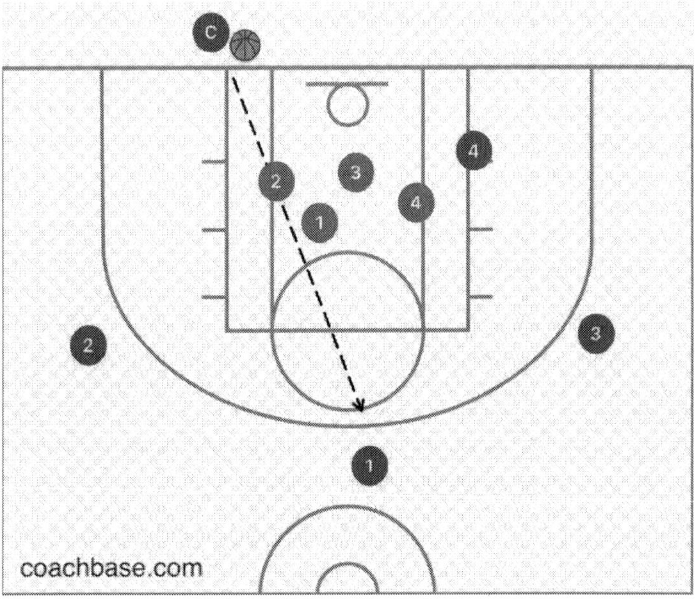

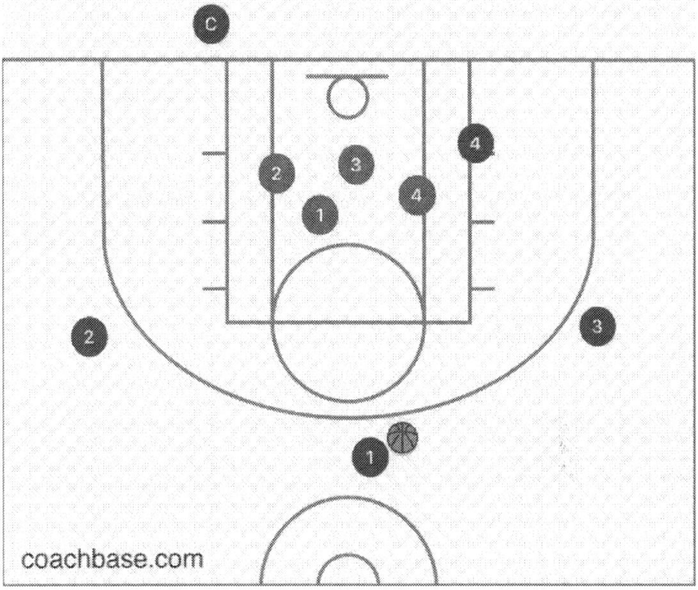
C
2
3
4
1
4
2
3
1
coachbase.com

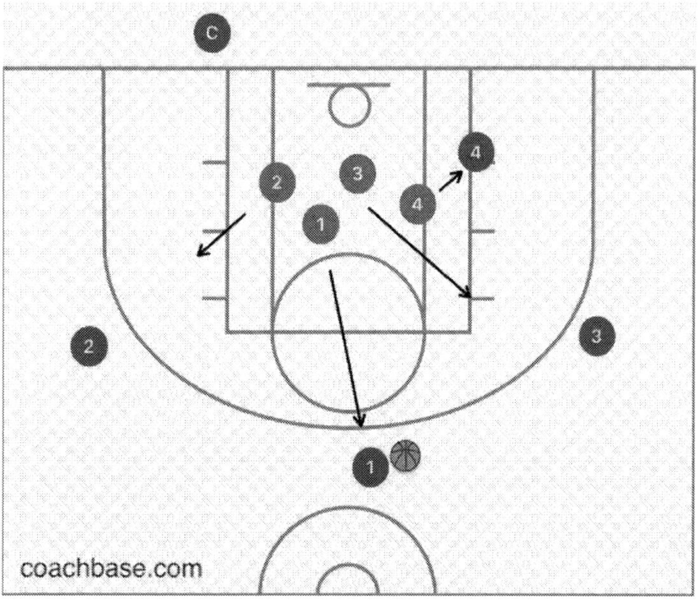
C
2
3
4
4
1
2
3
1
coachbase.com

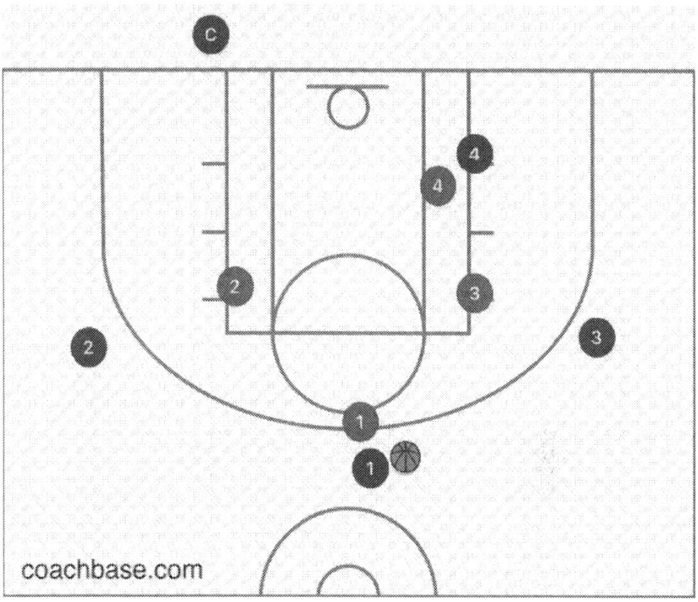
C
4
4
2
3
2
3
1
1
coachbase.com

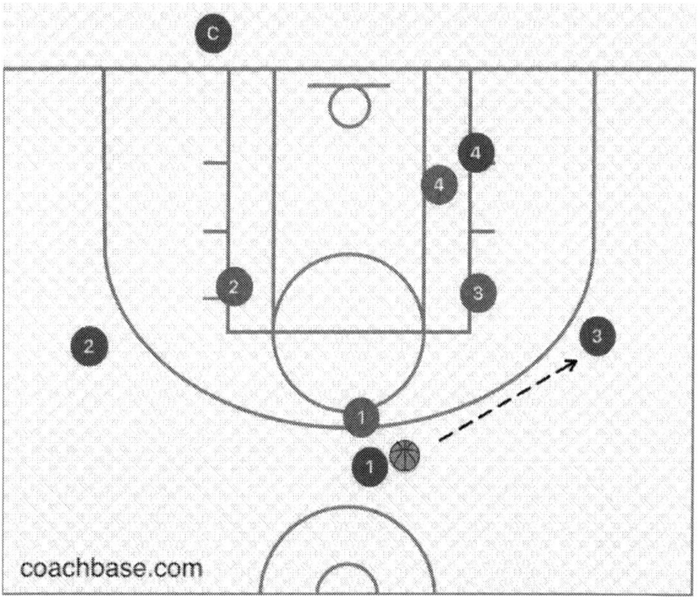
C
4
4
2
3
2
3
1
1
coachbase.com

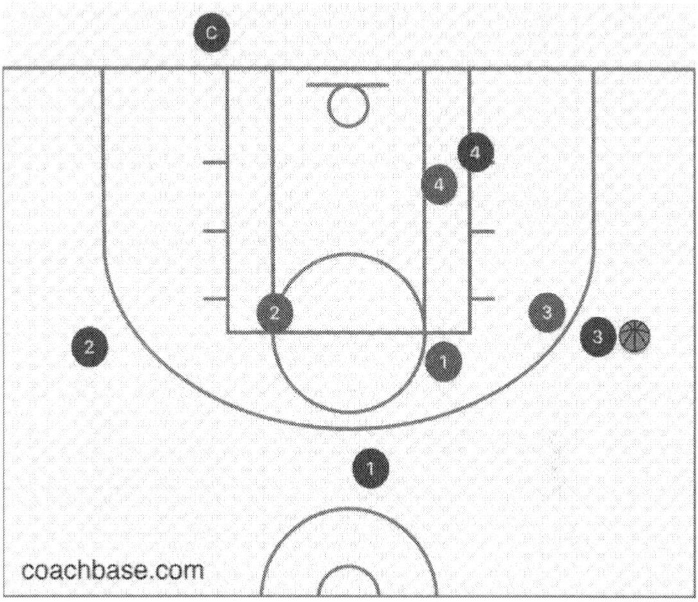
C
4
4
2
3
3
2
1
1
coachbase.com

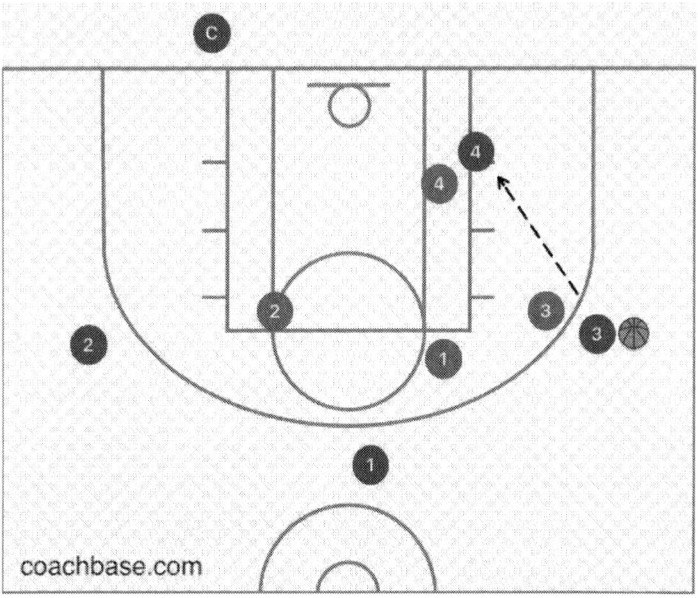
C
4
4
2
3
3
2
1
1
coachbase.com

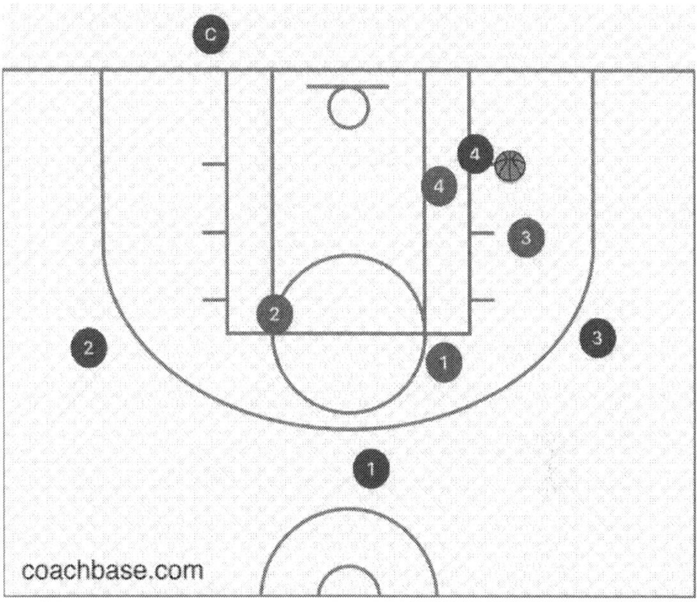
C
4
4
3
2
2
1
3
1
coachbase.com

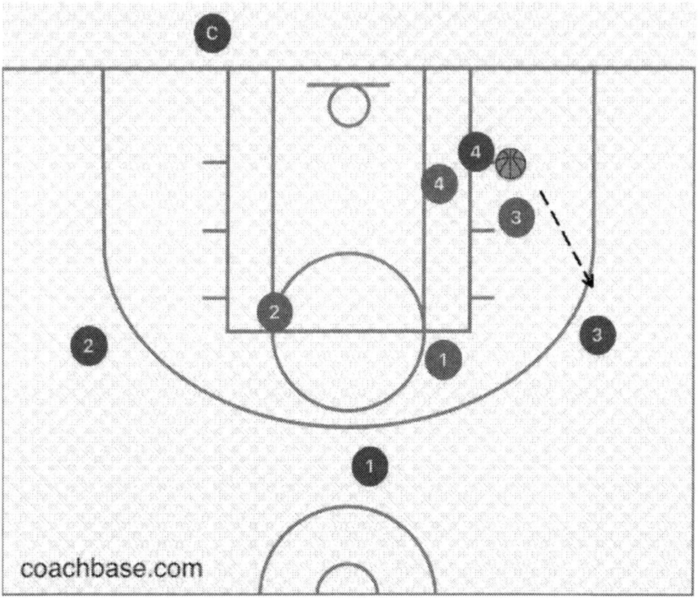
C
4
4
3
2
2
1
3
1
coachbase.com

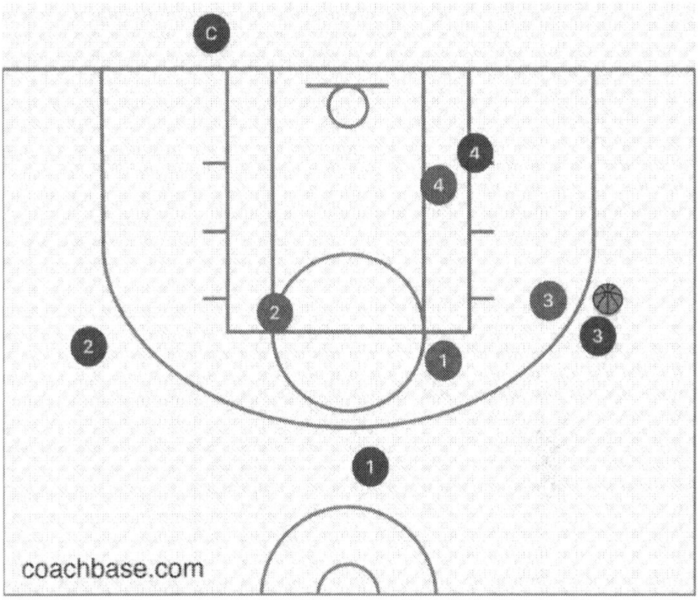
C
4
4
2
3
3
2
1
1
coachbase.com

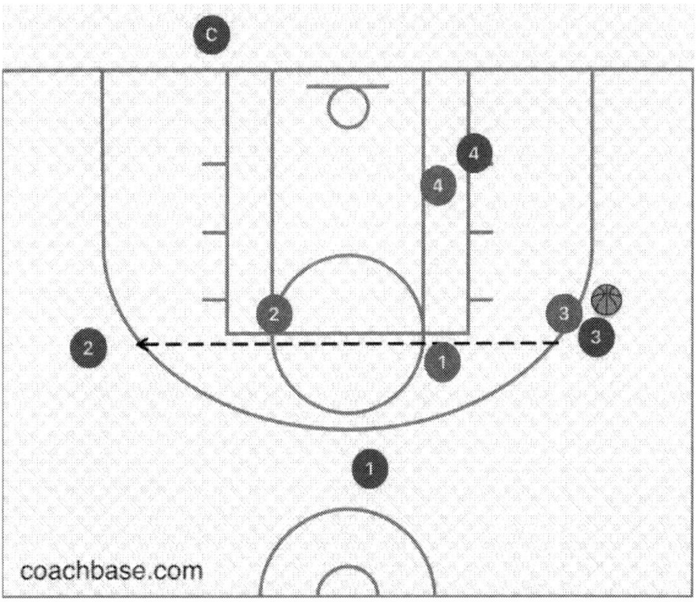
C
4
4
2
3
3
2
1
1
coachbase.com

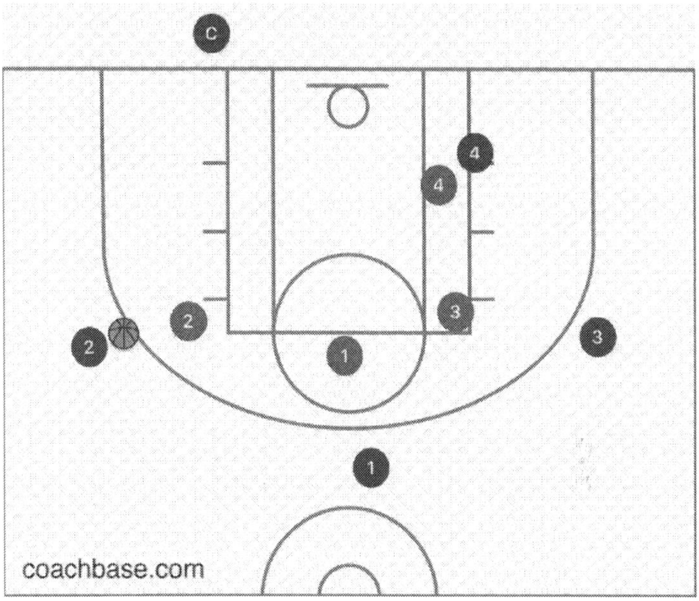
C
4
4
2
3
2
1
3
1
coachbase.com

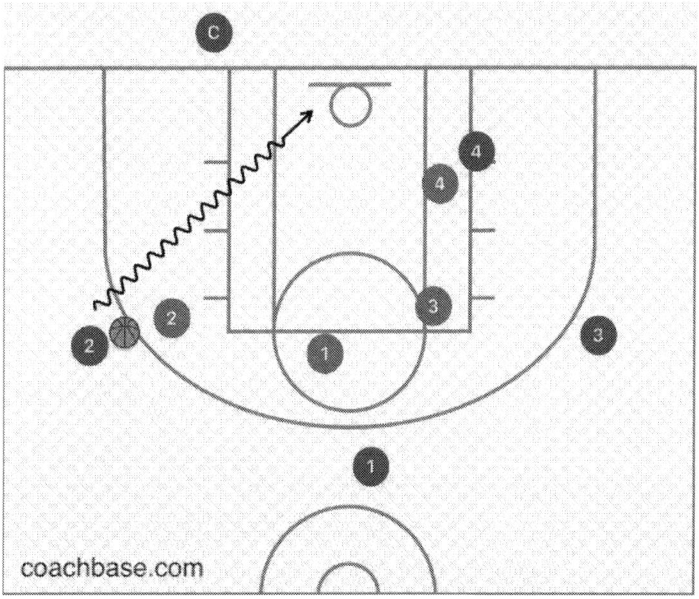

This drill focuses on choking the post when it gets entered into the post and then turning into a live four-on-four.

- Start with pass coach to one; defense closes out
- Offense must pass the ball to the wing
- Then the wing must pass the ball to low post
- Defense chokes the post, post throws ball back to wing
- Go live four-on-four

Defending Cross and Down Screens

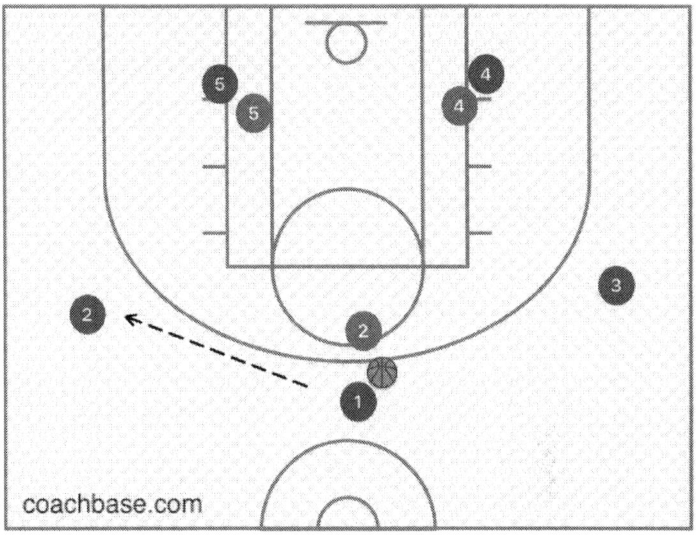
5
5
4
4
3
2
2
1
coachbase.com

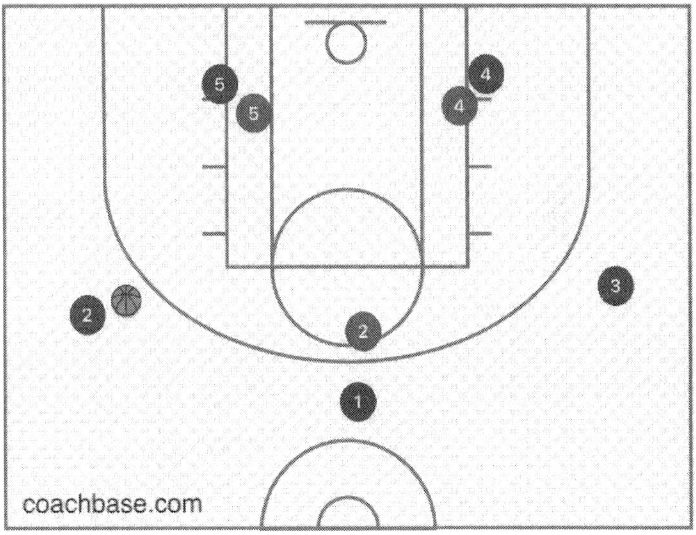
5
5
4
4
3
2
2
1
coachbase.com

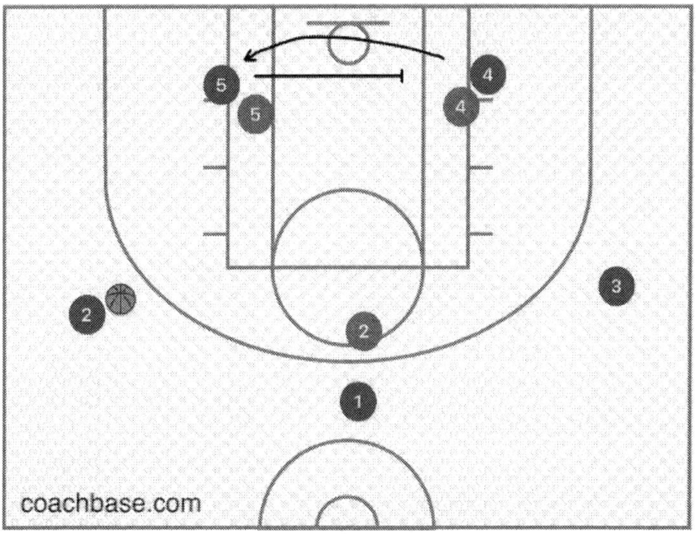
5
5
4
4
2
2
3
1
coachbase.com

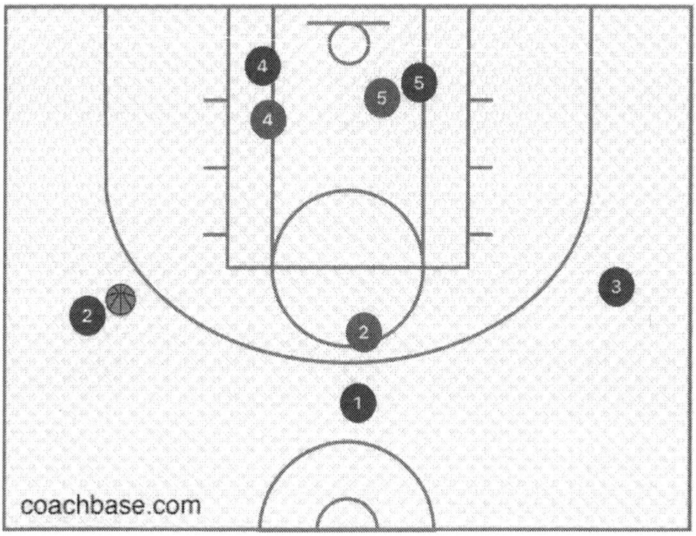
4
4
5
5
2
2
3
1
coachbase.com

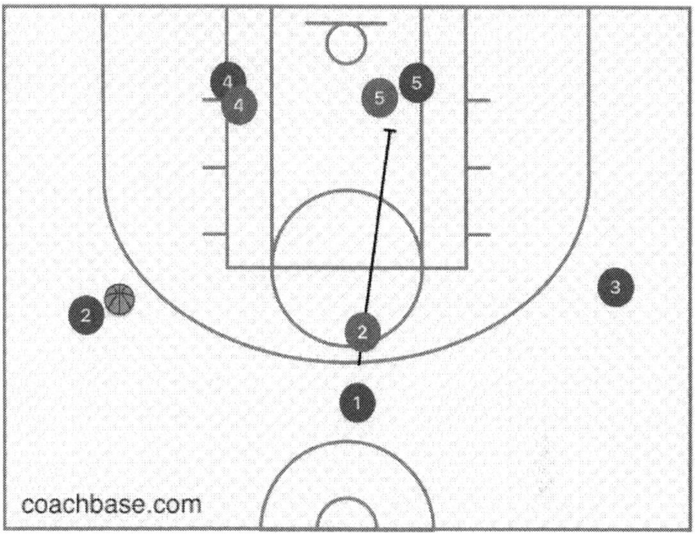
4
4
5
5
2
3
2
1
coachbase.com

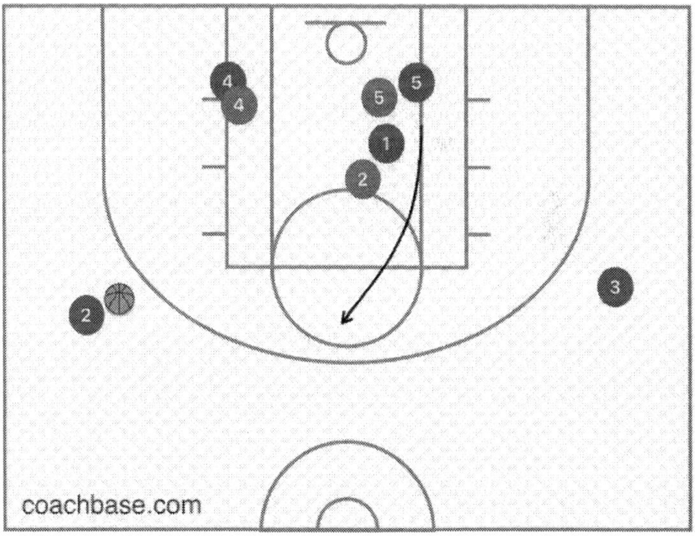
4
4
5
5
1
2
2
3
coachbase.com

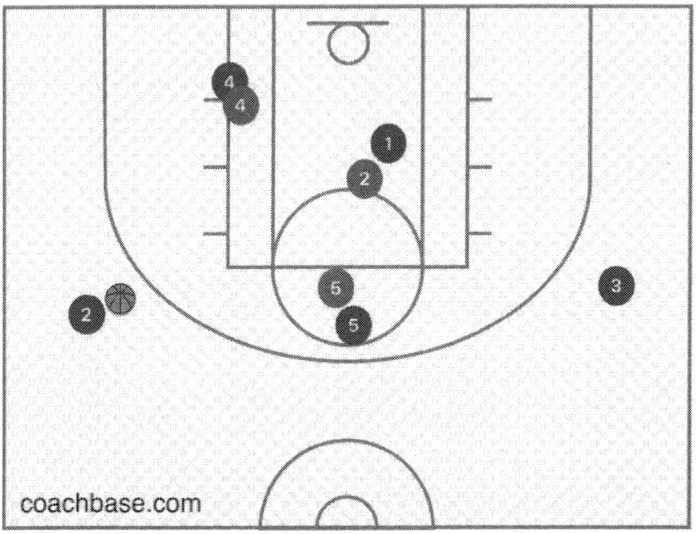

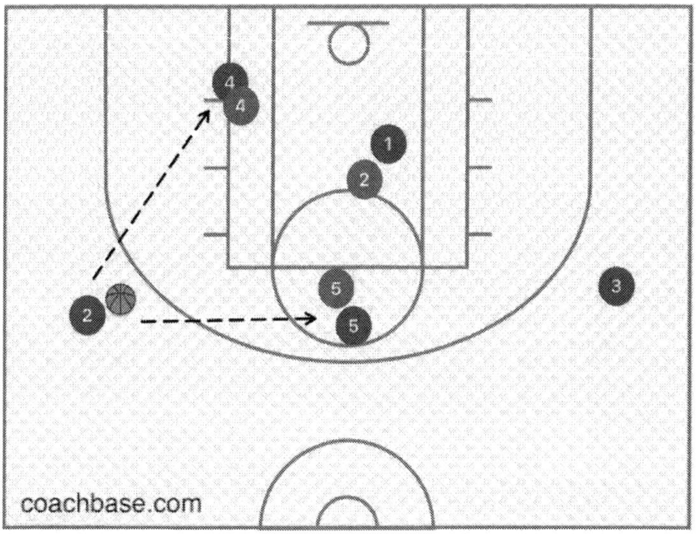

This drill is for defending cross and down screens.

- Two coaches on the wing, one player at the top and two players in low post
- Ball goes to coach on wing. Players can cross screen or down screen for each other
- Once ball is passed to a player, go live

Focus

You need to talk about how you want to cover your screens. Go over or under.

5

Man-to-Man (Denial) Defense

Denial defense is the opposite of pack-line defense. Its principle lies in the assumption that the defender can guard their opponent. The two key rules that reflect this are the 'no middle rule' and 'no help defender one pass away rule.' The advantage of a denial defense is that it is higher pressure than the pack line defense, leading to potentially more turnovers and better defense against long-range shots.

Man-to-man defense is great for youth teams because the skills are highly transferable to higher levels. In this defense, the defender is largely accountable for defending one opposition player but there will also be some help in the form of switches. The downside is that unlike a zone, you won't be able to hide weaker players.

Denial Defense Rules

There are five key rules:

1. No Middle Penetration

When the opponent is at the wing or at the top of the key, you must drive them baseline or sideline. No middle penetration is allowed.

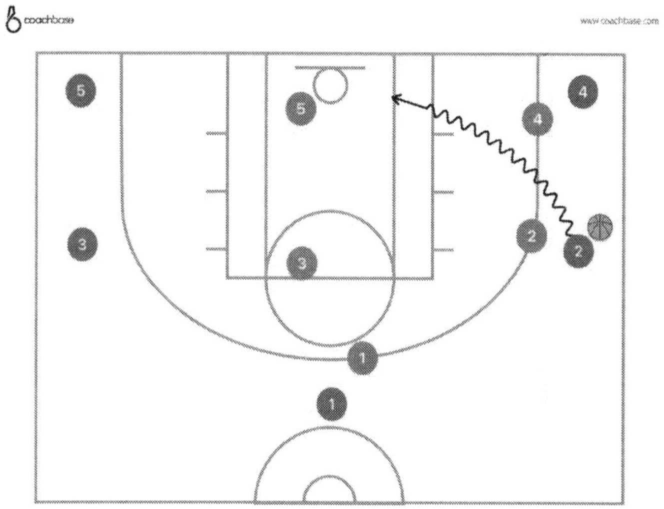

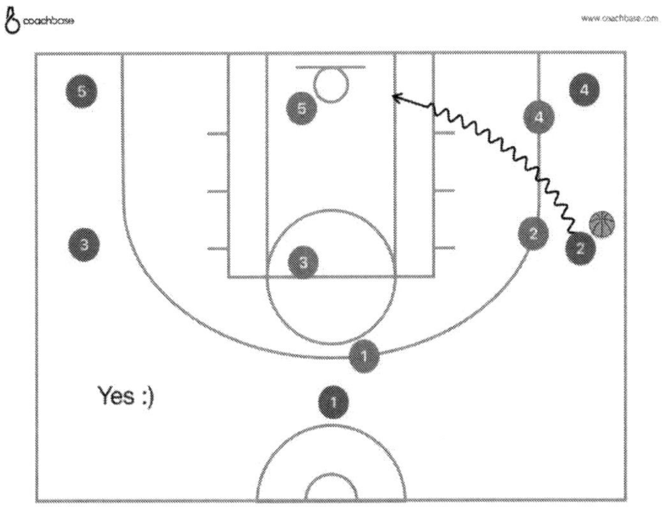
coachbase
www.coachbase.com
Yes :)

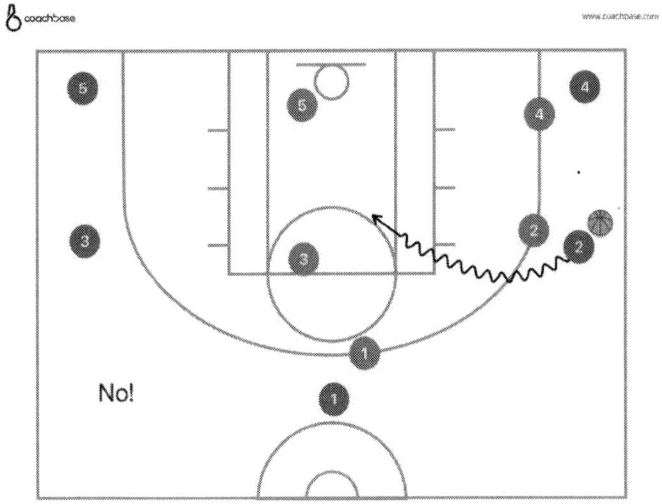
coachbase
www.coachbase.com
No!

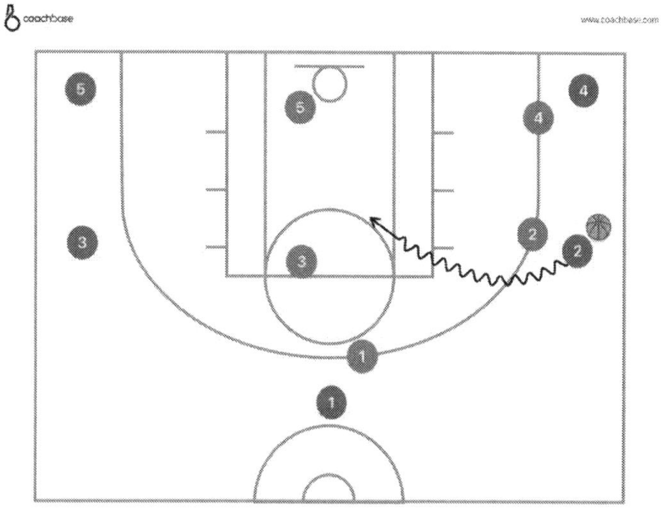

Why don't we allow middle? It is because there's help one pass away and the help defender has to come from two passes away. If the dribbler gets to the middle, it's easier to find the open man from that position than the sideline or baseline. That is why you'll see players like Chris Paul purposely getting to the middle so that have more options to pass.

The simplest way to enforce this is to teach your players to position their hips to drive the opponent to the sideline or baseline.

2. No Ball-Reversals

Since the defense shifts when the ball shifts, ball reversals will expose a lot of gaps on offense while the defense is catching up. That is why it is paramount your players deny the ball one pass away. Denial in this context means they put a hand up between the ball handler and the player they are guarding.

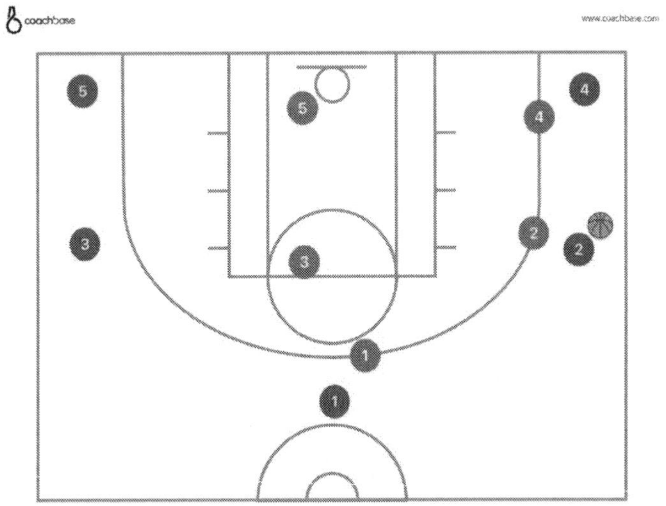

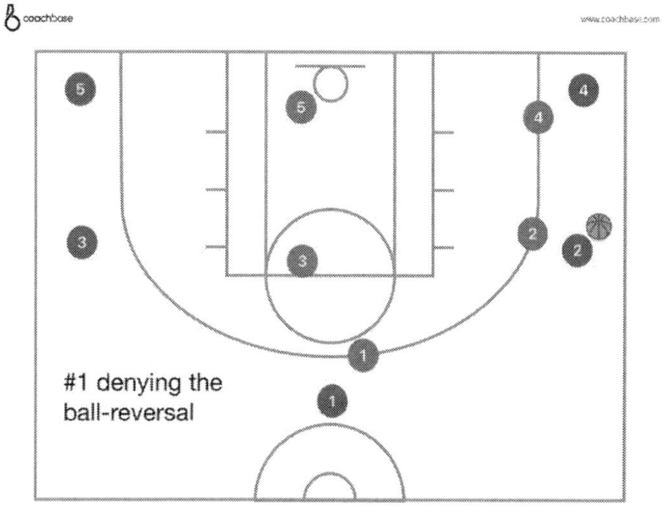
coachbase
www.coachbase.com
5
5
4
4
3
2
2
3
1
#1 denying the
ball-reversal
1

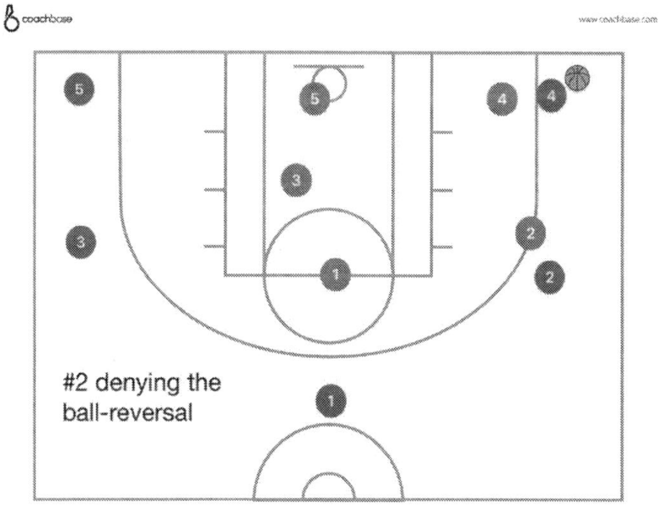
coachbase
www.coachbase.com
5
5
4
4
3
3
2
2
1
#2 denying the
ball-reversal
1

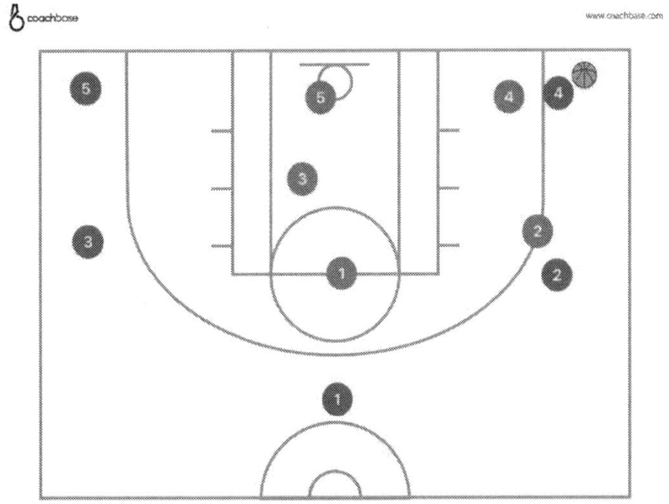

3. No Help from Defenders One Pass Away

This is the biggest difference between the pack-line defense and the man-to-man defense.

In the pack-line defense (which I often recommend), the players one pass away from the ball are helping in the driving lanes by taking away dribble penetration. This allows the ball to be passed around the perimeter.

In man-to-man defense, since the players one pass away from the ball are denying the pass to their player, this leaves driving lanes open and means the on-ball defender is more accountable for keeping the player with the basketball out of the lane.

If an opposition player does attempt to drive down the middle, the player one pass away can quickly ‘stunt’ in their direction to get the offensive player to pick up the dribble, but they can never fully help.

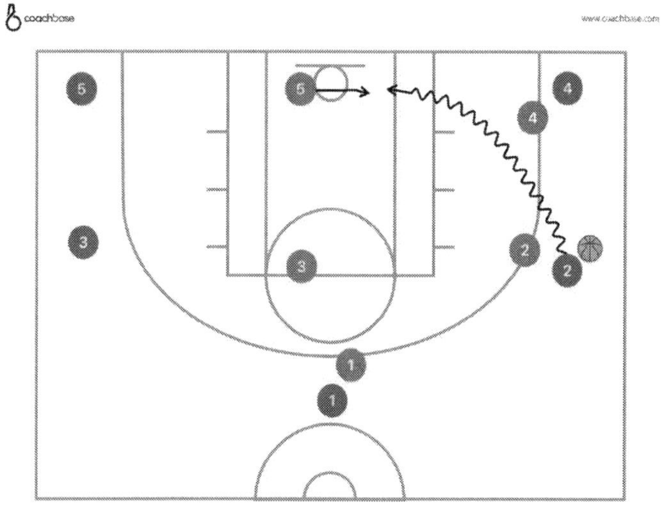

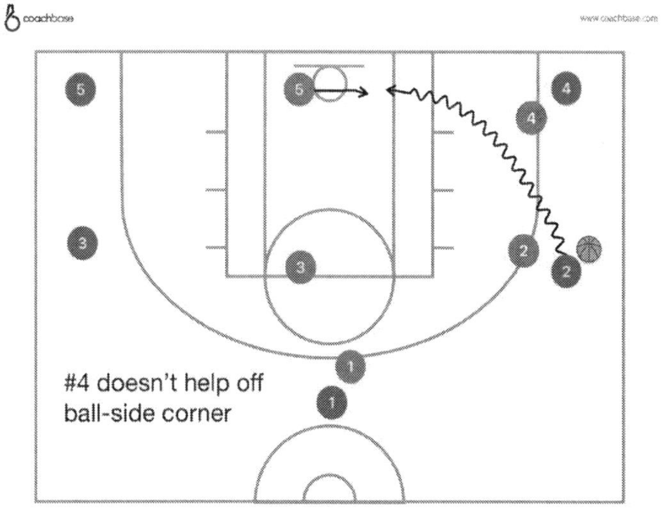

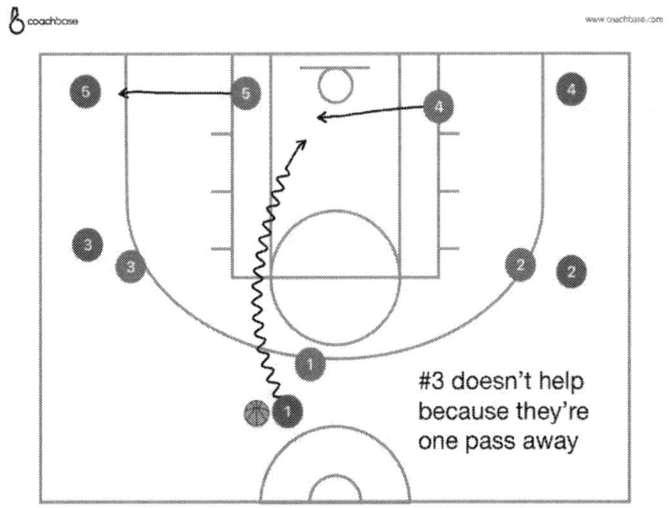

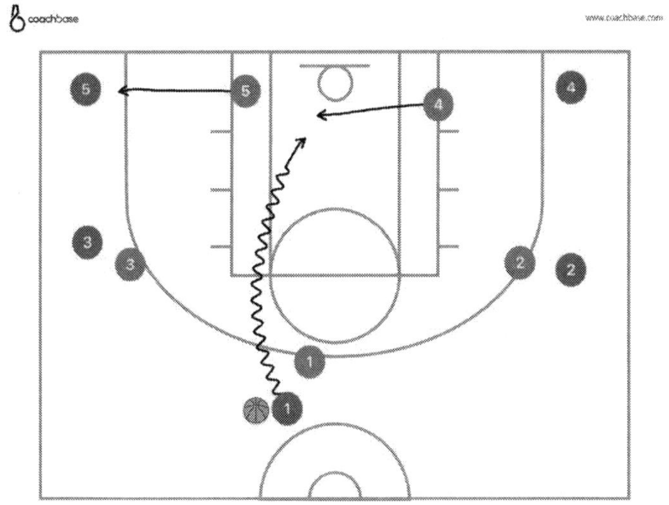

If they do, it will often lead to an in-rhythm jumper or an offensive drive after a difficult closeout.

4. No Face Cuts

A defensive player must never allow their opponent to cut across their face in between them and the ball. The 'no face cuts' rule will most commonly occur when the offense performs a 'pass-and-cut.'

When an offensive player makes a pass to a teammate (they will still happen even if we're denying them), the player defending the passer must immediately 'jump to the ball' to force their opponent to cut behind them instead of in front.

This rule is also important when playing defense off the ball to stop players from flashing to the ball to receive a pass.

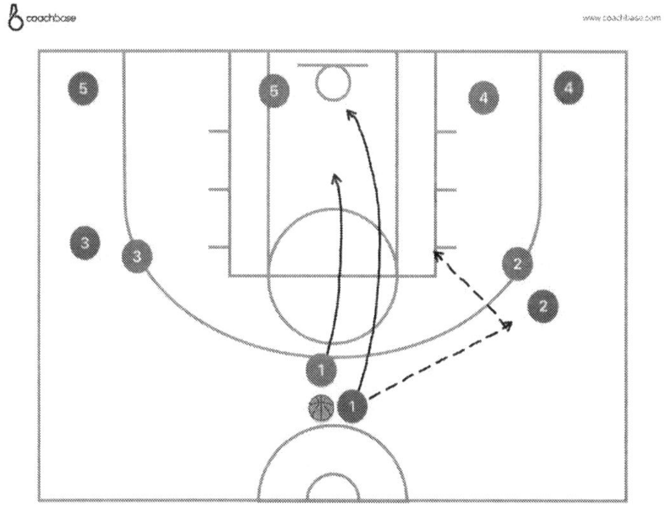

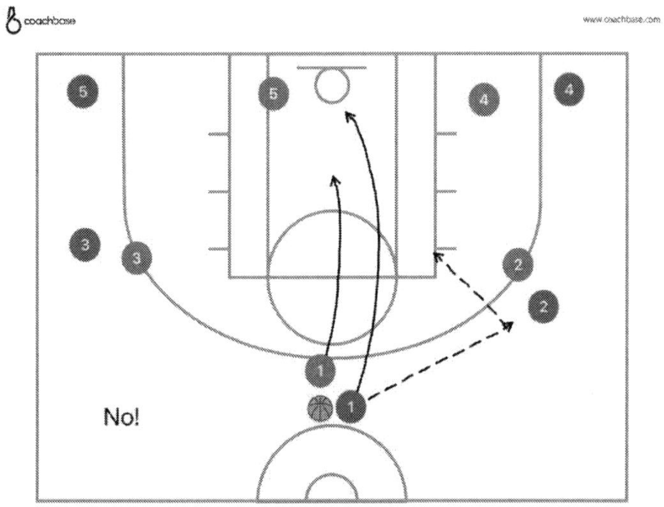
coachbase
www.coachbase.com
5
5
4
4
3
3
2
2
1
1
No!

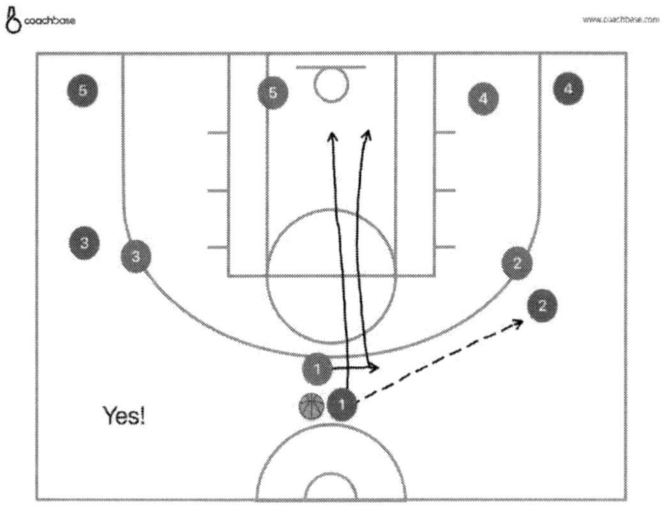
coachbase
www.coachbase.com
5
5
4
4
3
3
2
2
1
1
Yes!

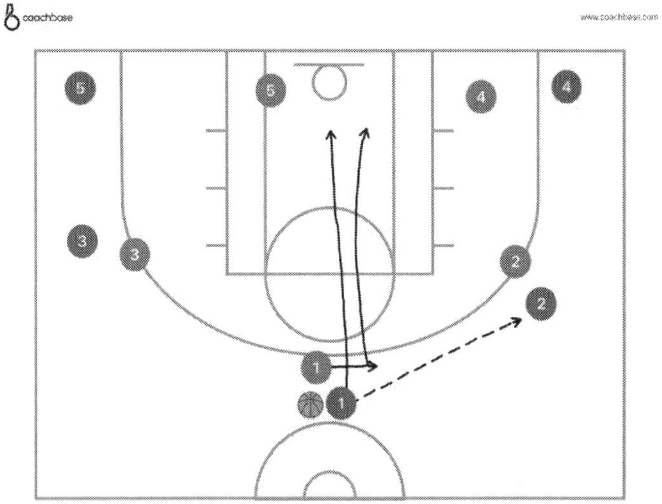

To put it simply, a defender must always stay between their man and the basketball whenever they're playing off-ball defense.

5. Move When the Ball Moves

The final rule is to ensure that players are playing correct off-ball defense. Whenever the basketball moves, every defensive player on the court should be adjusting their positioning. This means they need to deny when the ball is one pass away and go to the help position (halfway between ball and their man) when two pass away.

By keeping the importance of this in mind, players will learn that they must stay alert at all times and anticipate passes that they may be able to deflect.

As the great Don Meyer puts it: "Positioning, anticipation, and technique create quickness. Therefore, you can always get quicker."

This is incredibly important because the difference between a steal and an open layup or a missed steal and a breakdown of the defense can be a fraction of a second.

Man-to-Man Defense Positioning Basics

There are three positions you can be in when you're on the court playing man-to-man defense:

1. On-ball defense
2. Deny defense
3. Help defense

In this section I'm going to talk about each of them in detail and what's required of a player when they're in each role. Each player understanding all of these roles is crucial to good team defense. Being out of position by even a small amount can be the difference between blocking a shot or giving an easy layup. Positioning is everything.

On-ball Defense

The role of the on-ball defender in a man-to-man defense is to contain the offensive player while influencing them toward the sideline and baseline. While containment is the ultimate goal regardless of where the ball is on the floor, if the defensive player is going to get beat, we want it to be toward the baseline instead of the middle. This is why the on-ball defender slightly overplays the middle.

It's imperative that all defenders on the court have the ability to contain their man consistently. If not, dribble penetration will break down your defense very quickly. In fact, I never encourage on-ball defenders to reach in for steals unless the offensive player mishandles the basketball. There is a far higher chance of them getting called for a foul than getting a steal.

Here are the five keys to playing great on-ball defense:

1. Desire to Be a Great Defender

The biggest differentiator between a great defender and an average defender is that a great defender *wants* to be a great defender.

A player with this desire is willing to stay down in a stance the entire possession, chase their opponent around the court, dive on any loose basketball to gain possession, and take a charge if they're in the proper position to do so, etc.

2. Stay in a Balanced Stance

An on-ball defender must stay in a balanced stance at all times so that they're ready to react to the offensive player as quickly as possible. This means they should stay low, keep their chest up, and place an even amount of weight on each leg.

1. Slightly overplay the middle to force the offensive player sideline or baseline
2. The player defending on the basketball should have their head in line with the opponent's shoulder on the side you don't want them to drive
3. Keep an arm's length distance at all times
4. The defender should be able to stick out their arm full length in front of them and just be able to touch the player they're defending
5. Keep your eyes on the opponent's chest
6. It's very easy for an offensive player to fake with their head, eyes, or body. The spot on a player that is most difficult to fake with is their chest.

One Pass Away - Denial Defense

Any player one pass away from the basketball should be in a denial stance to deter any pass to their player. A denying defender should have one hand and one foot in the passing lane at all times, their chest should be facing their direct opponent, and they should be looking over their lead shoulder to see both the basketball and their man. This is important to note because I see far too many coaches teaching their players 'ball-you-man' stance when one pass away.

The reason this is the wrong stance is because if your opponent was to suddenly backdoor cut, the denial defender would need to do a full 180-degree turn to defend it. However, if your defender backdoor cuts when your chest is toward the player and you have a hand and leg in the passing lane, all it requires is the defender flicking their head around and the sliding in the deny position toward the rim.

The purpose of this is that we want to remove all easy passing options from the player with the basketball. This is why the man-to-man defense is an aggressive defense.

The distance a denial player should be from their man will depend on the distance the offensive player is away from the basketball. A good rule of thumb would be close enough to ensure you can close the distance and pick off the pass if a lob is thrown over the top.

Once again, the three keys to great denial defense are:

1. One hand and foot in the passing lane
2. Chest toward your direct opponent
3. Eyes over lead shoulder to see both

Two Passes Away - Help Defense

Any defender two or more passes away from the basketball is playing help defense. This requires the defender to be in a 'ball-you-man' stance. This means that the defender is pointing one hand at their opponent and one hand at the basketball. They must be able to see both with their peripheral vision at all times.

The position of a help defender will vary depending on where the basketball is on the court and where their direct opponent is on the court at that time. When the basketball is on the weakside and below the free-throw line, the players two passes away will often be in either 'high-I' or 'low-I.'

This is an important concept to understand so I'll give you a brief introduction here. When the basketball is on either of the wings or in one of the corners, there should always be two help defenders with at least one foot on the split line (the line down the middle of the court).

1. *A help defender close to the rim in the paint (low-I)*
2. *A help defender near the free-throw line (high-I)*

By establishing these two help defenders, it makes it much easier for the defensive players to understand their roles and rotations on drives to the rim by opposition players. Here are a few diagrams to give you an example:

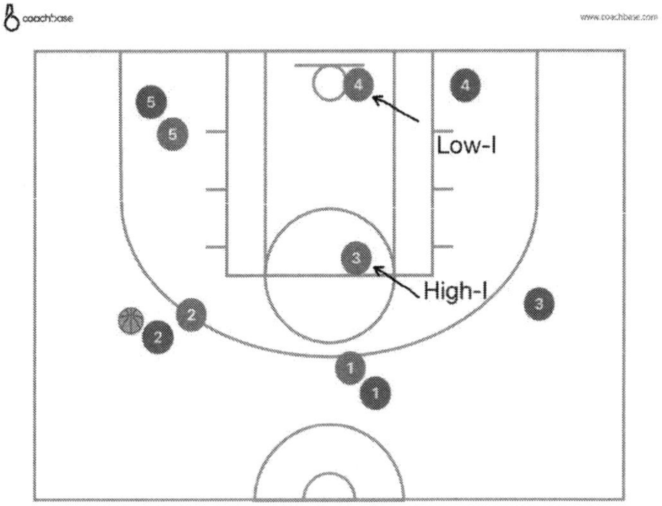

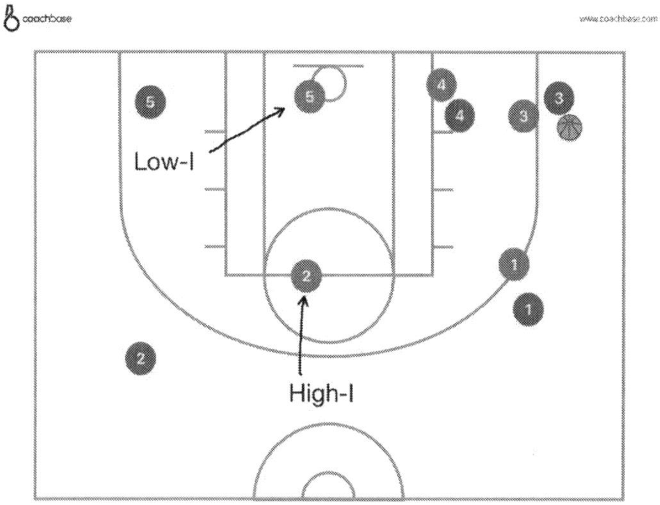

How to Run the Man to Man defense

Now let's get into how your team will actually run the man-to-man defense during a game! First, I'll talk about the positions the players should be in when the ball is in different areas of the court. After that, I'll break down what rotations must occur on the floor when there is dribble penetration from the offensive team.

Basketball Top of the Key

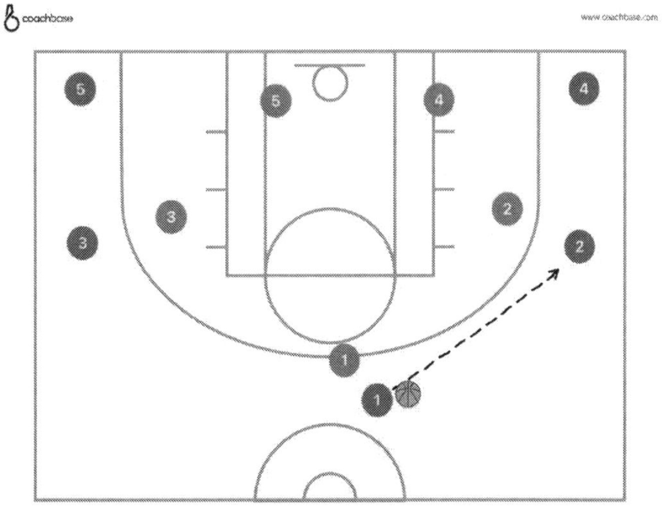

Whenever the basketball is within the lane lines at the top of the key, the team has one goal: get it out of there! As soon as the basketball is dribbled over the half-court line, the point guard defender (x one) immediately starts forcing the dribbler to the sideline by angling their defensive stance.

At the same time, the wing defenders (x two and x three) pinch in and allow the pass to be made to a player on the wing. (Note: when the basketball is at the top of the key this is the only time that players one pass away and don't deny the pass.)

As for the help defenders (x four and x five), both of them have a foot on their respective lane line. The goal when the ball is at the top is to get the basketball committed to one side of the court. This can happen either with the point guard dribbling to one side or passing to a player on the wing.

Let me take a minute to explain why we allow the basketball to get from the top to the wing.

When the basketball is at the top of the key, the man-to-man defense is at its most vulnerable. The reason for this is because on a drive through the middle of the lane, the defenders can be confused about who should help and who should stay attached to their player.

The confusion will often lead to easy layups and open shots because ball-side and weak-side has not been established. However, when the basketball is established on one side of the floor, players on the floor know whether they're in help or deny positions and what their responsibilities are, thereby making help and rotations much quicker and easier.

Ball on the Wing

When the basketball gets to the wing, the most important thing is that you don't allow the ball to be reversed back to the top of the key.

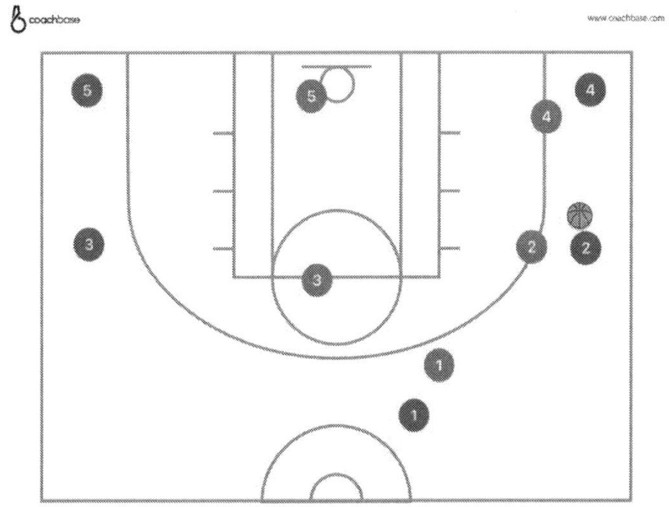

The player defending one pass away toward the top (x one) must be in complete denial position. The on-ball defender (x two) should be playing on the high foot of the player with the basketball to take away the middle drive and force them to drive toward the baseline if they choose to dribble.

If the offensive player does attempt to dribble middle, the on-ball defender should only slide vertically to force them to the top of the key.

As for the corner defender (x4), they should be in full denial as they're one pass away from the basketball. (Side note: Although I don't recommend it for youth teams, there can be a benefit to allowing the pass to the corner to occur since it removes even more offensive options.)

Looking at the help defenders, x three and x five should have a foot on the split line as the basketball is at the free-throw line extended or lower. This puts them in the best position to help, but still gives them time to recover and perhaps get a deflection if the players with the basketball decides to throw a skip pass.

Basketball in the Corner

Once again, when the ball is passed to the corner, the most important thing is that we don't allow the basketball to be reversed to the wing.

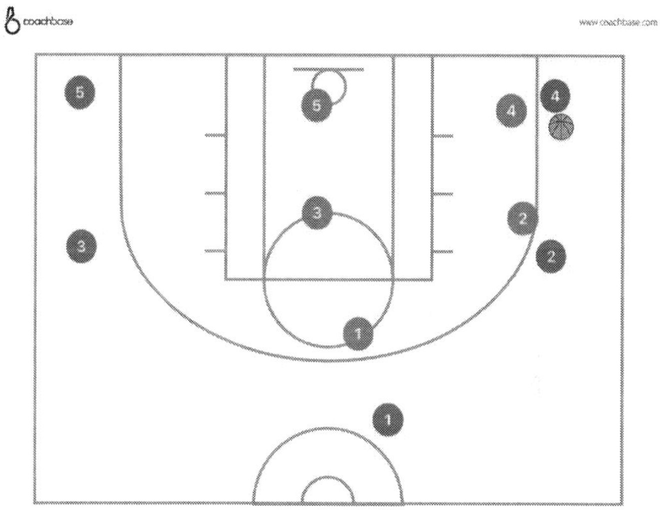

The player one pass away to the wing (x two) must be in complete denial and not allow the pass to be made to the wing.

The on-ball defender (x four) must aim to contain the player in the corner, but by overplaying the high side if x four is beaten off the dribble, it must be toward the baseline because there is help waiting.

The player in low-I (x five) is in a help position anticipating the drive from the player with the basketball. The player in high-I (x three) is in a help position and is preparing to drop down and rotate if four drives the basketball and x five needs to help.

The final player (x one) is in ball-you-man position and are as low as possible while still being able to intercept a pass to one.

Dribble Penetration and Rotations

If your players are not able to make the correct rotations when an offensive players drives the basketball, you will have a very ineffective man-to-man defense. Make sure you constantly drill the following rotations each and every practice.

Top of the Key Drive

As explained in the previous section, dribble penetration from the top of the key through the foul line is the hardest penetration to defend when playing man-to-man defense. We never want to let it happen. It can often occur against a great point guard if the player defending the dribbler is playing too close to their man or if we allow ball reversals and rotations and closeouts are poor.

Knowing this will occasionally happen, your players must know how to best defend it. Here's how to do it:

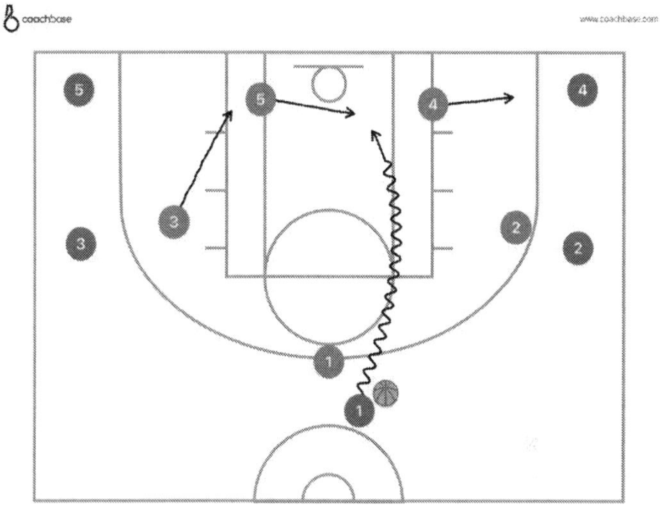

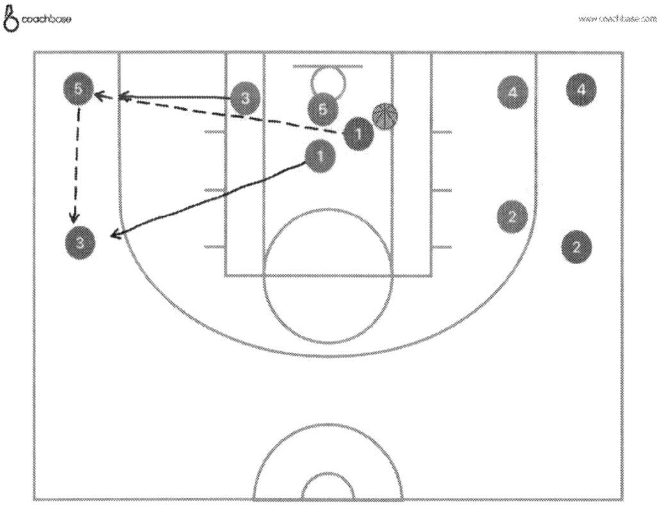

When the defender at the top of the key is beat and the dribbler gets into the lane, whichever defender is the lowest on the weakside must step across to defend the ball. X three doesn't help on the drive since they're one pass away. They can quickly stunt to try to make the driver hesitate or pick up the ball, but they must not leave their direct opponent.

Since help always comes from the weakside, x four must step out and take away the corner three-point attempt. The player that must help is x five since they're the lowest on the weakside. When x five steps up to help, x one must immediately rotate down and will now be the player that closes out on the basketball if the pass is made across court to three or five.

Wing Baseline Drive

When the basketball is on the wing, our ball side and weakside are clearly established and this is great for the defense.

On the baseline drive from the wing, if there's an offensive and defensive player in the corner (x4), they do not help off a ball-side corner player.

Remember: help always comes from the weakside.

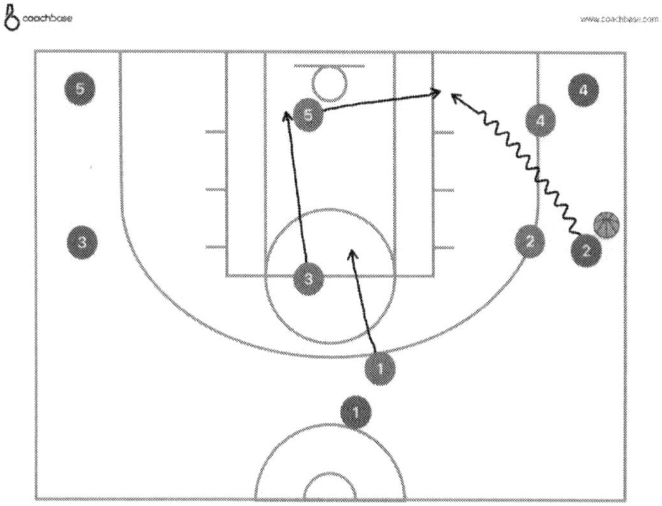

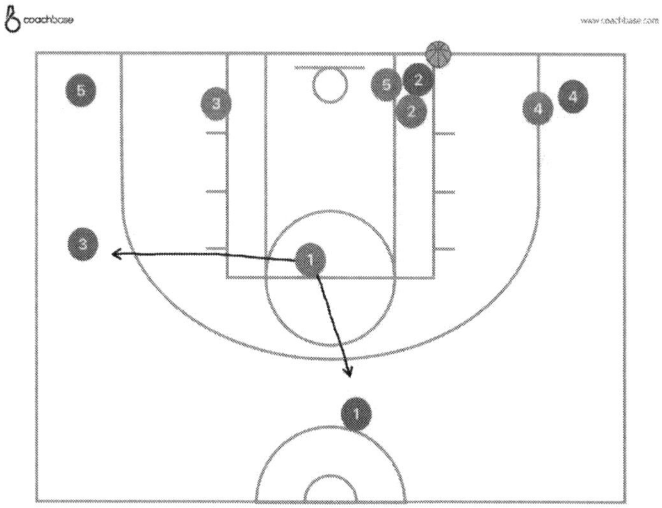

The player at the top of the key (x one) is denying the ball reversal. Then, since the basketball is on the free-throw line or lower, we have high-I and low-I established in the key.

Low-I (x five) helps on the drive and meets to trap the dribbler just outside the paint. X five and x two trap the offensive player if they pick up the dribble. High-I (x three) must rotate down and prevent the pass to five in the corner. The final defender (x one) drops down and positions themselves so that they can intercept a lob pass made to either three or one, or defend either of them if the skip pass is made over the top.

Wing Middle Drive

The middle drive from the wing is a bit more difficult and not a drive the defense ever wants to give up. If the on-ball defender is correctly playing on the high side of the player with the ball, they should be able to take a large slide or two vertically and cut off the drive or draw a charge.

If the on-ball defender has been caught out of position, the next goal is to force the offensive player to dribble to the top of the key. If the on-ball defender has really been caught out of position and the drive is inevitable, the lowest weakside player must step across and challenge the shot and the correct rotations must take place.

X three can quickly stunt on this drive with their back to the basketball in an attempt to make the offensive pick up the ball as long as they can quickly close out on their player without giving up the shot. They should never fully commit to a trap as it will leave the wing shooter open.

This can be a difficult rotation, because if the dribbler crosses over the split line with their dribble the help defender (ball-side and weak-side) changes.

Take a look at the following diagrams to see the differences and the rotations:

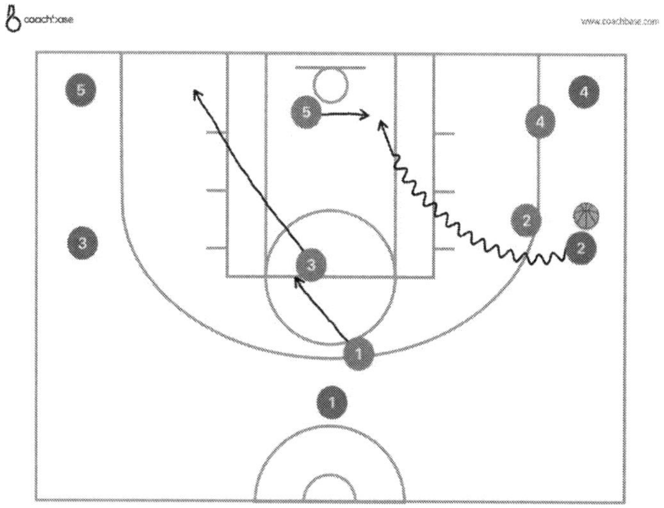

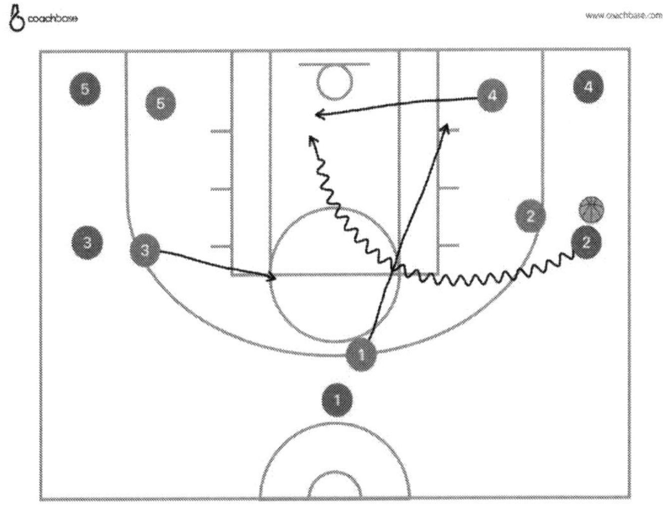

As you can see, allowing the middle drive ends up very problematic and confusing for the defense, so make sure it never happens!

Corner Baseline Drive

The rotations on baseline penetration from the corner are very similar to wing penetration:

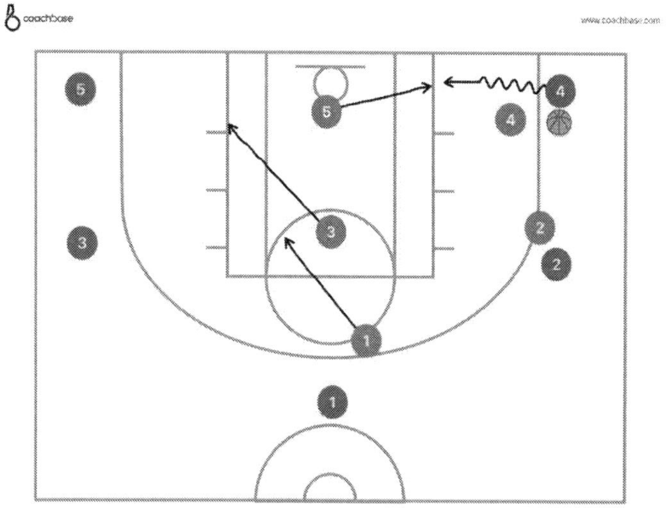

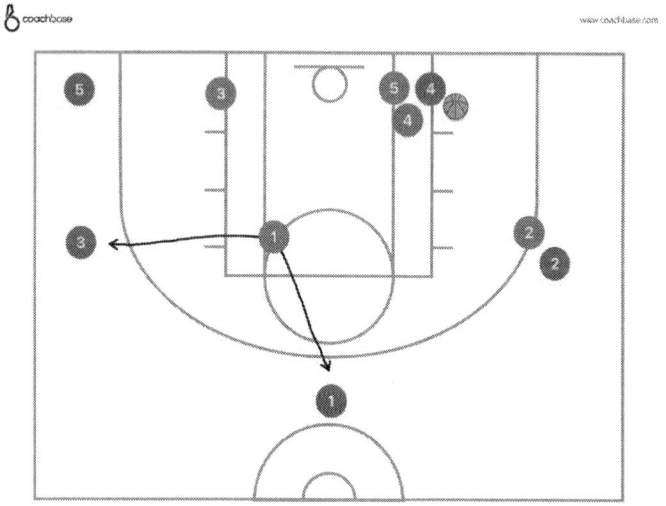

The defender playing on the wing player (x two) makes sure to deny the easy reverse pass back outside. The player in low-I (x five) is responsible for stepping across to set a trap with x four if the player with the ball decides to drive baseline to the basket. If this occurs, x three drops down and cuts off the passing lane to the player x five was defending.

Finally, x one drops and now has two offensive players they must position themselves in between. If the interception pass is there, go for it. If not and the skip pass is made, x one is responsible for closing out on either one or three.

Drive with Low-post Defender

Dribble penetration from the corner or wing while there's an offensive player in the low post is not common but can happen. Here are the rotations when it does occur:

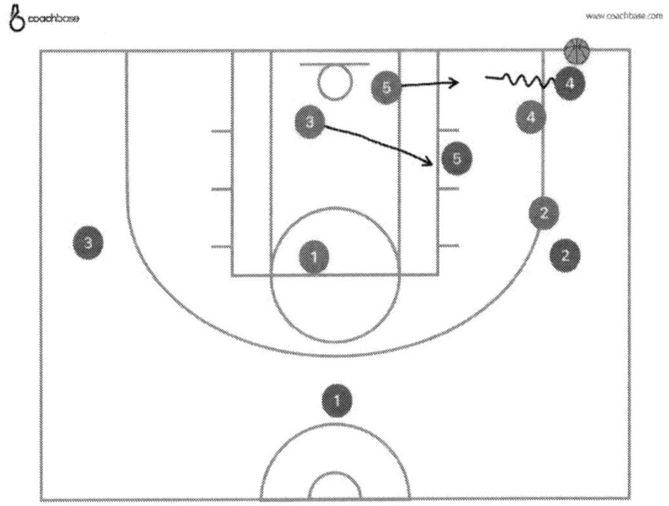

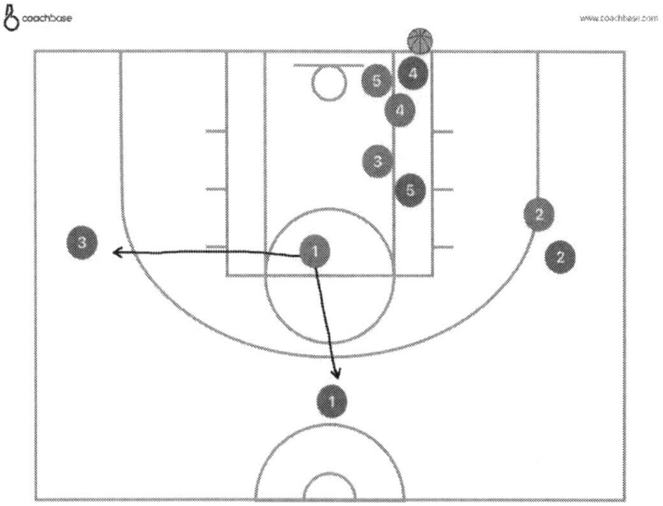

Since we half-front on the low side when there's a player in the low post, it's easier for the low-post defender (x five) to take one step across and trap the dribbler on the baseline with the on-ball defender (x four).

To take away the pocket pass to the low-post player, the defender in low-I (x three) must step across and guard the pass to the low-post player.

The defender in high-I (x one) must then drop and they're responsible for being in position to either intercept a lob pass or closeout on either one or three.

To not give four an easy pass out of the trap, x two must continue complete denial of the outlet pass to two.

Drive with High-post Defender

When there are offensive and defensive players in the high post, the defender does not help out on the drive as they're too far away and all it takes is a pocket pass for an open jumper. Instead, low-I (x three) steps across and traps the dribbler with the on-ball defender (x four) just below the low block.

The defender in the high post (x five) denies the pass to the high-post player and doesn't help. The player denying the retreat pass (x two) continues to deny the pass outside. This leaves high-I (x one) to drop in and is now responsible for intercepting the pass or closing out on three or one.

Skip Pass Rotations

On any skip pass, the most important thing is that the player closing out on the player who receives the ball closes out in a banana cut so that there's no middle penetration.

Every player on the team must be committed to sprinting to their next position on the flight of the basketball. Often it's not the closeout player who is too slow, it is the players who were previously on the ball-side not sprinting into help positions quickly enough.

Also, depending on what level you're playing you might want to run the shooter off the three-point line if they're a good shooter.

Here are a few diagrams to show you closeout rotations:

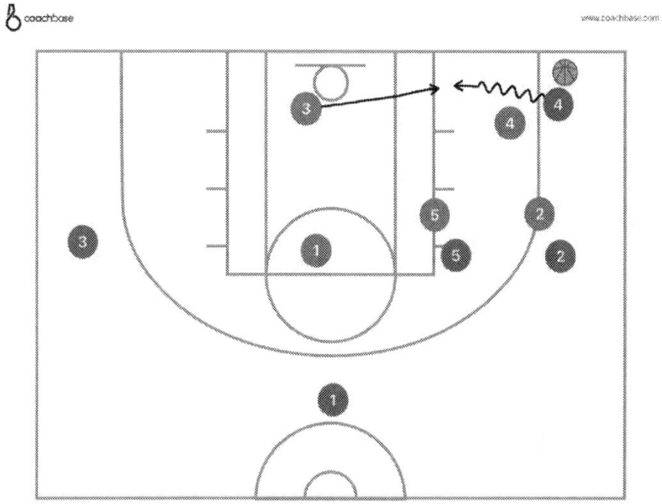
coachbase
www.coachbase.com
3
4
4
5
2
3
1
5
2
1

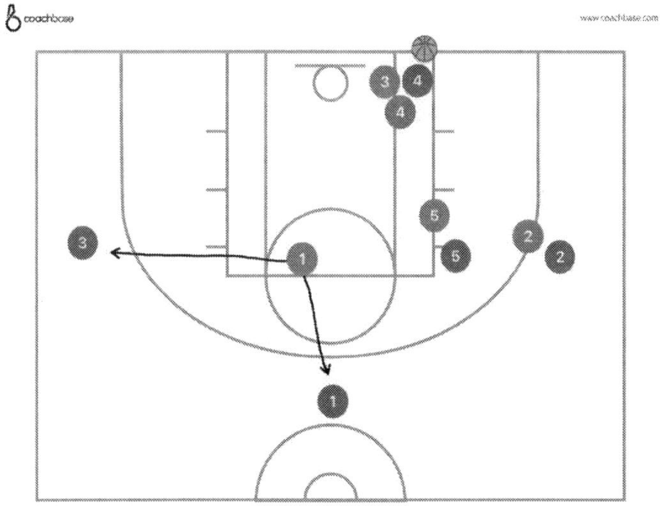
coachbase
www.coachbase.com
3
4
4
5
2
3
1
5
2
1

Advanced

Top to Wing Pass

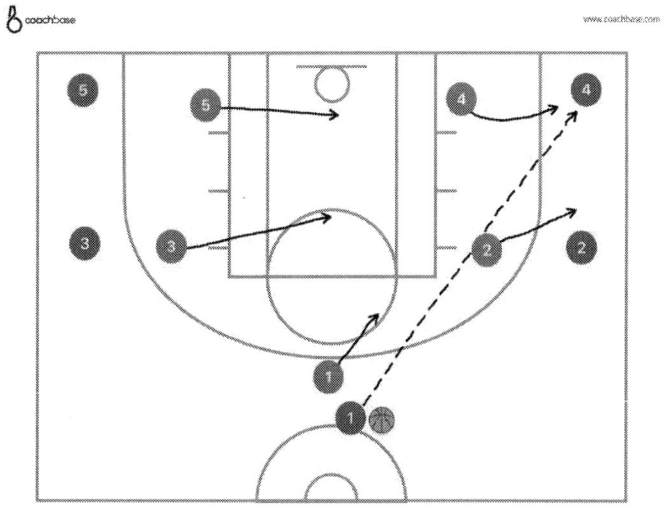

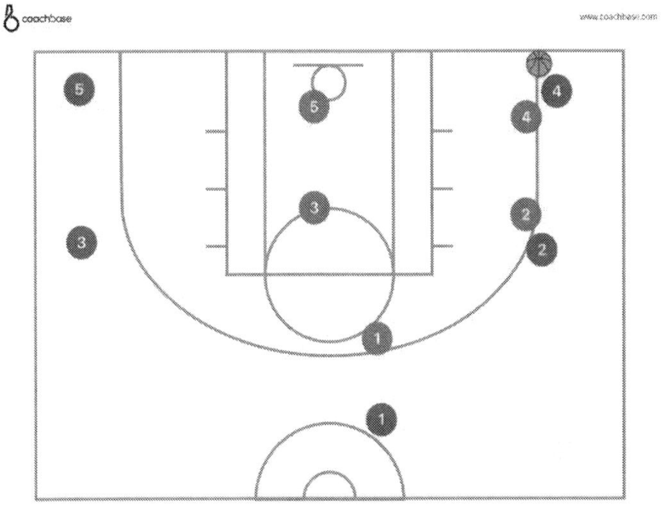
coachbase
www.coachbase.com
5
5
4
4
3
2
3
2
1
1

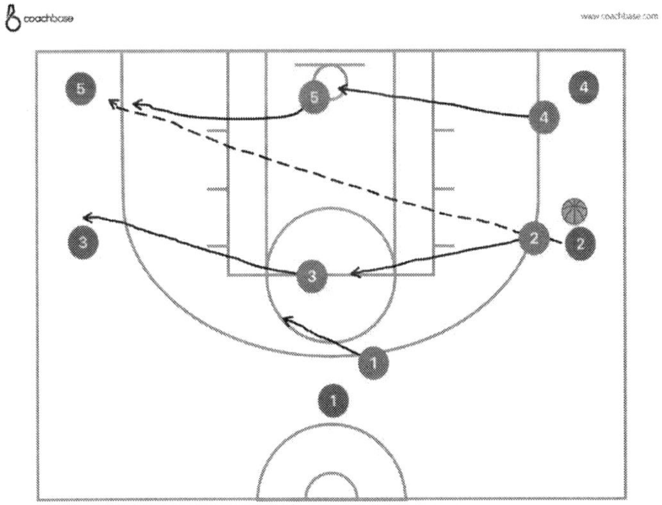
coachbase
www.coachbase.com
5
5
4
4
2
3
2
3
1
1

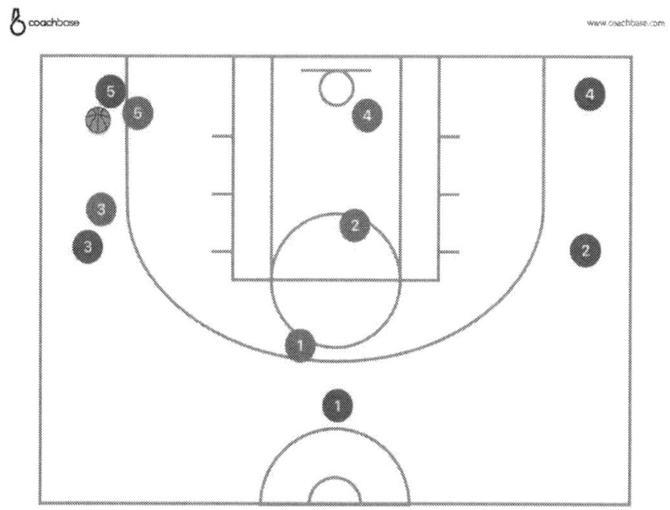

Should you allow it? In the guide above, I break down the variation allowing the pass from the top of the key to the wing because I believe it to be the most effective way to play man-to-man defense.

Since the man-to-man defense is most vulnerable from the top, why would we want to keep the ball there by denying the pass to the wing? But there are other ways to do it. For example, Is it easier to simply make a denying one pass away a universal rule, including from the top?

Here are a few ways why you might consider denying this pass to the wing:

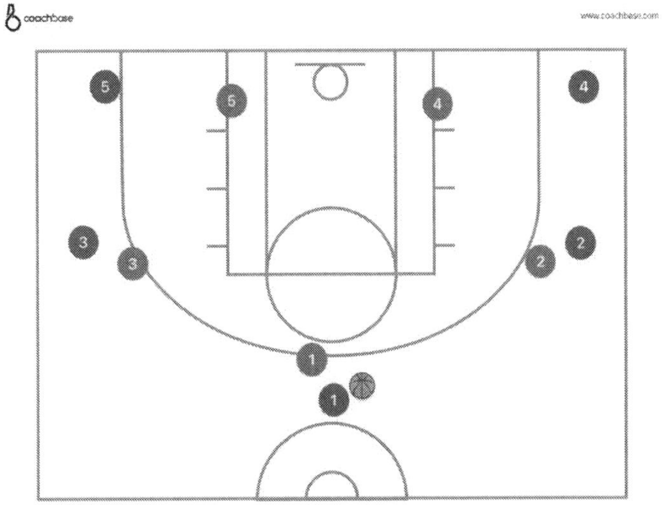

1. *Players can sometimes get confused when exactly they should allow the pass and when they should deny it*
2. *It is another rule for players to remember*
3. *Sometimes putting more pressure on the point guard is a good thing!*
4. *Most teams begin their offense with a top to wing pass. By denying it, you will often disrupt the opponents offense.*

Since there is no right or wrong answer to choosing to deny or allow the pass, each coach must decide individually after looking at the pros and cons. Basically, it's up to you!

Defending the Post

Knowing how your team is going to defend the post is crucial to a great man-to-man defense. You must have a consistent system that's based on the strengths and weaknesses of the post players on your team.

But before we get into any of that, here's the main rule for defending the post: don't let it get there! Allowing the basketball to get into the post is bad news for any defense. It will often lead to part of the defense collapsing or a silly foul by a post defender.

Before we discuss the ways to defend the post, here are three tips to keeping the basketball out of there in the first place.

1. Beat them down the floor

By beating the opposition post player down the floor, it takes away their ability to establish a strong early position that can result in a quick pass inside and an easy score.

2. Great On-ball Defense

Guards pressuring the player with the ball can go a long way to discourage the pass inside to the post player. Every on-ball defender should be active with their hands in the passing lane and tracing the ball.

3. Push Them Off the Block

If a post player does establish position on the block, a post defender can move them further out by keeping their arm bar locked while pushing the offensive player out with the strength of their lower body.

Positioning to Deny the Post Player

There are many different ways to deny the pass into the post, but here are my preferences (I'm not a fan of fronting the low post):

1. Basketball above the free-throw line.

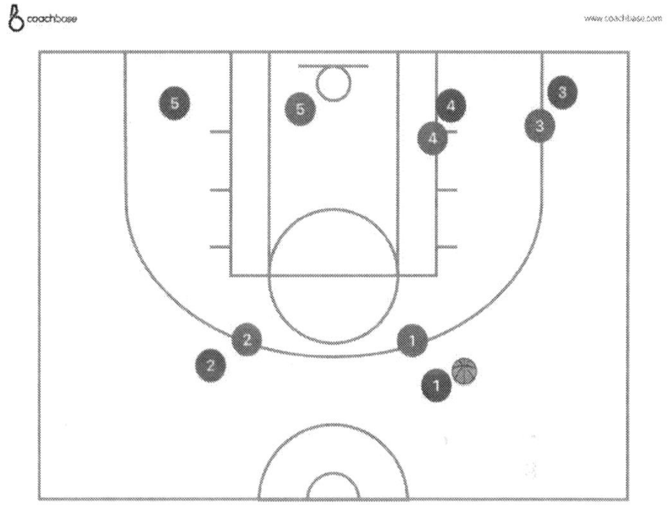

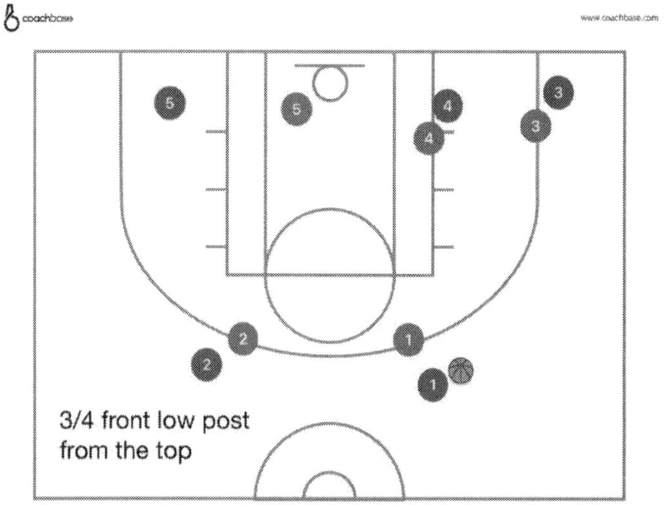

When the basketball is above the free-throw line, the post defender should be three-quarters front keeping themselves on the line between the ball and their opponent.

For the offensive team to make this entry pass, it would have to be very accurate and the post defender will still have time to establish a position between them and the basket. Also, keep in mind that there is a player in low-I who can pick off any passes made over the top.

2. Basketball below the free-throw line.

When the basketball is below the free-throw line, the post defender should half front from the baseline side.

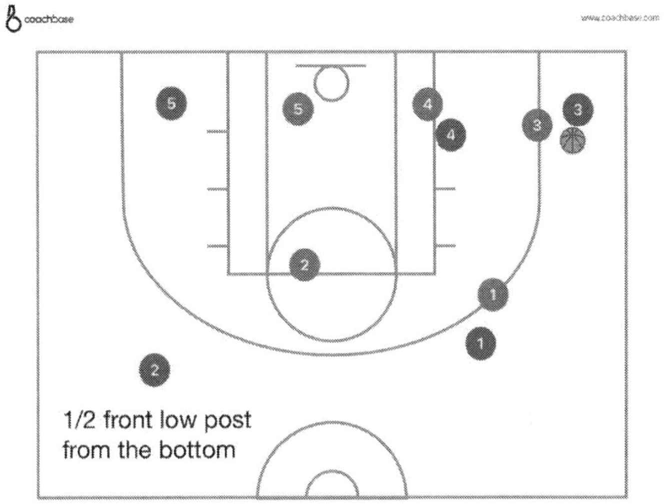

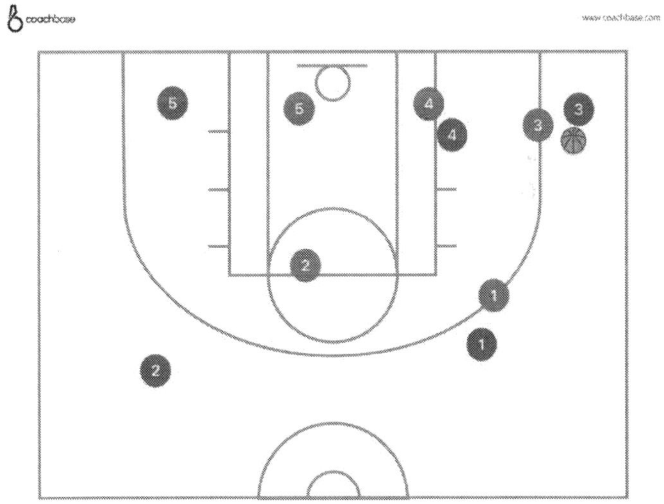

By doing so, they're in the perfect position to help on any baseline drives. Also, since the pass is now shorter, only half-fronting the offensive player will allow the defender to still be able to establish a position behind if they're unable to get a deflection on the pass inside.

Trapping a Dominant Low-post Player

There will be times when you come up against such a dominant low-post player that you have no choice but to send help and trap them in the post. When this happens, I recommend sending trapping with the player in the low-I help position. Here's how it works:

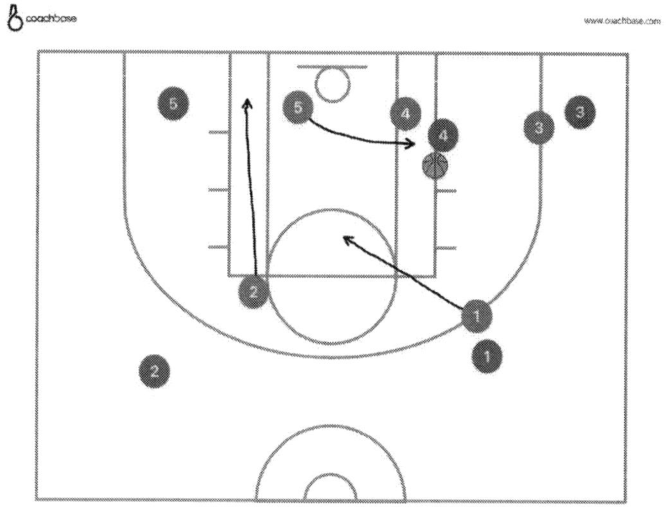

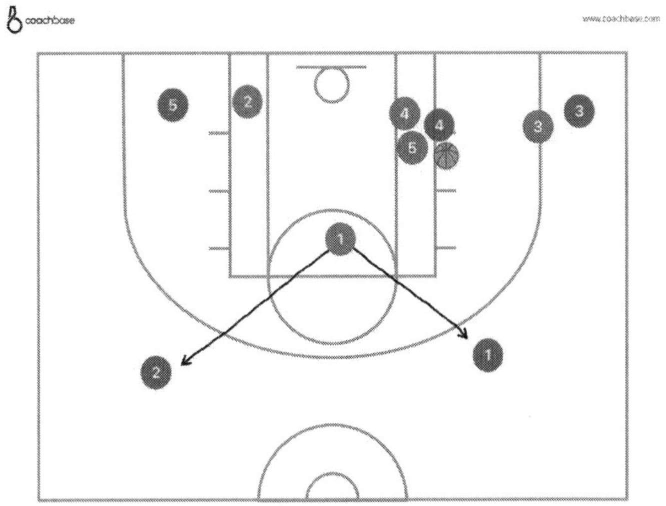

When four receives the pass in post, x four must immediately establish position behind. Then x five will sprint across and set a trap on the high side with x four.

X two drops to defend five and then x one drops and becomes the interceptor. Their role is to pickoff any passes made to one or two. If none are available for steal or deflection, they're the first to close out to whoever receives the outlet pass.

On the ball-side, x three never allows the simple pass out and is in complete denial while the basketball is in the post.

Transition Defense

You can never have a great man-to-man defensive team if you're not a great transition defense team. Educate your players on the importance of this and then get them to buy in and commit to transitioning back quickly after each offensive possession.

The secret to being a great transition defense team is that your players must know how many people are going to the offensive boards and how many are going to immediately retreat on any shot attempt.

The worst possible thing a player can do after an offensive shot is to stand and watch, neither transitioning back on defense or attacking the offensive glass. Most coaches refer to this as being in 'no man's land' – a place a player never wants to be!

Here's what I recommend when running the man-to-man defense:

Send three players to the offensive glass and send two players back on transition defense immediately after the shot.

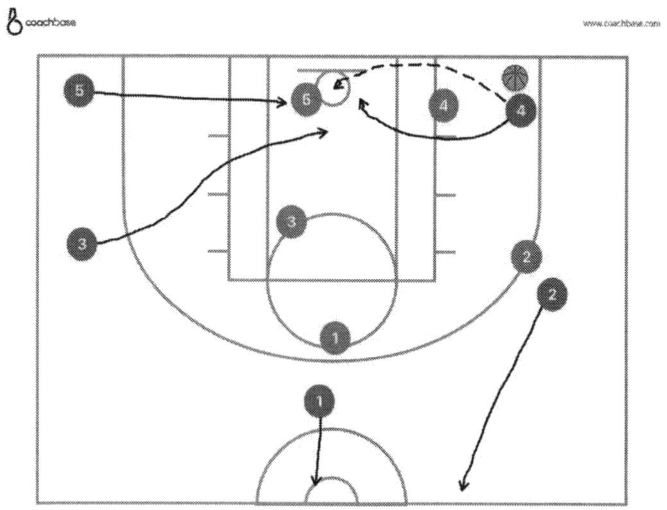

As the two players transition back, the goal is to establish a top defender and a bottom defender. The bottom defender protects the rim while the goal of the top defender is to slow down the basketball and give the players that were competing for offensive rebounds time to recover on defense.

This is the method I've found the most success with, but it might not necessarily be the best option for your team. For instance, if you have a very small team that never gets offensive rebounds, you could send all five players back immediately after each shot in an effort to never give up any transition baskets. There are numerous NCAA teams that currently do this.

Defending Baseline Out of Bounds Plays (BLOBs)

Inbounds plays often provide great scoring opportunities for the offensive team. They have well-thought-out plays and are in the perfect position to run them.

The main goal when defending baseline in-bounds plays is to get the opponent to throw the ball to the top and set up their main offense. If you can do that, you've successfully defended the BLOB.

Defending a baseline in-bounds while playing man-to-man defense can be done in two ways:

1. Stick to Man-to-Man Defense

If you're going to stick to the man-to-man defense on baseline inbounds, there are a few things you must be prepared to do to stop the opponent from getting an easy score:

- Position the in-bounds defender near the rim. The main

goal here is to take away the easy pass and score under the rim and force the opponent to pass out to the wing. Depending on where the in-bounds pass takes place, the in-bounds passer's defender should position themselves along the lane line connecting to the baseline to take away the under the rim pass.

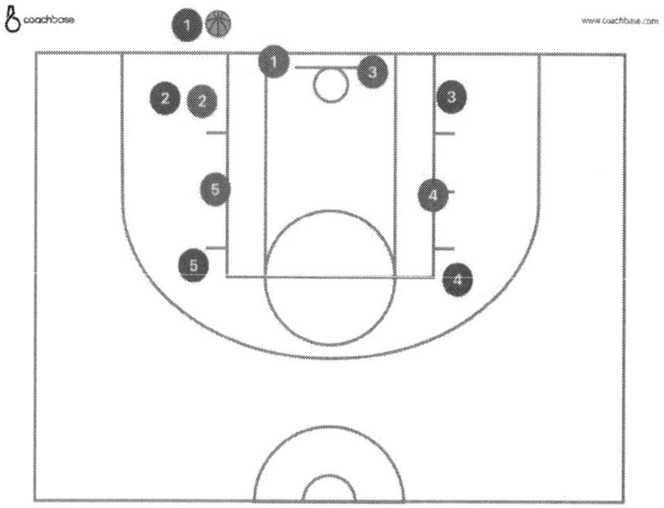

- Switch everything. Since the up-screens and cross-screens can be difficult to defend on BLOB plays, I often recommend that teams switch everything. The key is for defenders to stay below the offensive players and keep themselves on the basket side of their opponents.

2. Run a two-three zone.

Depending on the level of basketball you're coaching and the rules of your league, you might consider running a two-three zone on inbounds plays.

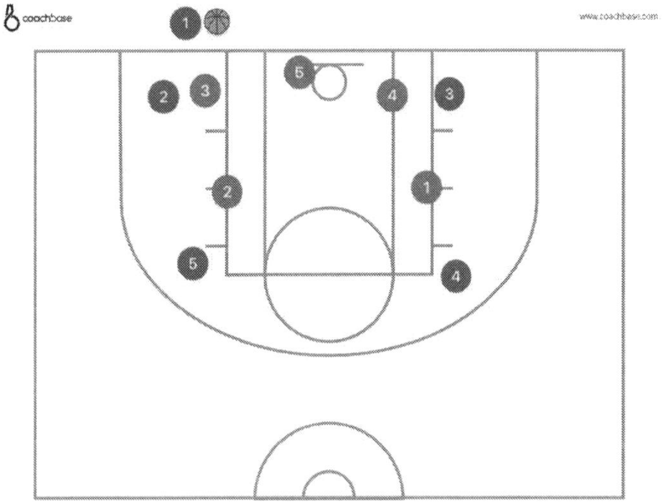

Once the play has been in-bounded to either the wing or the top, players switch straight back into their man-to-man defense. The reasons the two-three zone works so well on BLOBs is because it floods the key with defenders and doesn't allow the easy baskets under the rim that can often occur when playing man-to-man defense.

Defending the Pick and Roll

The pick-and-roll is arguably the toughest action in basketball to defend against. When playing man-to-man defense, there are a few ways you can choose to defend this action:

1. Fight Over the Screen

This is my recommended method of defending against the pick-and-roll.

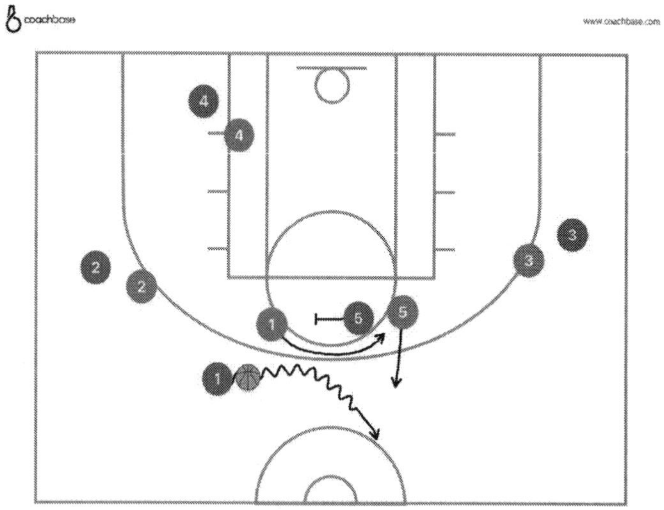

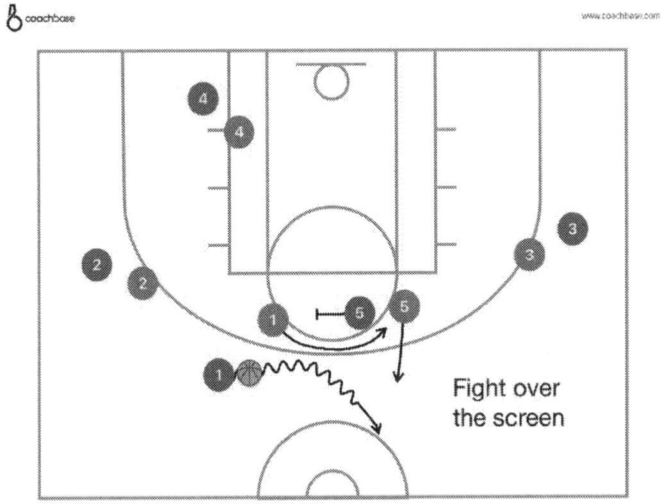

my recommended method of defending against the pick-and-roll.

This requires the screener's defender 'hedging' out high and forcing the dribbler to take a few extra vertical steps that allows the on-ball defender to fight over the screen and recover back in front. This can be difficult for youth players, but hedging and fighting over screens are great habits for players to get into at a young age as it will be a very important skill when they're older.

2. Switch the Screen

Another option a coach has at their disposal is to switch on any pick-and-roll.

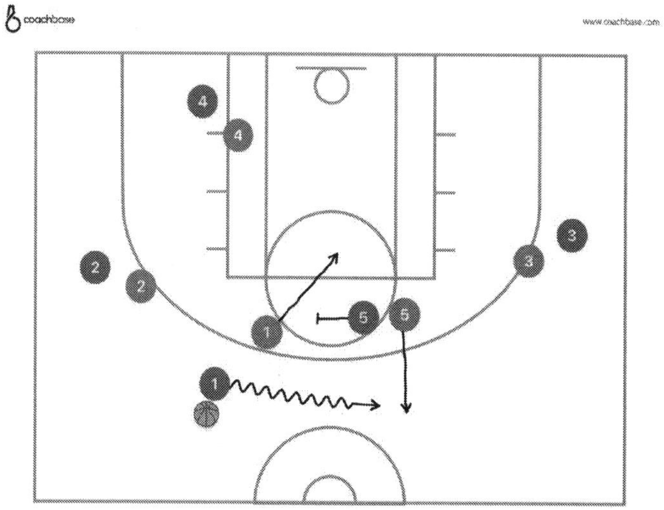

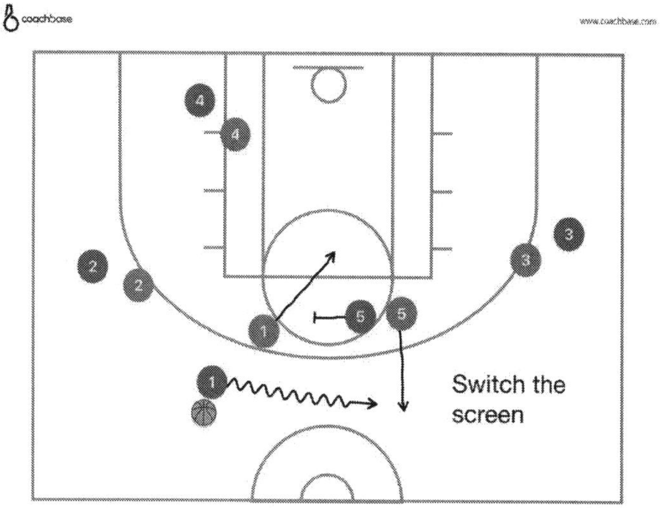

As the name implies, this simply means that the defenders hold their positions and swap the offensive player they're guarding. This can be problematic if you end up with small player defending a big player or vice versa, but at the youth level players aren't often experienced enough to take advantage of it.

3. Go Under the Screen

To go under the screen, the screener's defender can take a quick step back to give the on-ball defender room to squeeze past the screen and immediately establish position in front of the dribbler.

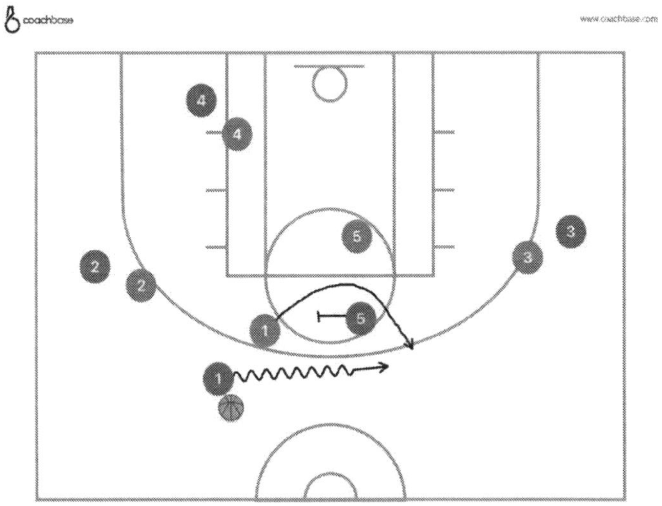

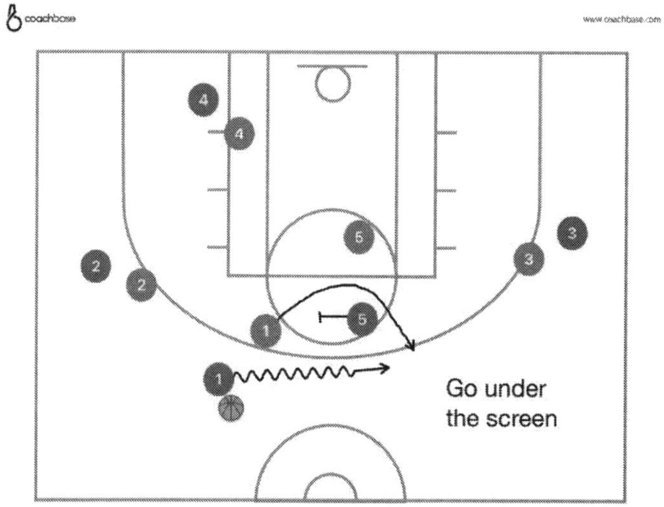

While this is probably the easiest way to do it, I do believe players are missing out on the important skill of learning to fight over screens and how to hedge.

Conclusion

The five main man-to-man defense rules:

1. No middle penetration
2. No ball reversals
3. No help one pass away
4. No face cuts
5. Move when the ball moves

The man-to-man defense is one of the best defenses you can run with your team no matter what level you're coaching. With nearly all high-level basketball teams using this defense, the skills that are learned in man-to-man defense are crucial for all players to develop from the earliest age possible. Sure, it can be difficult to teach, but they payoff for your players will definitely be worth it in the long run. If you're a coach that puts developing players over winning youth basketball games, then this defense is for you!

6

One-One-Three Zone Defense

It is a common coaching saying that 'defense is the best offense,' but Scott Drew's Baylor Bears and their one-one-three zone take that concept to a whole new level. Watching them play defense has you unsure which team is meant to be attacking. Their guards harass opposing ball handlers, their wings are lengthy and quick to trap, and their center is an intimidating presence in the paint.

And it's working. In 2016, the Baylor Bears held opponents to just 0.9 PPP and an astounding 0.71 PPP in the half-court. Anyways, enough chat – let's break down the one-one-three zone defense!

Personnel and Organization

So the first thing you need to know about the one-one-three zone defense is that unlike most zones your goal is not to pack the paint. Rather, it's about getting in the face of perimeter players and using rotations aggressively to allow the defense to recover, rather than give help outright.

Keeping that in mind, let's look at what the players do:

1. 'Patrick Beverley,' your quickest guard whose main goal is to harass the opposing team's primary ballhandler from half-court and to prevent middle penetration.

2. 'Chris Paul,' the guard with the best basketball IQ, needs to deny the high post, make rotations to trap the wings, and otherwise cover any holes in your defense. One and two will rotate positions over the course of a possession.

3 and 4. 'Jimmy Butler', 'Paul George', your athletic, lengthy wings. These players need to be great at defending one-on-one, rotating quickly to trap and deny passes to the corners (defending the corner three is a weaknesses of this defense, but more on this later).

5. 'Deandre Jordan,' your shot-blocking center. This player

defends the post and erases any perimeter mistakes at the rim.

As the ball is brought up following a make:

- One goes to meet the ballhandler at half-court
- Two stands at the high post to guard any player there
- Three and four stand high and wide, outside the three point line between the second block and free-throw line, ready to deny any pass to the corners
- Five stands in the paint. If there is a post player he goes to guard them, otherwise he patrols the restricted area, moving closer toward the corner rather than being dead center

Key Principles

1. **Everyone must communicate** – with so many rotations, the defense is in constant movement. Communication is key.
2. **Everyone must rebound** – not many players are in the paint so boxing out is key.
3. **Ball pressure at all times** – this will force mistakes and turnovers.
4. **Hard closeouts with hands high** – there are no 'soft' closeouts in this defense. Players need to get into the face of their man.
5. **Defender stays on man until called off by teammate** – some closeouts require a teammate to bump and then retreat to guard another player. No leaving the ball until called.
6. **Always guard the high and low posts** – the one and two must communicate constantly to make sure someone is

always protecting the high post.

7. **No middle** – force the ball handler baseline.

One last note on defensive philosophy – this defense, while it has some built in traps it isn't about creating steals. Baylor plays at one of the slowest paces in the nation so they don't get a ton of breakaway fast breaks. Instead, each good rotation denies the offense open looks and forces them into taking contested shots with the shot clock counting down. Any steals you get are going to be by players forcing passes that aren't there.

Defensive Rotations

Now let's look at how the one-one-three responds when the ball is passed to different areas.

Slot-to-Slot Pass

Many offenses, including the dribble drive motion, and four-out one-in offense have two guards in the slots (area directly above the lane line). In a slot-to-slot pass, the one and two guards most rotate between guarding the high post and the perimeter.

1. One is forcing the defense baseline and tries to make the slot to slot pass as difficult as possible
2. On the pass, two anticipates and closes out on the perimeter.
3. One sinks back to guard the post
4. Meanwhile, the strongside wing (four) moves to deny the

pass to the corner. The weakside wing (three) moves in to be inside and deeper than the deepest man on his side of the court. He gets ready to run out and intercept any skip pass

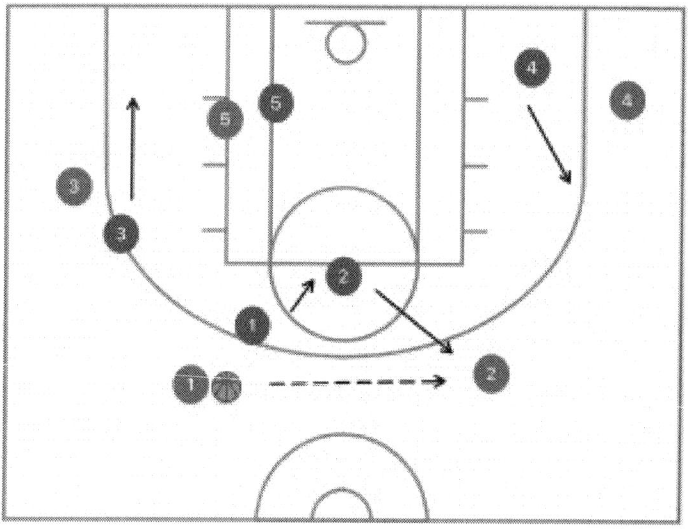

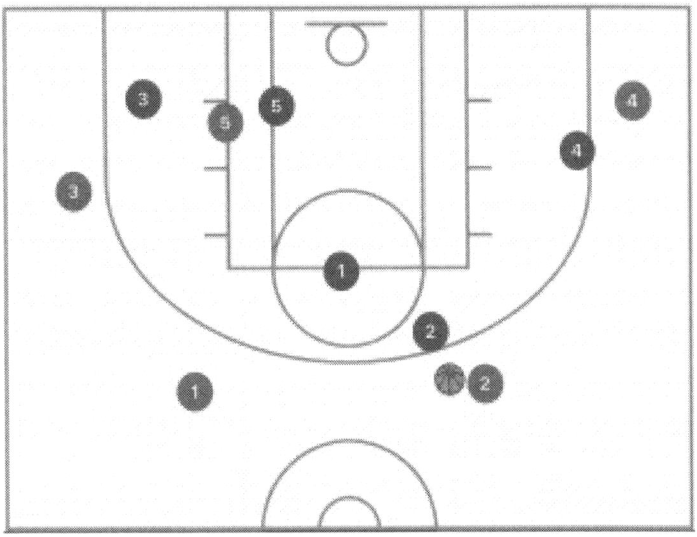

Coaching Points

Four and three can help close out on top players, depending on how high the offense is (e.g. in the high post-spread offense). When this happens, three closes out until two can rotate over before running back to his man. Five stays in the low post but anticipates the pass to the corner and close out.

Slot-to-Wing Pass

On the pass to the wing from the top, everyone must be ready to move the ball:

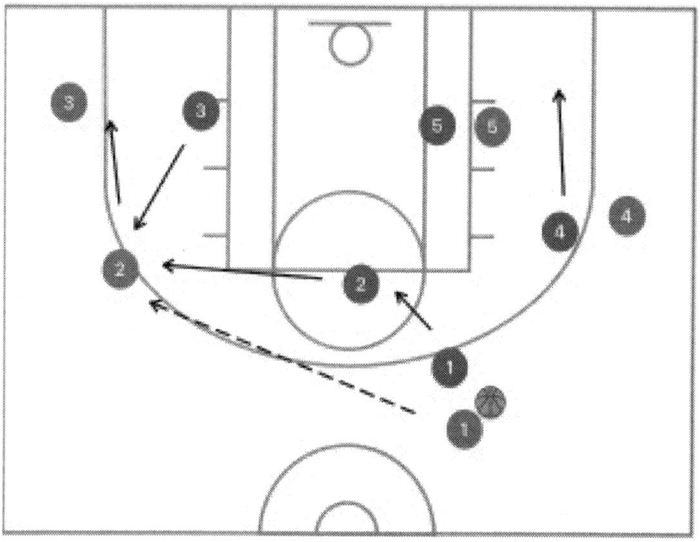
3
3
5
5
4
4
2
2
1
1

.

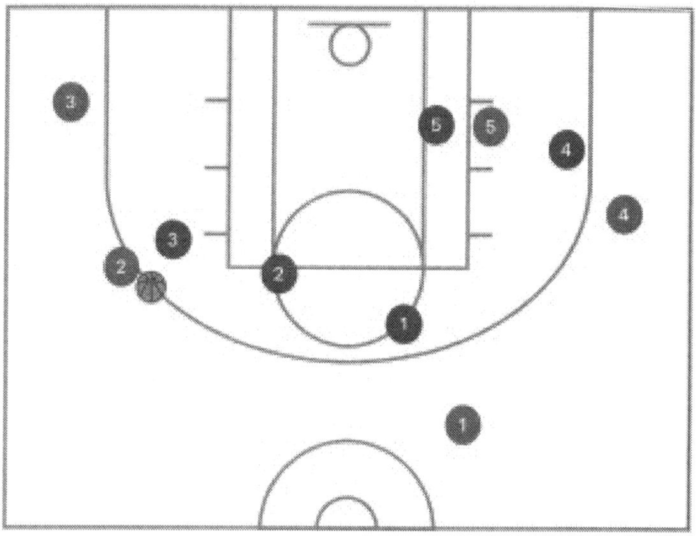
3
5
5
4
4
3
2
2
1
1

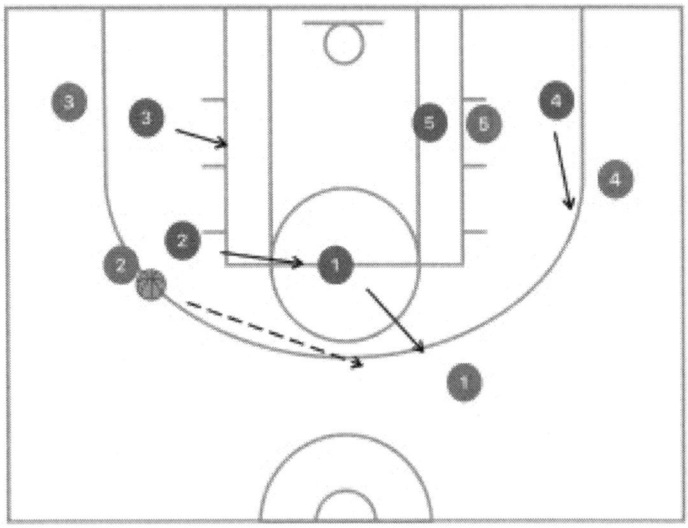

1. Side wing (four), quickly hedges giving two time to rotate over
2. One drops down to guard the high post and the weakside wing, three also moves down to be as deep as the lowest player on the offense
3. Five tries to push his man out of the low post if he's fighting for post position
4. Once two is on his man, four drops back down to his man

Coaching Points

- If there's no corner, four can just guard his man one-on-one on the wing, remembering to force baseline
- Once this happens, you want to keep the ball on that side of the floor. Two should deny middle and make the reverse pass difficult

Wing-to-Corner Pass

If the ball gets into the corner you want to be aggressive in ball denial to try and force a risky long skip pass.

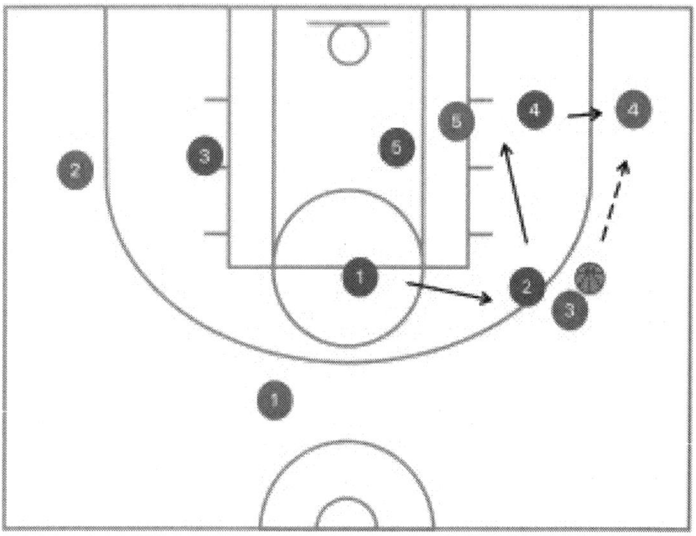

1. Four, the ball side wing closes out on the corner
2. If there's a big in the low post, five guards him from behind while two sinks down to front him and deny the entry pass
3. One rotates down to the wing to cover the reverse pass
4. Three, the weakside wing, steps in and sags toward the baseline and gets ready for a long skip pass. When it comes, he must steal it

Coaching Points

- The weakside wing sags below the lowest man on the weakside (either the low post or corner) to get full vision of the court – it's easier to run and look forward than behind you. This is to also to ensure the ball doesn't get skipped to the corner
- When the ball is in the corner you want to make it difficult to reverse it – don't allow a quick straight-line pass. Force a risky skip or a lob by closing out with active hands to deny the ball
- When the ball is in the wing and corner, the one-one-three looks like a two-three zone with a post double team

Ball Reversal from the Corner

When the ball is finally skipped, you must scramble to rotate. Ideally, this is a skip pass back to the top because you're denying the pass to the wing and the cross court skip pass will get picked off.

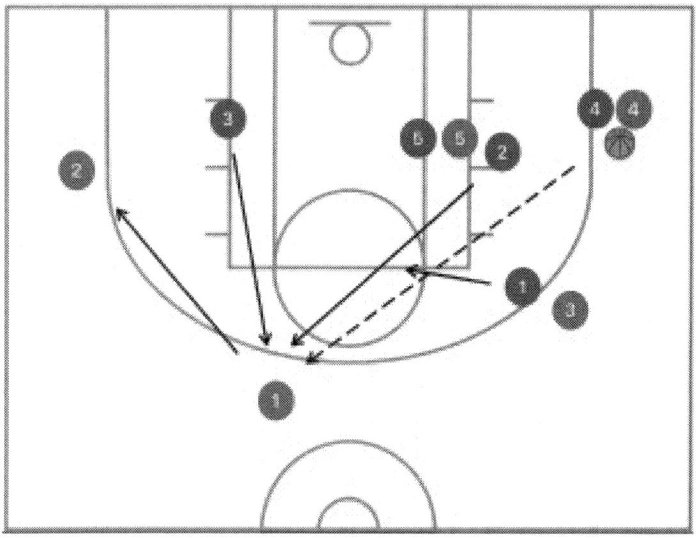
3
4
4
5
5
2
2
1
3
1

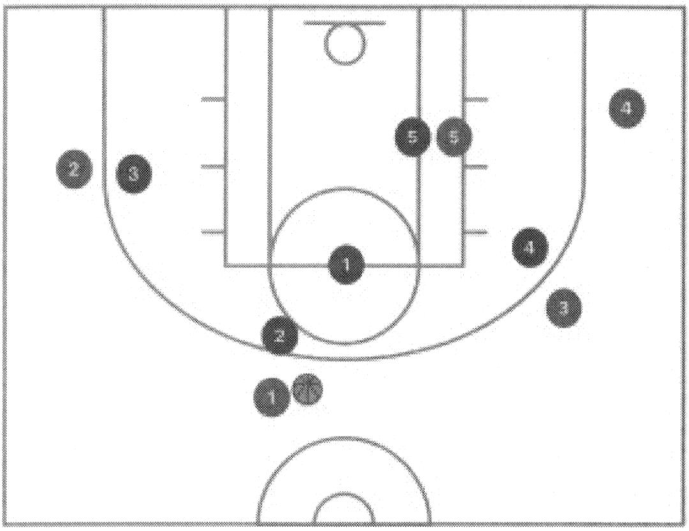
4
5
5
2
3
4
1
3
2
1

1. The weakside wing – three – moves when the ball is in the air to bump up top
2. The guard closest to the middle, two (who has been denying the post) closes out to the top so that three can drop back to guard his spot on the wing
3. One, who has been denying the wing, moves back to the middle to guard the high post
4. Five goes back to guarding the rim while four, who is on-ball in the corner, can move back to the wing

Coaching Points

Communication between players closing out is key. You want a call such as "off" or "mine" to let the help defender know that he can rotate back to his spot.

Advanced Tactics

These are just the basic rotations for when the ball is passed around the perimeter. Here are some more trapping tactics for different situations:

High Post Entry Trap

As with any zone, it's dangerous when the ball is in the high post. The one-one-three uses an aggressive two guard trap to get the ball out of there.

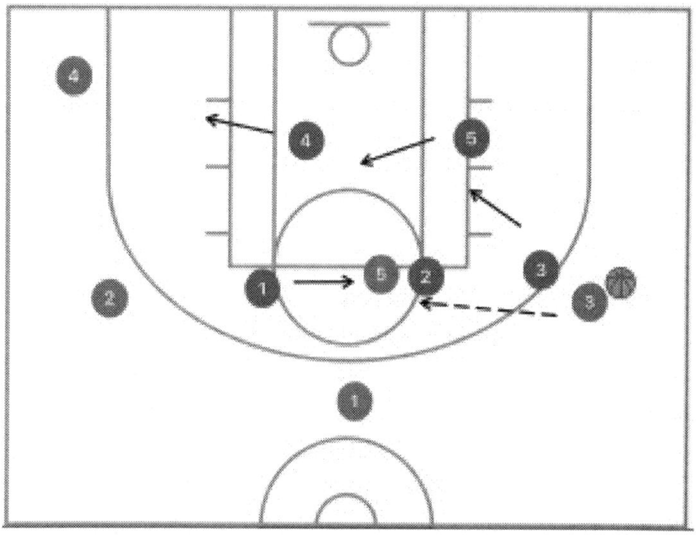

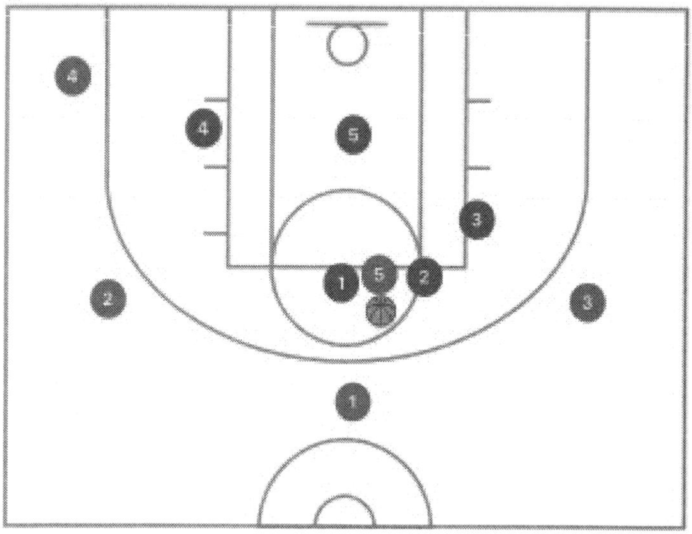

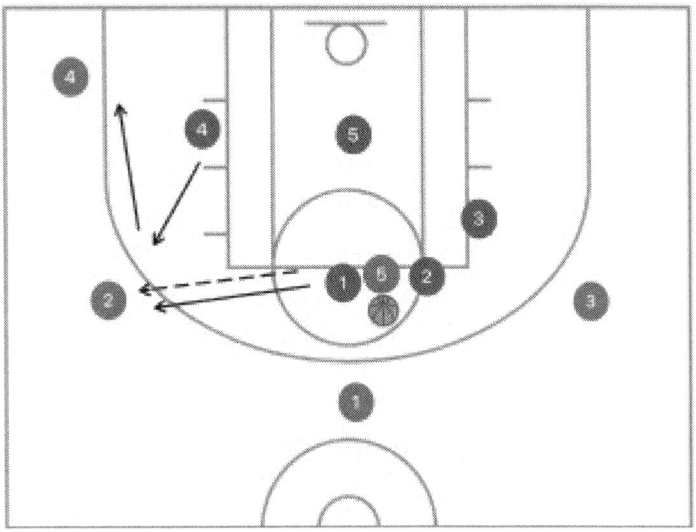

1. The ball is in the wing. As the wing is the last player on the strong side (three), the strongside wing is guarding him
2. On the pass to the post, one drops down to double the post with two. Three steps back to protect the paint but is ready to close out
3. Five – the center – steps up to protect the basket in case of a drive
4. Four – the weakside wing – moves to the low block to get ready for a close out to the corner

Coaching Points

Note that in the diagram above, one is lower than weakside wing to prevent that skip pass in this situation. If the ball was passed to the top, two would close out, one would guard the high post, and four would step up to the wing.

Short Corner Trap

Baylor Bears will always trap if the ball is passed to the short corner. Everyone drops down and makes it difficult to get the ball back out.

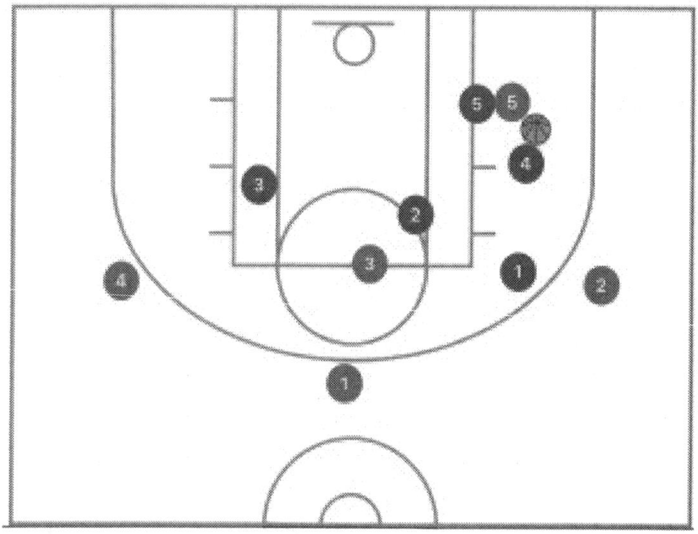

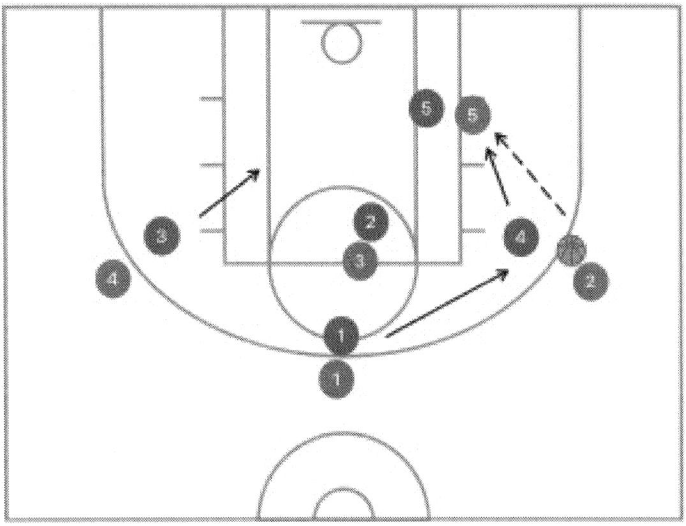

1. When the ball is passed from the wing, four leaves his man and drops down to trap with five
2. The weakside wing – two – steps ball-side to protect the paint
3. One and two both drop down closer to the ball to protect against cutters

Coaching Points

If the ball is passed back out to the wing, the nearest guard (two) can help until three recovers.

Pick-and-Roll Defense Notes

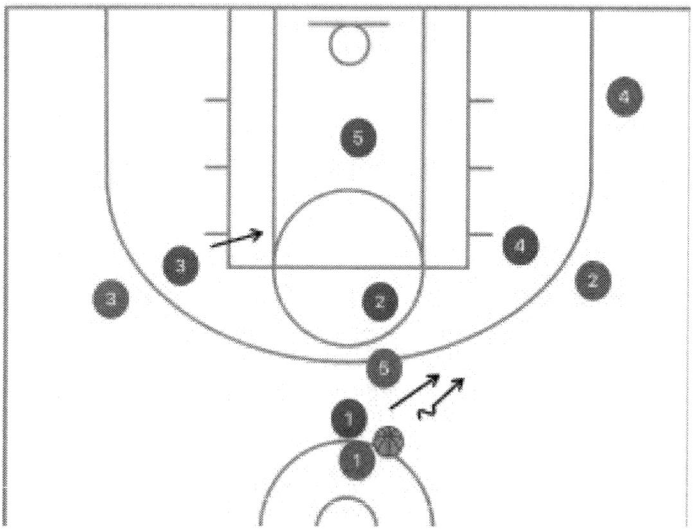

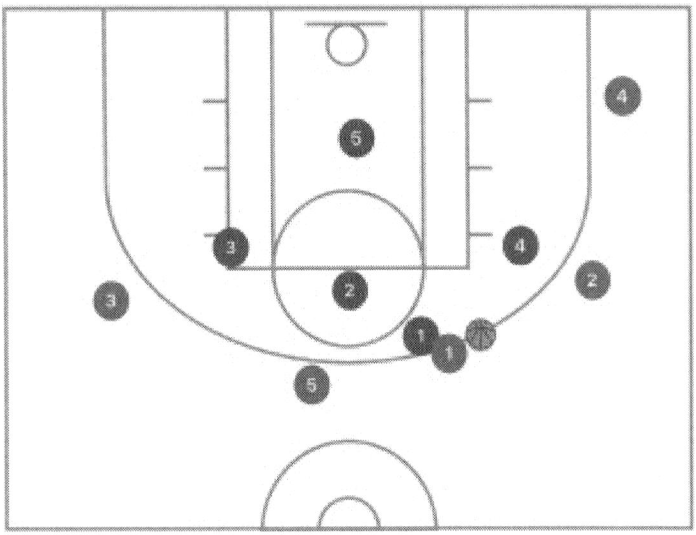

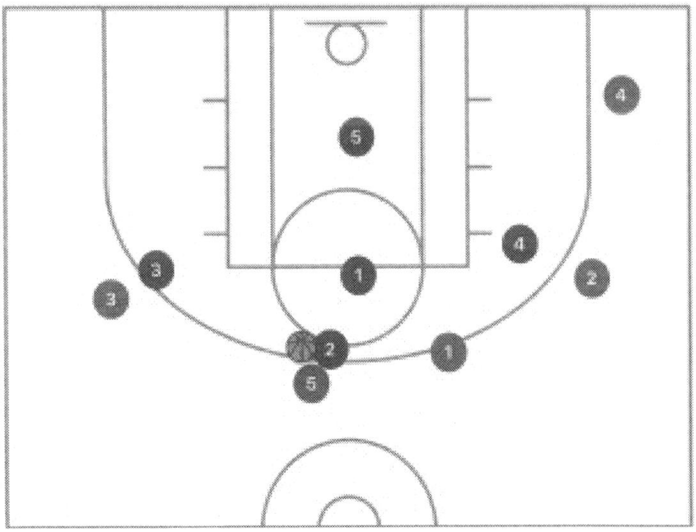

Baylor defends the high pick and roll with the one and two guards. As they're already stacked, they're in good position to guard it:

- One harasses the ball handler and follows him around the screen
- Two sags back to contain about three feet in front of the free-throw line (this depends on his or her quickness)
- The weakside wing (opposite to which direction the guard is driving to) puts a foot on the lane line to close up the driving lane

This is an unconventional approach as it can give up a size mismatch for speed but it is effective in containing dribble penetration. Giving up a contested jumper on the pop to the five is generally a good end result for the defense.

7

Havoc One-Two-One-One Full-court Press

We're going to break down Coach Shaka Smart's famous 'Havoc' press defense. As the name suggests, it's going to create havoc!

Coach Smart led an underdog VCU team to the NCAA final four in 2011 with less talent than many big-name teams use with this system. Is your team lacking in talent? Read on.

In every other sport, the defense plays defense for the entire length of the playing field. So why do we retreat to our own half and let the opponent casually stroll up the court? I love the full-court press because it gives each player more playing time and it's exciting! Famous coaches that run full-court press are team USA's Don Showalter and VCU's Shaka Smart. I'm going to breakdown why you should run the 'havoc' press and the principles to make it work for your team!

Pros of a Press

1. More Players Get to Play

This is particularly true in youth basketball, as you want your players to get playing time because you never know when a team member is going to get a growth spurt or suddenly improve over the summer. I even recommend having two units and substitute all five players each time. It also means that depth matters, so who's bench is better? Most teams have a significant drop off outside their starting five.

2. Exciting Style of Play Builds Chemistry and Everybody Gets Shot Opportunities

Every player will get a chance to score. It's fast paced and everyone is involved.

3. Keeps Teams From Running Their Offense (Especially If You're Shorter)

Press is difficult to prepare for because if players are not committed to it, it's very hard to simulate in practice. Even pressing teams find it difficult to break a press. Opponents get shots that they normally don't take at faster speeds than they normally take them, thereby forcing a tempo upon the opponent they're not accustomed to. If you're a short team, it's great for preventing the taller players from getting a close shot.

4. It Exhausts Your Opponents

Very few players like to be pressed. Over time, there is a cumulative fatigue effect because it's at such a fast tempo.

5. Great If Your Team Can't Shoot or Are Not Very Skilled

If you manage to force a turnover, it's usually in the opponent's half and often results in a layup. If your players aren't very skilled, it also helps because you're relying on defense for offense. Trade in effort and stamina for skill.

Cons of press

1. Effort and Stamina

This is an all-or-nothing system. It's very tiring and requires players to sprint. You'll need to coach effort and conditioning.

2. You Need Nasty Players

If your players are not aggressive then this is not for you.

3. Transition Speed

If your players are slow, this is not for you. Everything is about speed of transition. You need to force a high tempo.

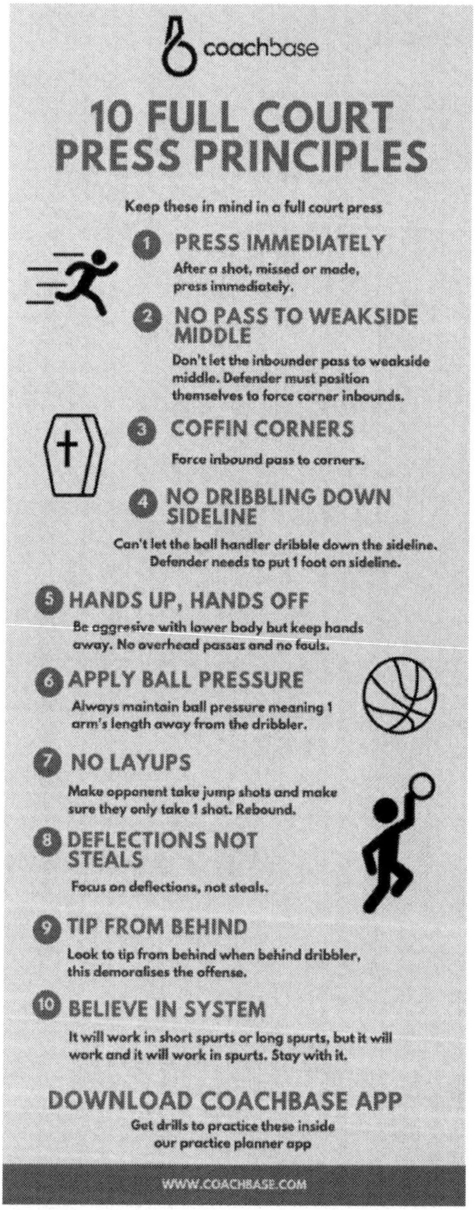
coachbase
10 FULL COURT PRESS PRINCIPLES
Keep these in mind in a full court press
1 PRESS IMMEDIATELY
After a shot, missed or made, press immediately.
2 NO PASS TO WEAKSIDE MIDDLE
Don't let the inbounder pass to weakside middle. Defender must position themselves to force corner inbounds.
3 COFFIN CORNERS
Force inbound pass to corners.
4 NO DRIBBLING DOWN SIDELINE
Can't let the ball handler dribble down the sideline. Defender needs to put 1 foot on sideline.
5 HANDS UP, HANDS OFF
Be aggresive with lower body but keep hands away. No overhead passes and no fouls.
6 APPLY BALL PRESSURE
Always maintain ball pressure meaning 1 arm's length away from the dribbler.
7 NO LAYUPS
Make opponent take jump shots and make sure they only take 1 shot. Rebound.
8 DEFLECTIONS NOT STEALS
Focus on deflections, not steals.
9 TIP FROM BEHIND
Look to tip from behind when behind dribbler, this demoralises the offense.
10 BELIEVE IN SYSTEM
It will work in short spurts or long spurts, but it will work and it will work in spurts. Stay with it.
DOWNLOAD COACHBASE APP
Get drills to practice these inside our practice planner app
WWW.COACHBASE.COM

Things to Bear in Mind to Keep You From Losing It

1. This is an 'all-or-nothing' system – it requires constant attention.
2. It will very often seem 'bad' early on; be patient with it and teach it well.
3. Sell the players on it by promoting it as 'our best offense' – explain that the harder they play on defense, the more shots they will get. If they can't handle that, find someone who can.
4. It will be described as 'hully gully,' 'jungle ball,' and various other terms and phrases, especially when it's very good or very bad, by both your opponents and your school board. Stick to it and see what they have to say at the season's end.
5. If you have a dog, he will still love you no matter what happens with it – if you don't have a dog, GET ONE!

11 Key Press Coaching Points

1. Ball pressure is crucial at all times. '–Press' means ball pressure (arm's length away).
2. Be patient – good things take time. It may work for long spurts of short spurts, but it will work and it will work in spurts. Stay with it, as there are some intangibles that are constantly in your favor if you allow them to be.
3. Deflections are KEY, even more important than steals. Aim for 20 per game, 10 by the half.
4. Set good traps and DON'T REACH! Spring to your teammate when trapping.
5. HANDS UP! HANDS OFF!

6. SPRINT out of traps! Square shoulders to point to where you're running.
7. Look to tip from behind when you are behind the ball. Aim for two–three steals like this each game.
8. Anticipate the next move of the opponent, read their position and eyes.
9. REBOUND and RUN!
10. Make opponents take jump shots. Be there when they shoot it; be there when they miss. Give them one shot or less.
11. HAVE FUN – winning is lots of fun!

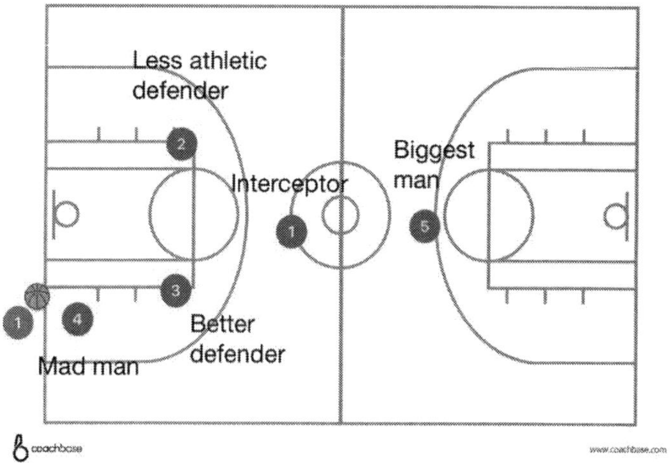

Personnel

Ideally, you'll need five energy players who can guard multiple positions. Players that are aggressive, long, and quick laterally are perfect for this defense.

1. **'Madman'** – this player is the 'heart and soul' of the system. You want a taller, mobile player with an aggressive and relentless attitude. Competitive spirit at this position, along with tremendous footwork, are of paramount importance. This position is filled first in the selection of personnel.

2. **A taller wing player** is desirable at this spot since it will involve numerous possible 'first traps.' He or she must be very good with their left hand. 'Lefties' have been very useful players in this spot.

3. **Smaller player** of the two wing players. Weaker of the two wings in regard to defending on the ball. Must exert patience when the ball is reversed, hence a player who finds it difficult to play hard for extended spurts fit nicely here. Anticipation should be better than three since this player will play more passes than the other wing.

4. **Point guard**. Often called 'interceptor' since basic responsibility is to play passes. Quickness and anticipation are of great value in this spot.

5. **Center** or bigger of the two posts. This player must protect the basket and become adept at defensive faking (stunting), thereby buying time for teammates to recover in defensive transition. They must also communicate with teammates as this player can see the entire press attack of the opponent.

First Trap

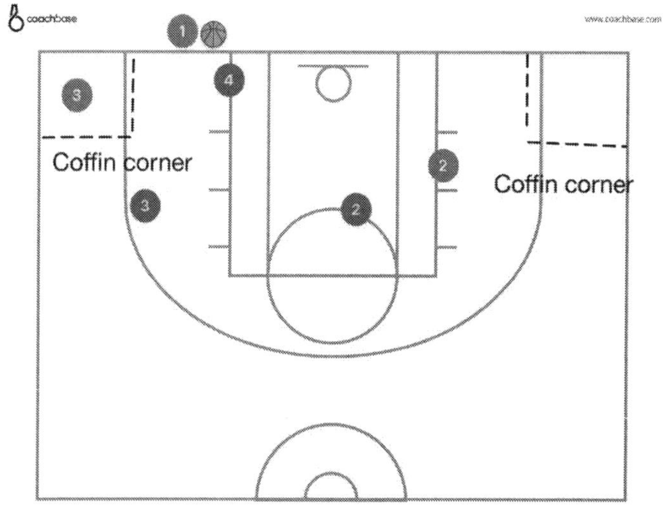

The madman has to angle themselves so that the pass does not go to the WEAKSIDE middle. All the other players must make sure the ball does not get inbounded to the middle.

Next we want the ball inbounded to the 'coffin corner' as indicated by the dotted line.

Once the ball gets inbounded, both the madman and three must trap the ball handler. (The term 'coffin corner' comes from the nickname for a very tight corner or decorative niche found in some staircases in Victorian houses.)

First Trap Key Points

- Three must NOT allow the ball handler to beat him/her down the sideline.
- Force the ball handler to pick up the ball and then immediately close the space to force the ball handler to pivot.
- Two must look at the ball handler's eyes and body to anticipate where he/she will pass the ball.
- The goal is not to steal the ball on the first pass but on the second.

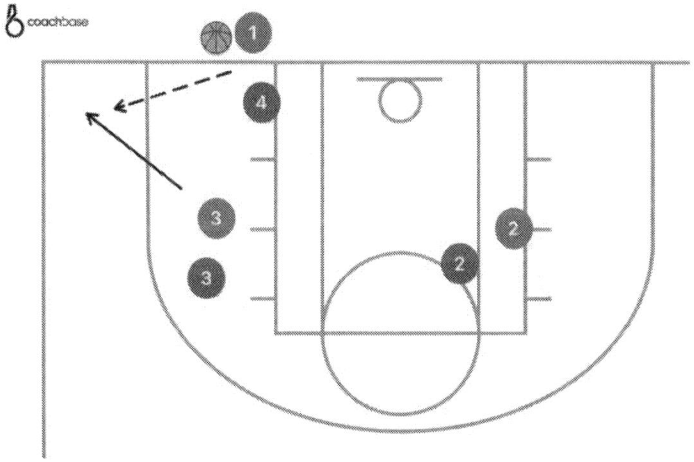

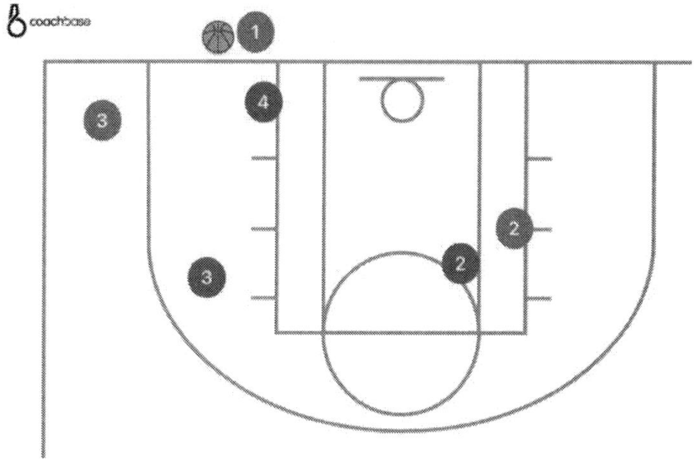
coachbase
1
4
3
3
2
2

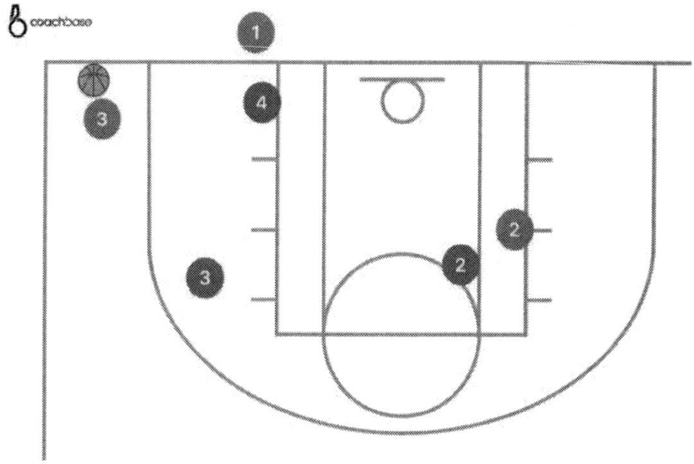
coachbase
1
4
3
3
2
2

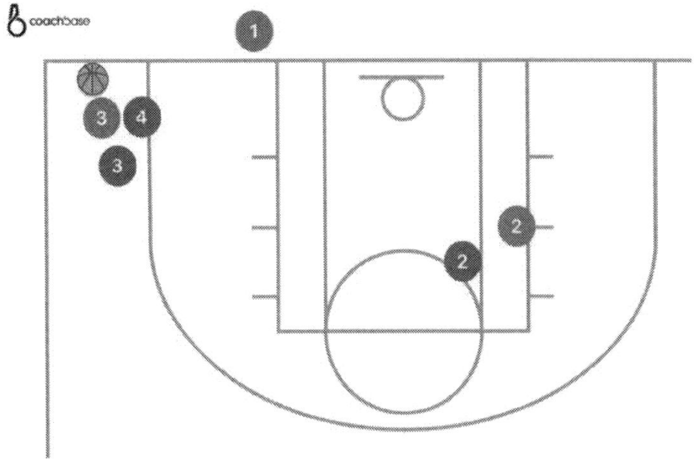

Second Trap

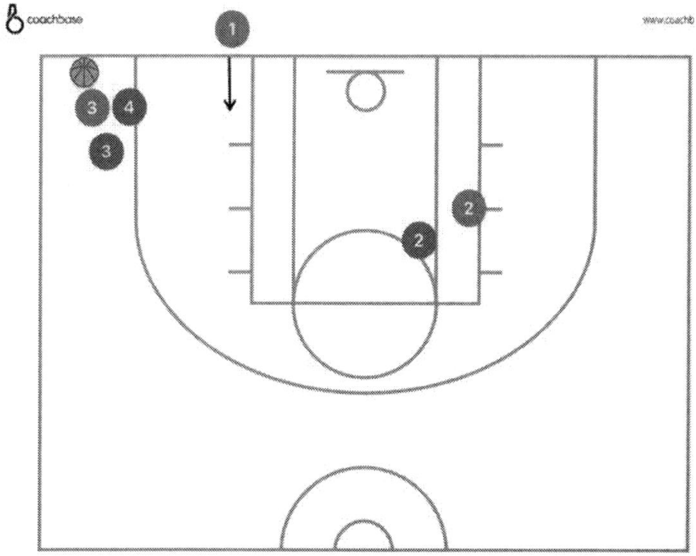
coachbase
www.coachb
1
3
4
3
2
2

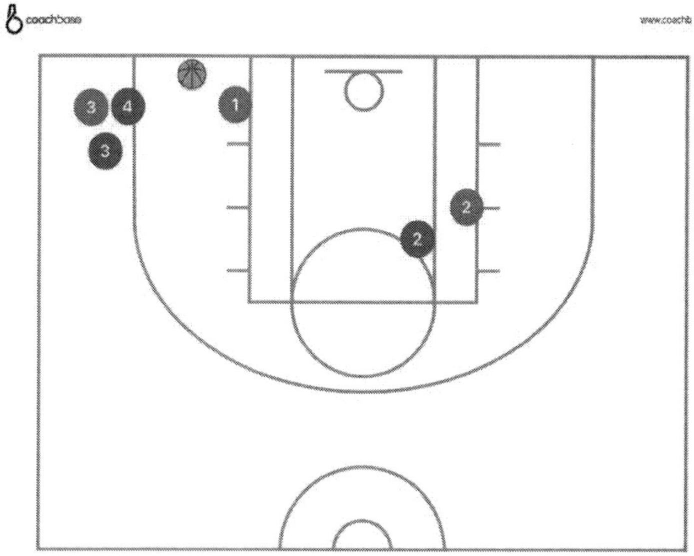
coachbase
www.coachb
3
4
1
3
2
2

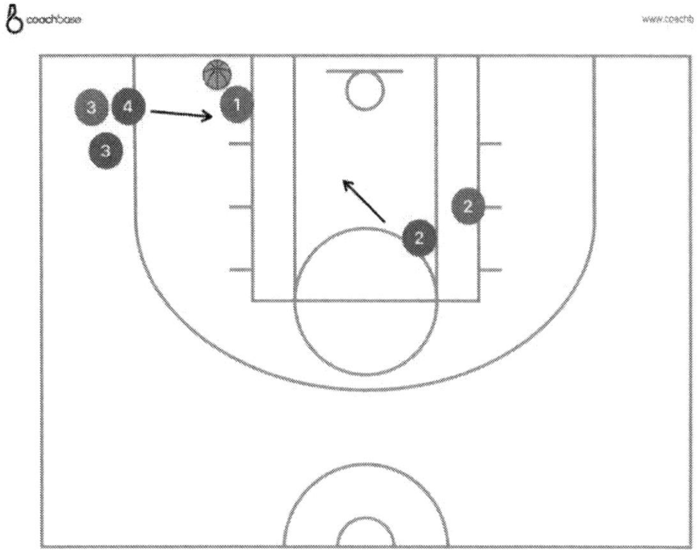
coachbase
www.coachb
3
4
1
3
2
2

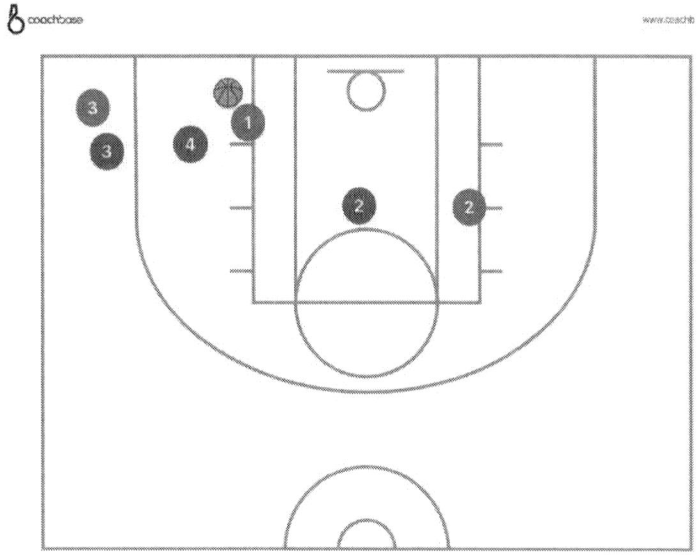
coachbase
www.coachb
3
1
3
4
2
2

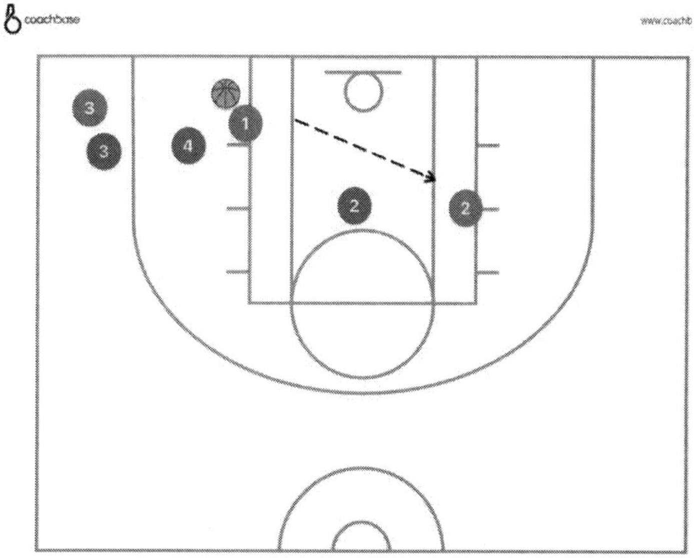
coachbase
www.coachb
3
3
4
1
2
2

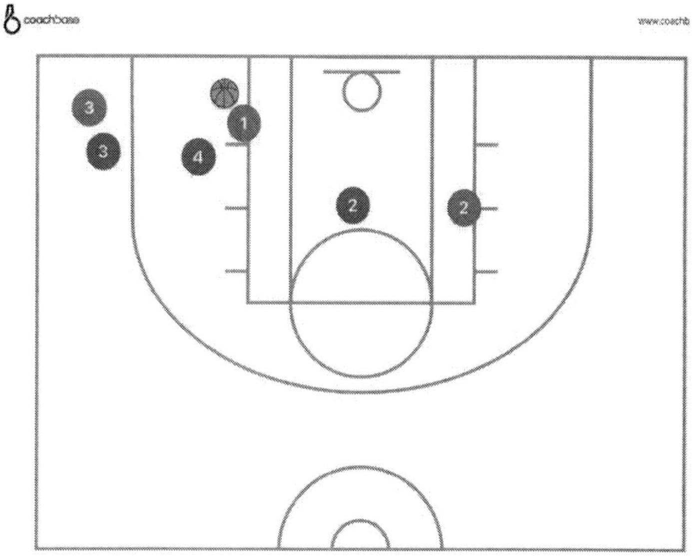
coachbase
www.coachb
3
3
4
1
2
2

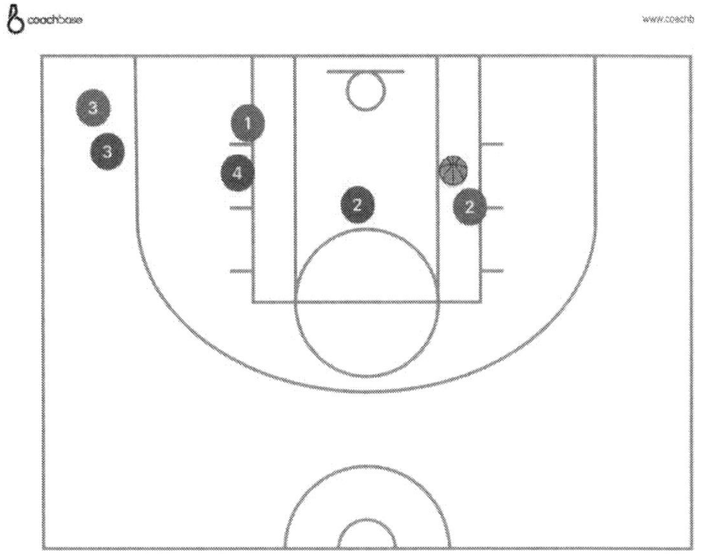
coachbase
www.coachb

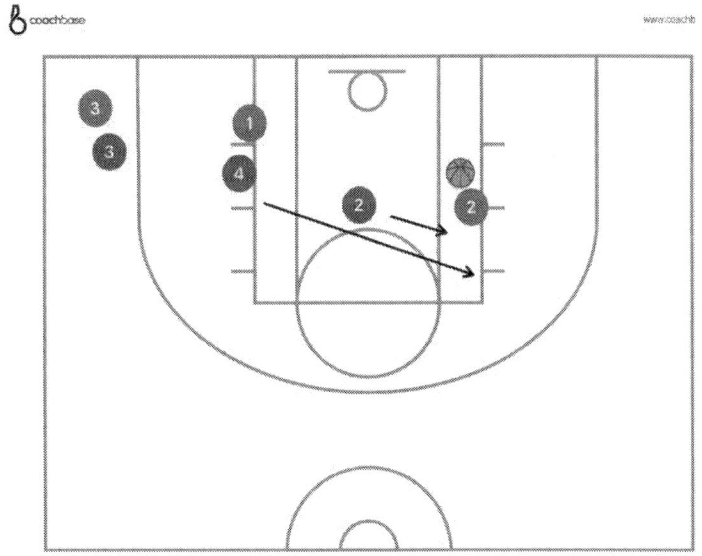
coachbase
www.coachb

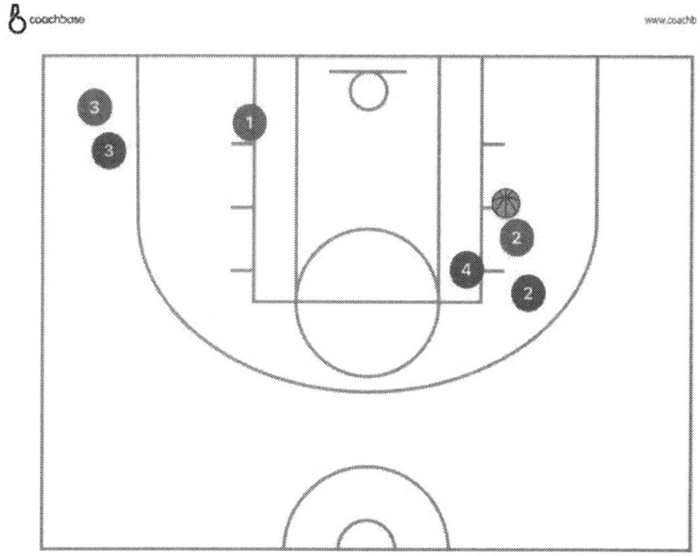

If the opponent manages to pass the ball back to the inbounder, it is two's responsible to defend both one and two. DO NOT trap one in the middle as it is difficult position to maintain and if they pass to two the press is broken.

Two needs to 'stunt' and pretend they will commit to the dribbler while buying time for the madman to recover.

If they swing the ball to the opposite two, then immediately trap. Ideally you want to trap around the half-court line area and use the baseline as an extra defender.

'Fix It' Situation

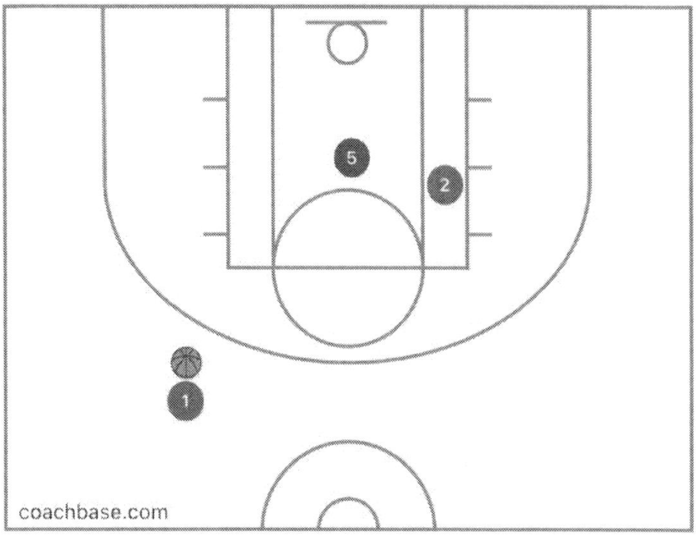
5
2
1
coachbase.com

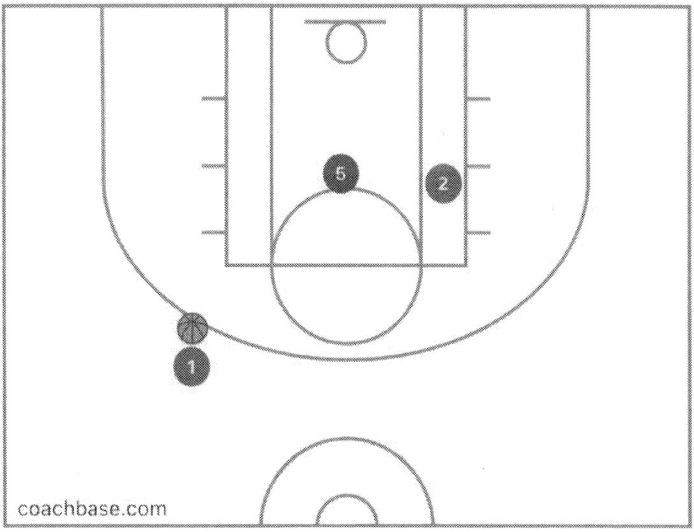
5
2
1
coachbase.com

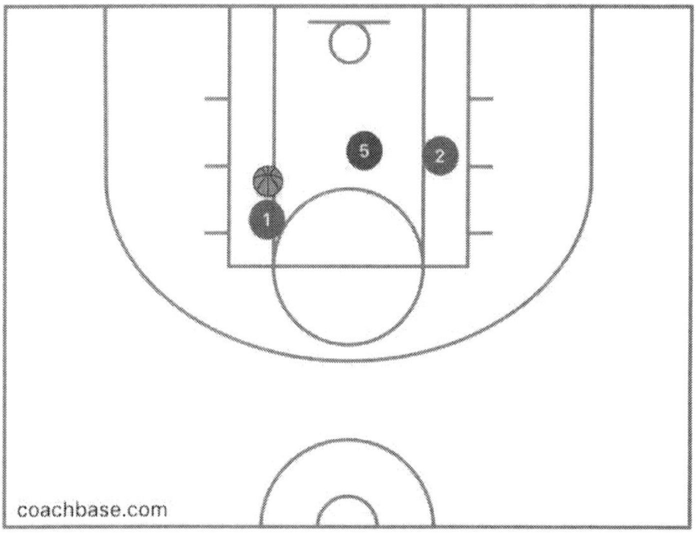
5
2
1
coachbase.com

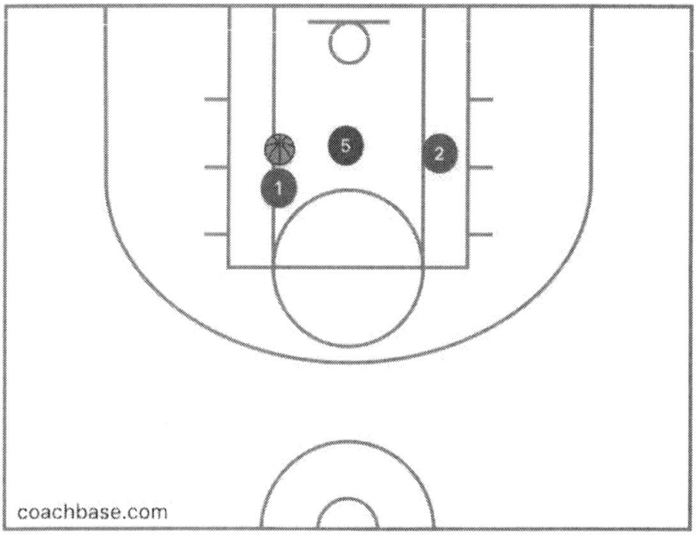
5
2
1
coachbase.com

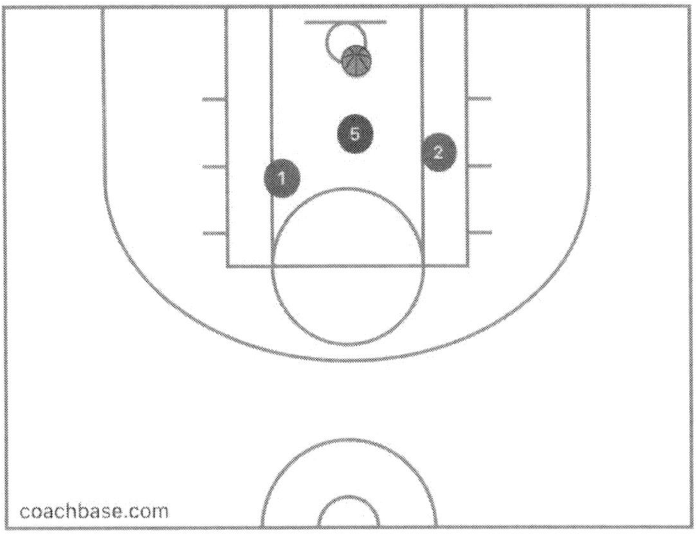

If they break the press somehow, immediately call out "fix it" and every man needs to sprint back. It doesn't matter who guards who, as long as the ball handler is being pressured and everyone has a man.

It's important that the opponent does NOT get a layup. It is five's responsibility to prevent layups and usually with a numbers disadvantage. Again, the five needs to 'stunt' (jab step) toward the dribbler to pretend they are committing to buy time for other teammates to come back.

Try to tip the ball from behind – aim for one-two tips from behind each game.

Finals tips:

- Do not allow the offense to break the press the same way twice.

8

Eight Drills for Building the One-Two-One-One Press

To implement this high-intensity defensive system, your players need to:

- Get comfortable in a defensive stance. Stay low – don't bob up and down. Ask them to imagine a ceiling they can't hit.
- Attention to detail when trapping. Practice two-on-one trapping. You should never let someone split your defenders. The two defenders need to communicate and also have their legs toughing (close together) to prevent a split.
- Toughness. Defense is 90% effort. These drills will be physically challenging, so stay focused and keep intensity high.
- When players get tired they can often foul with their arms. Move your feet and be aggressive with your lower body, not upper body.

Tip Drill

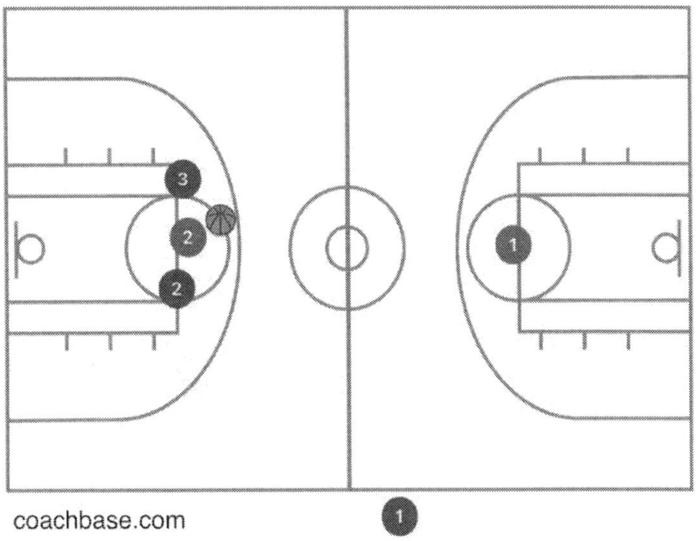

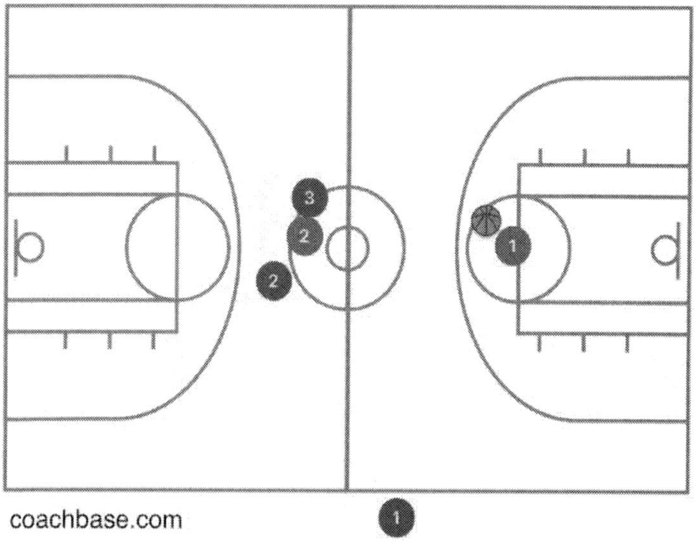
3
2
2
1
coachbase.com
1

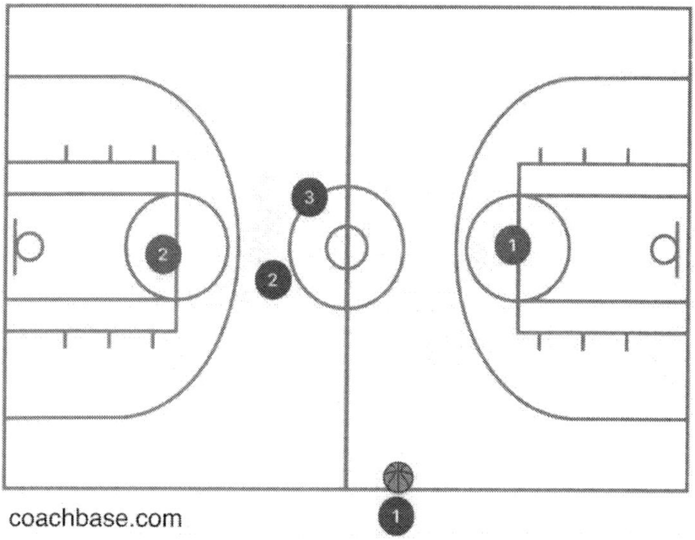
3
2
2
1
coachbase.com
1

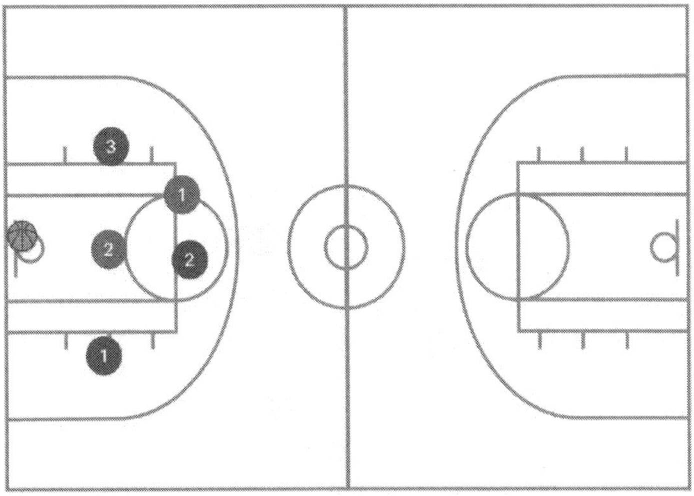

coachbase.com

Purpose

When your press gets beaten, a tip from behind will really deflate the offense. This drill simulates tipping the ball from behind and then into a three-on-two situation.

Instructions

- The ball handler starts inside the paint. He/she can only dribble with one hand
- The two defenders try to tip the ball from behind
- If the ball is tipped or ball handler reaches halfway, one must pick up the ball and pass to the player on the sideline
- Play three-on-two

Mirror into One-on-One

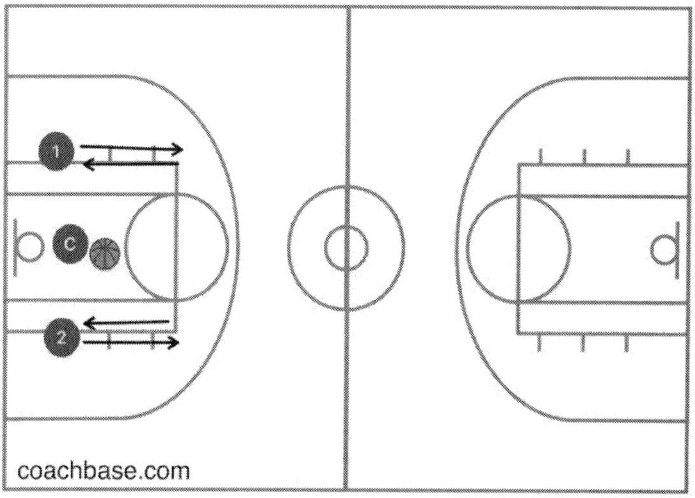

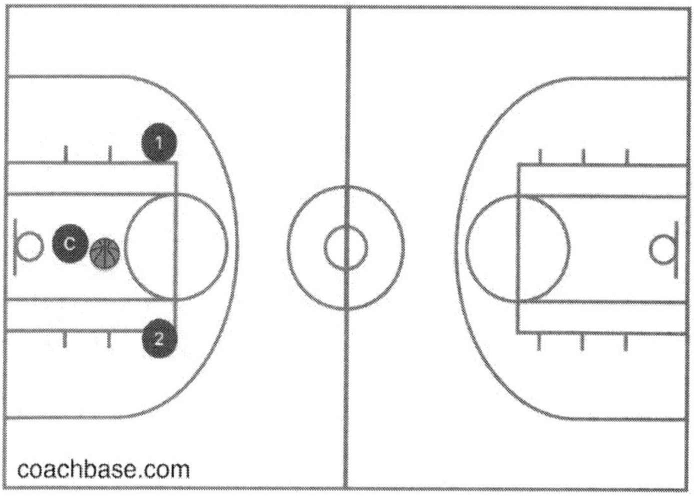

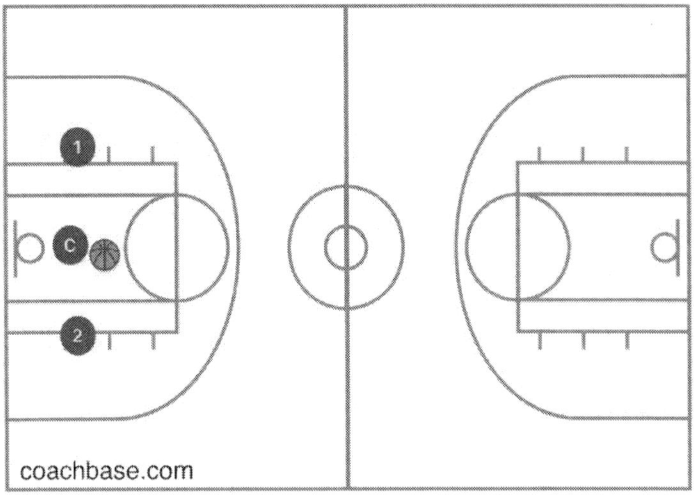
1
C
2
coachbase.com

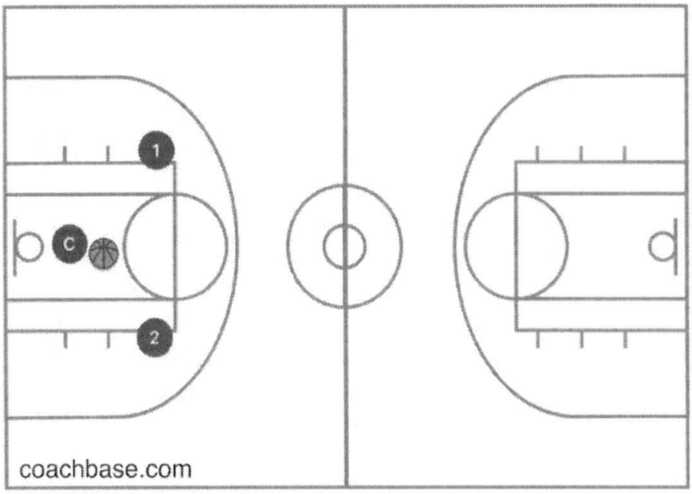
1
C
2
coachbase.com

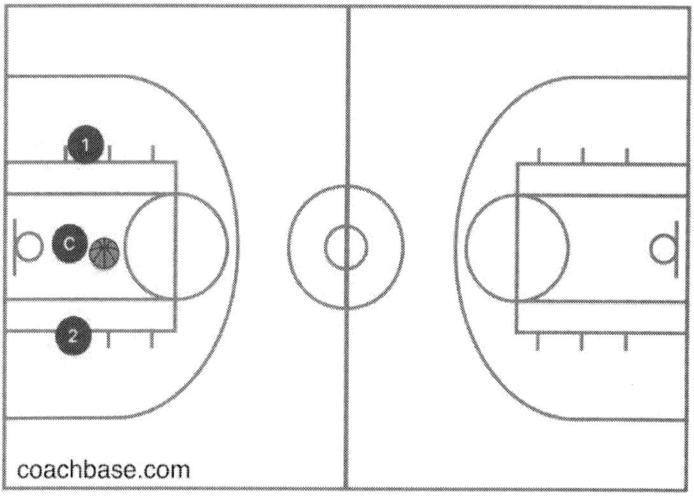
1
C
2
coachbase.com

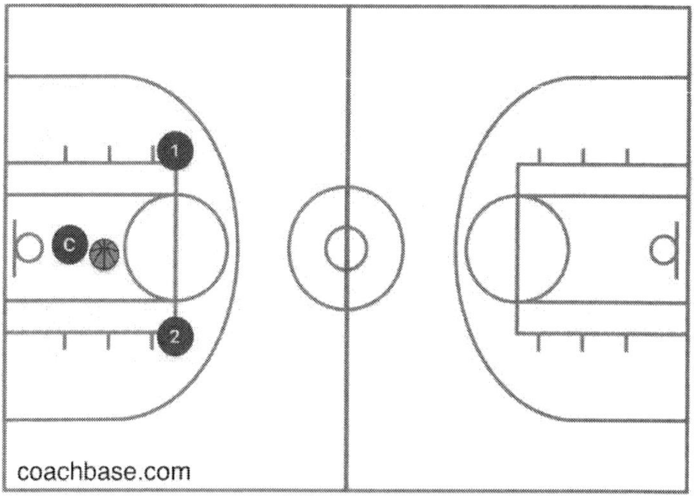
1
C
2
coachbase.com

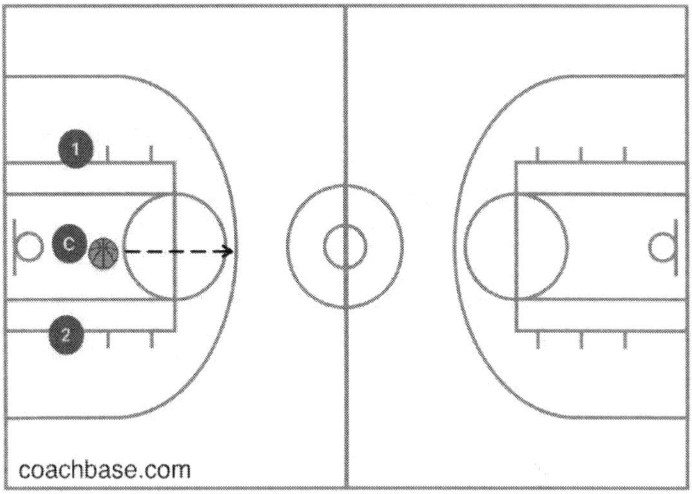
1
C
2
coachbase.com

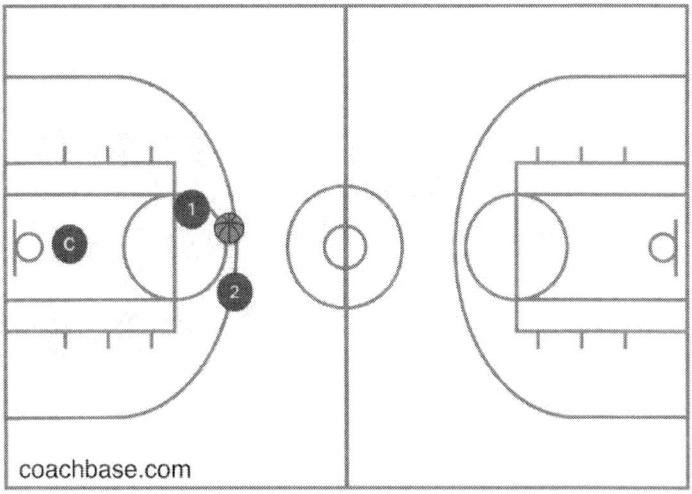
1
C
2
coachbase.com

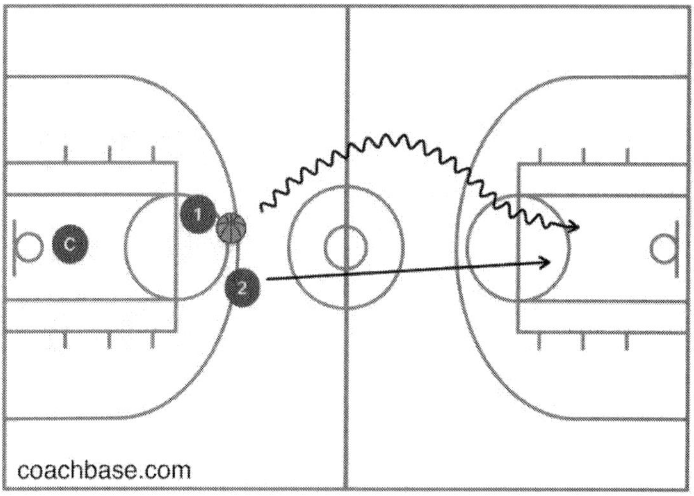
1
2
C
coachbase.com

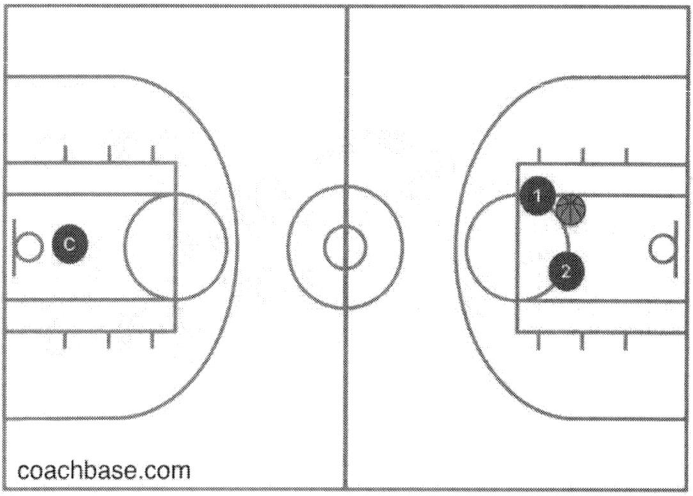
1
2
C
coachbase.com

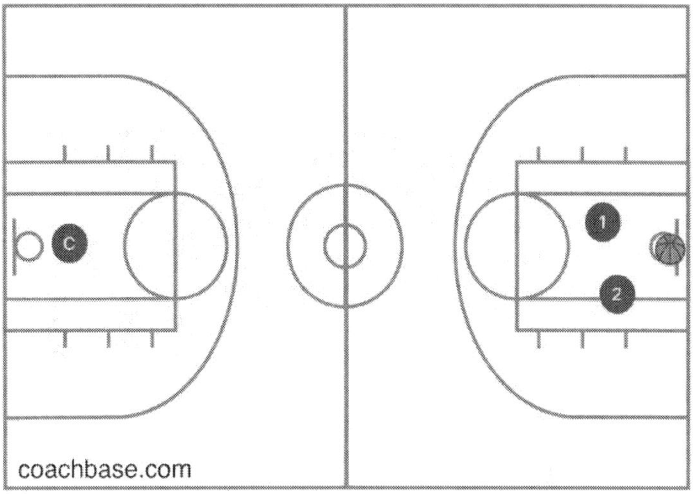

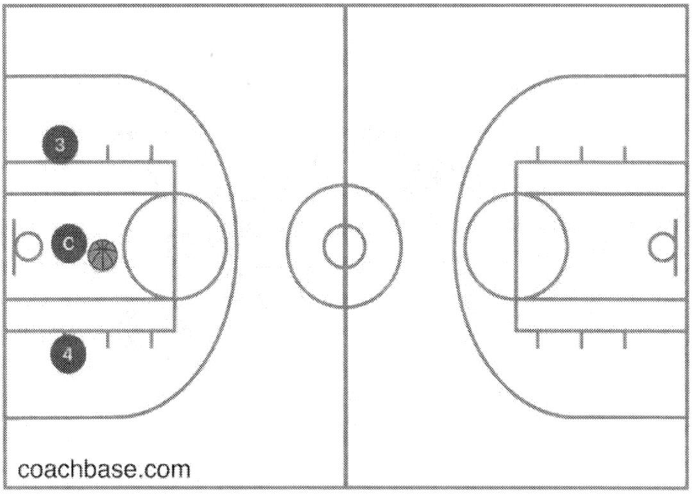

Purpose

This drill has two parts: mirror game and then into a one-on-one. Mirror defense is great for getting players into a defensive stance and moving quickly laterally; one-on-one is a great conditioning drill.

Instructions

- The coach holds the ball underneath the rim
- One player is defense, one is offense. The defense must 'mirror' the offense's lateral movements. The offense can only move laterally and tries not to let the defense mirror them.
- Coach will randomly throw the ball onto the court
- The two players must fight to get the ball. The person who takes it is offense
- Play full court one-on-one.

Two-on-One Stunt

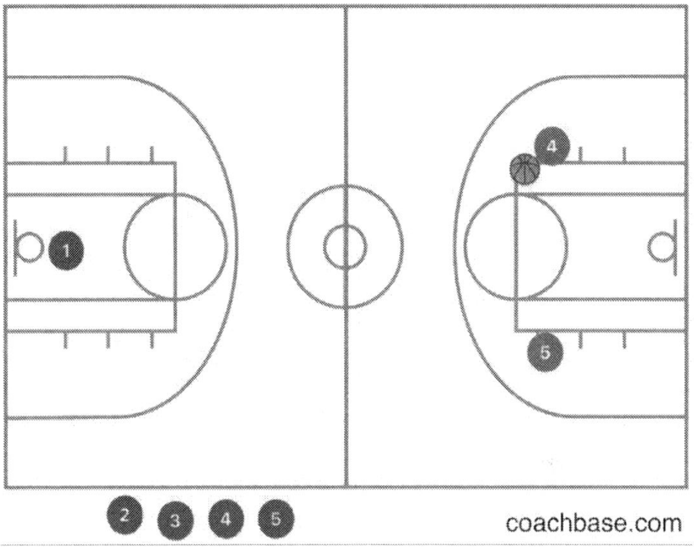
4
1
5
2
3
4
5
coachbase.com

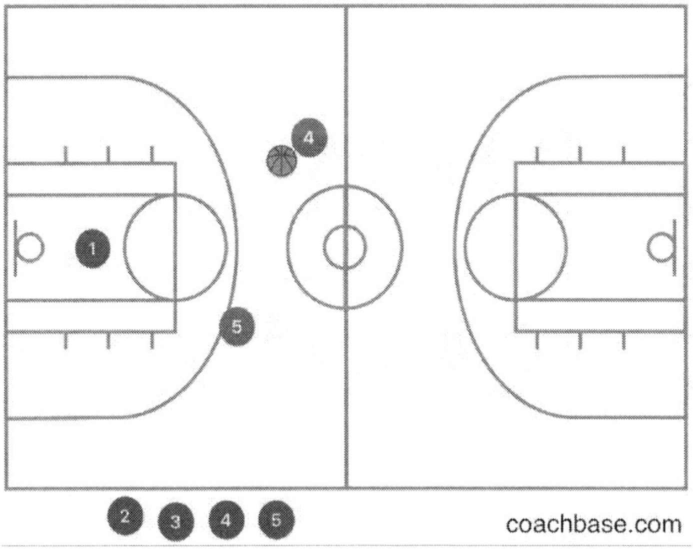
4
1
5
2
3
4
5
coachbase.com

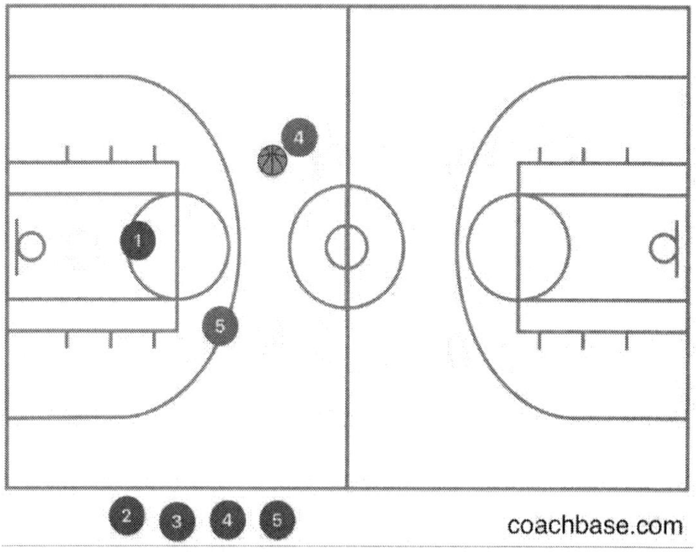
4
1
5
2
3
4
5
coachbase.com

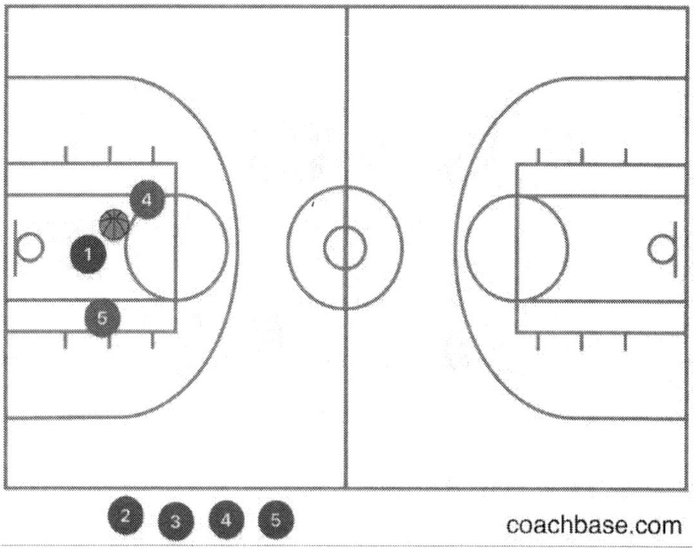
4
1
5
2
3
4
5
coachbase.com

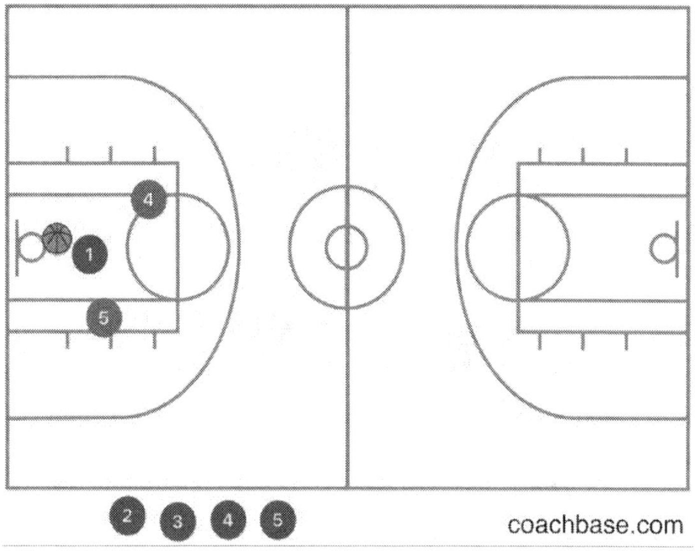
4
1
5
2
3
4
5
coachbase.com

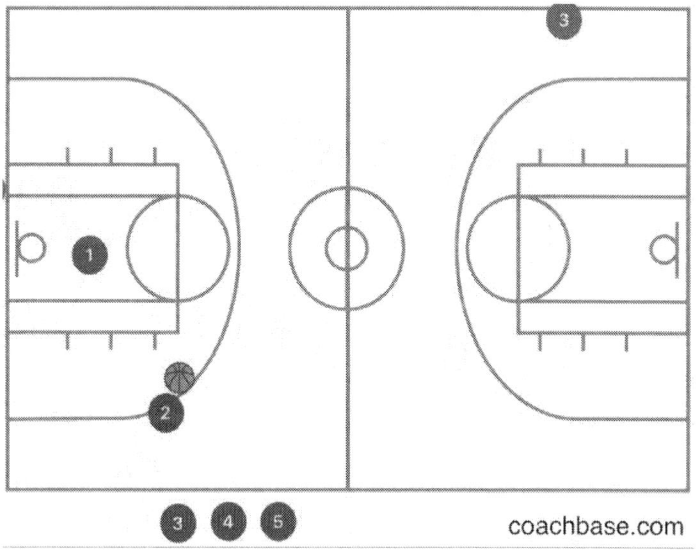
3
1
2
3
4
5
coachbase.com

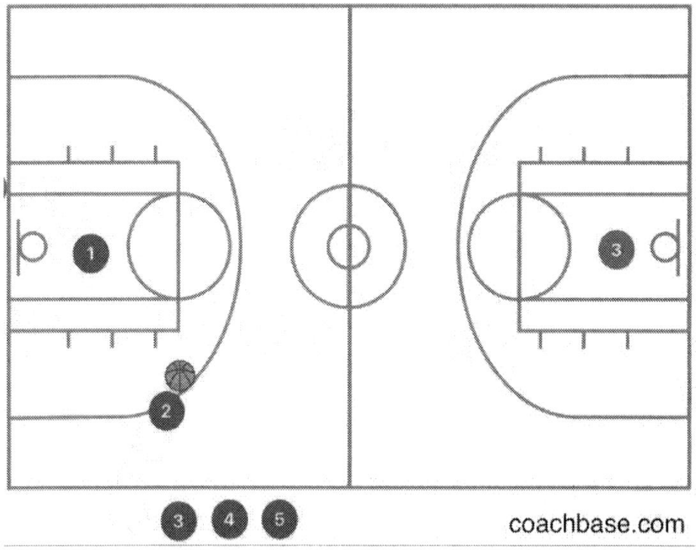
1
3
2
3
4
5
coachbase.com

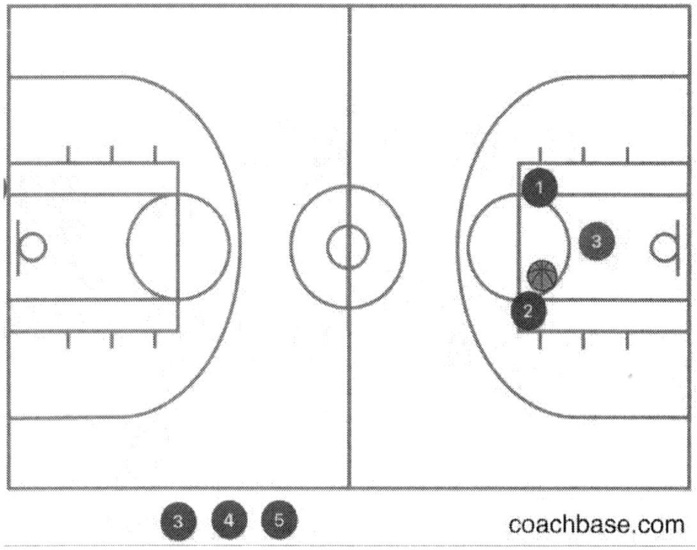
1
3
2
3
4
5
coachbase.com

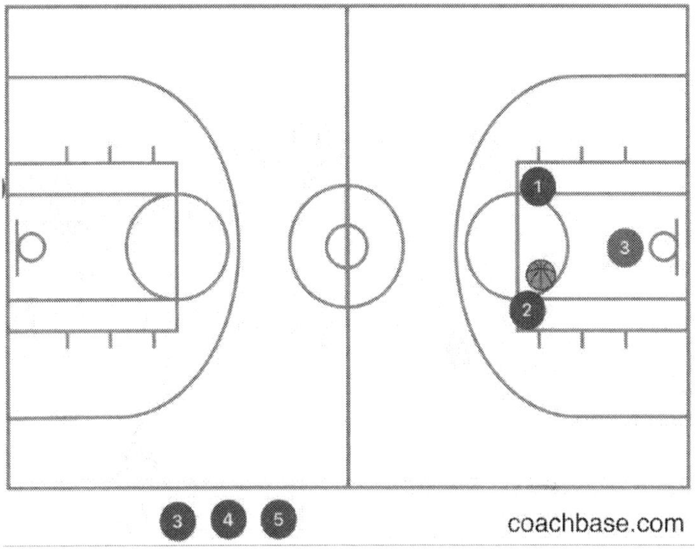
1
2
3
3
4
5
coachbase.com

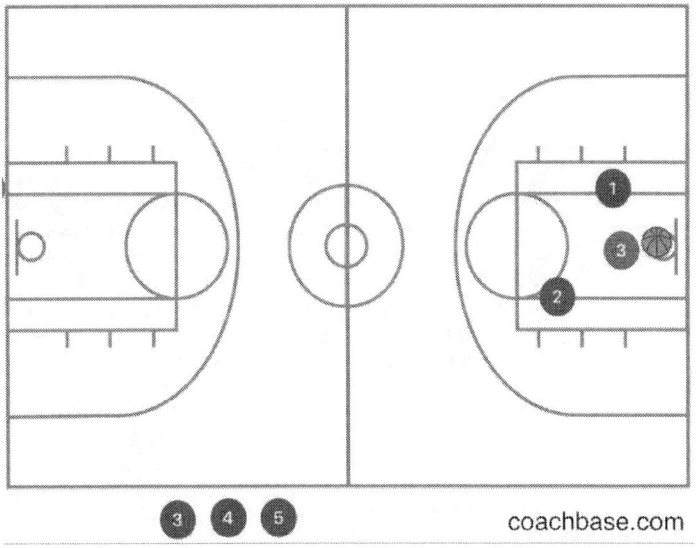
1
3
2
3
4
5
coachbase.com

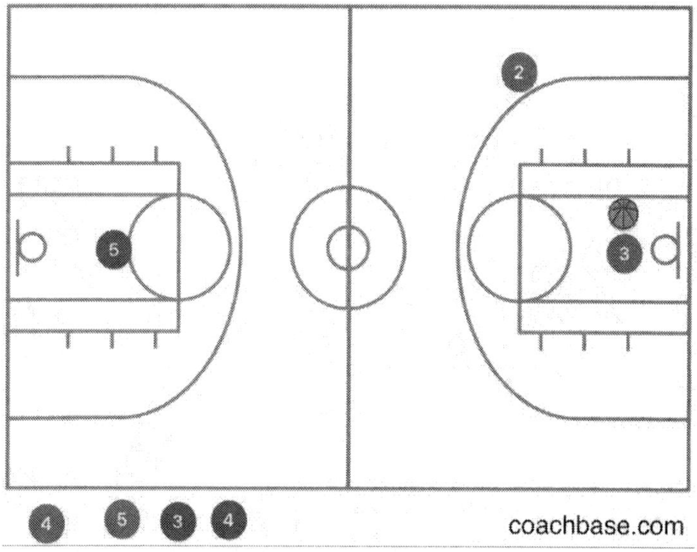
2
5
3
4
5
3
4
coachbase.com

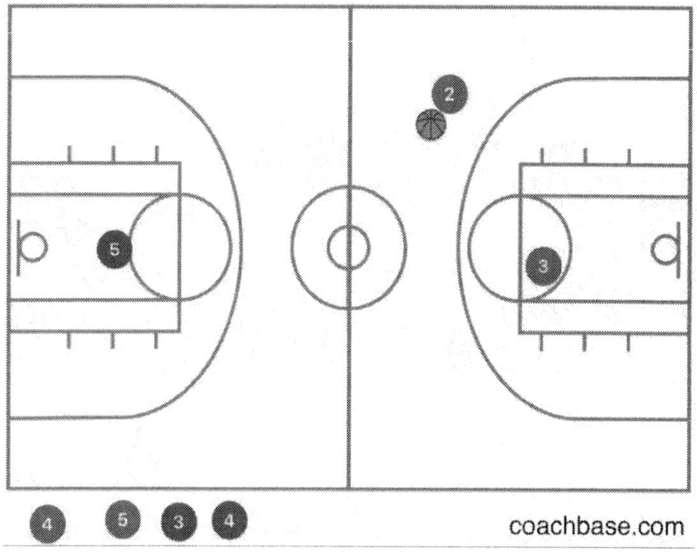
2
5
3
4
5
3
4
coachbase.com

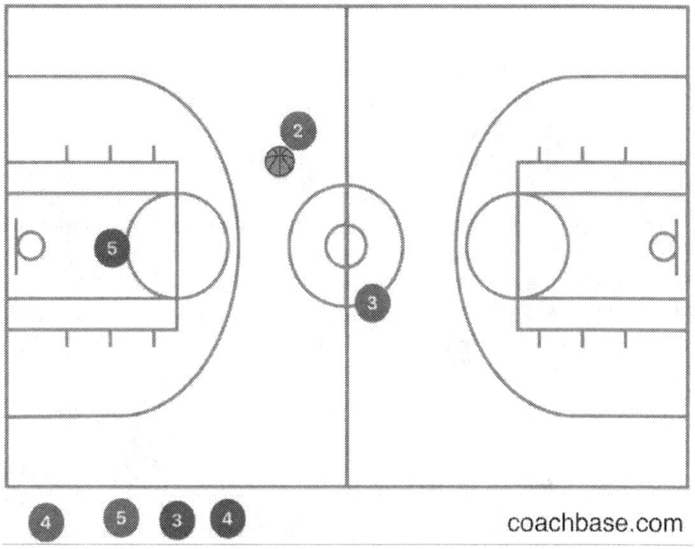

Purpose

One of the cardinal rules of the press is no layups. A lot of time you'll have a numbers disadvantage when the offense breaks the zone. This is when you want to stunt, meaning you want to pretend to commit by making a jab step.

Instructions

- Play two-on-one. The defender tries to prevent a layup
- Have two lines lining up along the sideline. Join in for two-on-one

One-on-Two into One-on-One

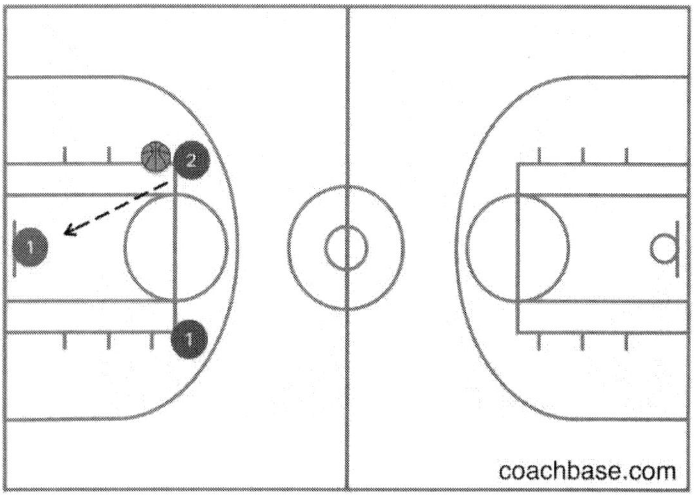

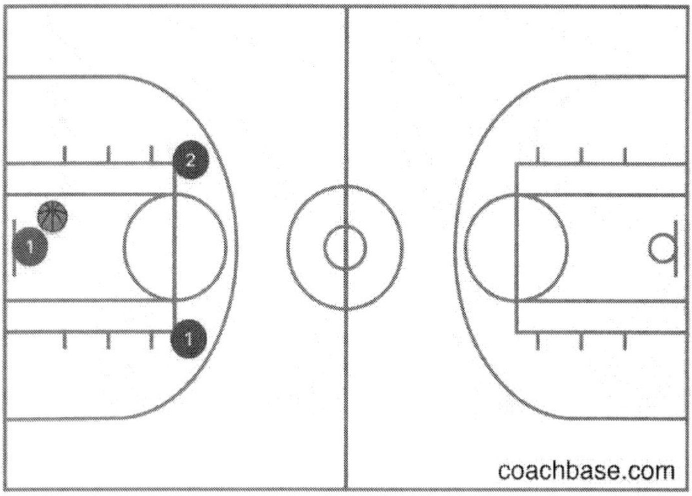

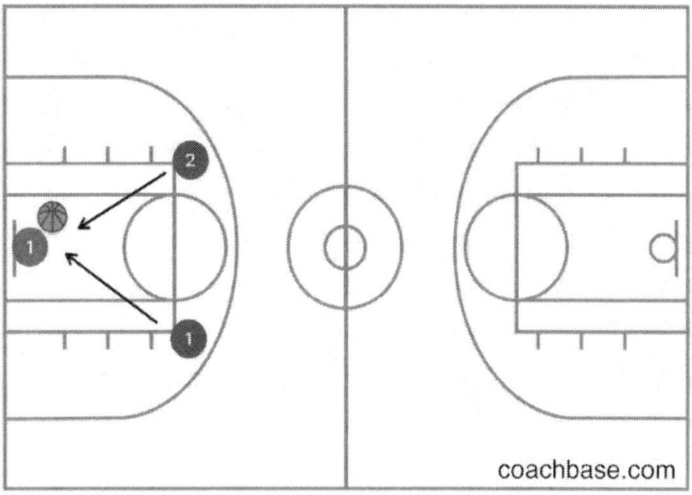
2
1
1
coachbase.com

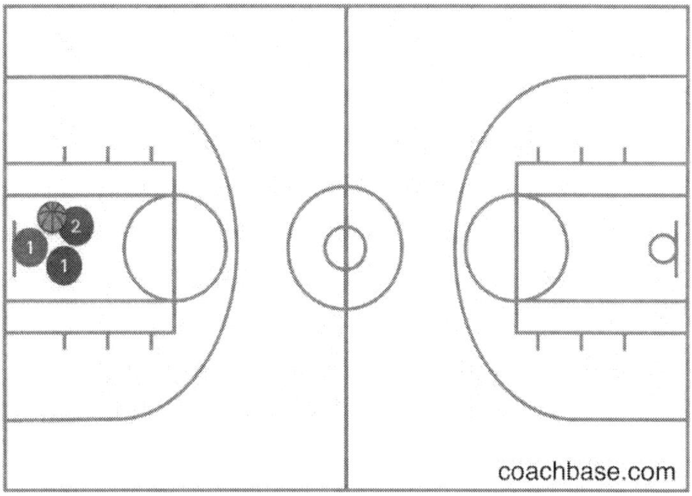
2
1
1
coachbase.com

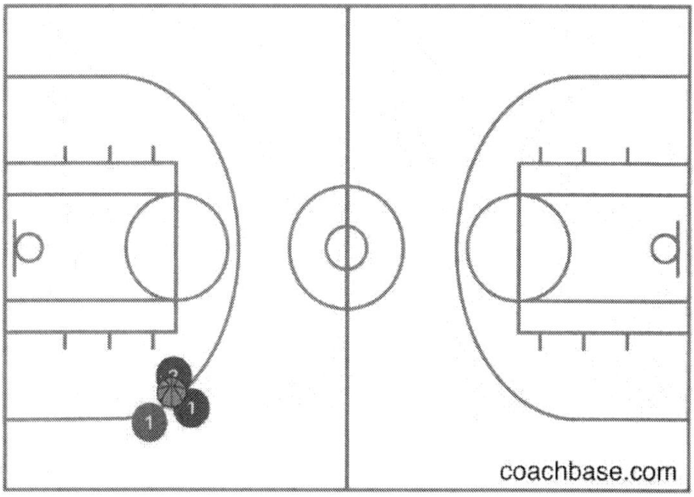
coachbase.com

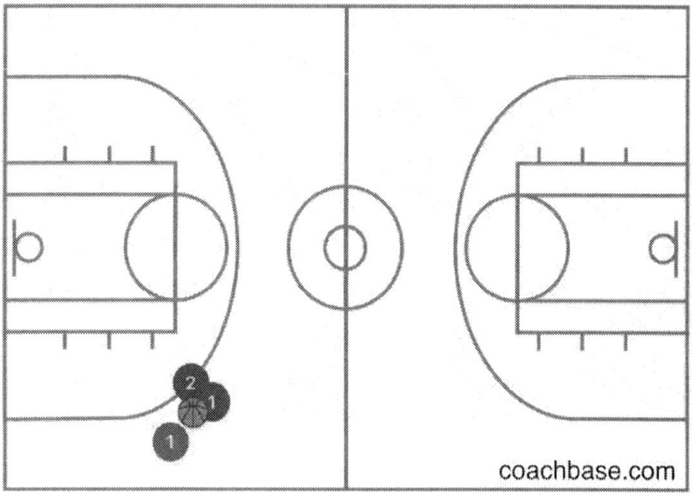
coachbase.com

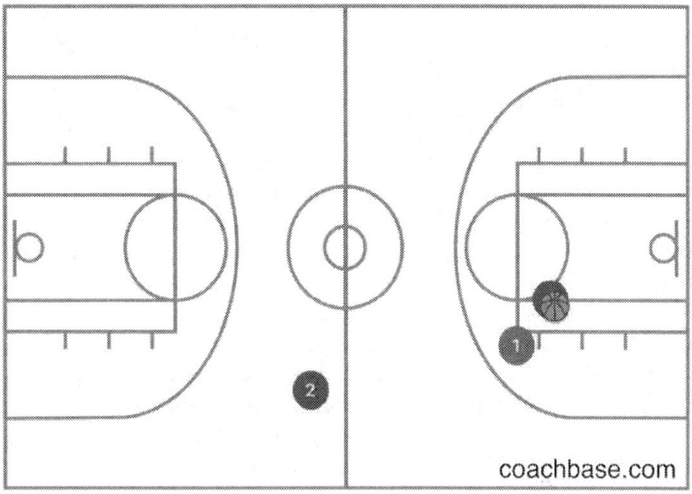

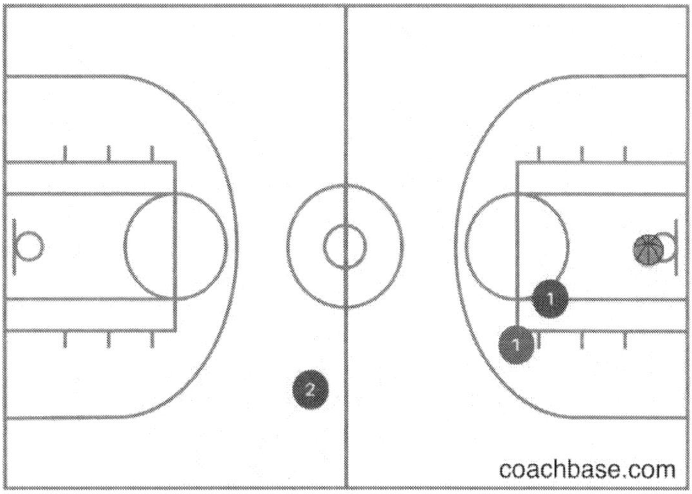

Purpose

In this press, it is important to trap the ball handler, especially in the coffin corner. Practice trapping and not letting the ball handler split the defense or beat the defenders down the sideline. Force the ball handler middle.

Instructions

- Two defenders at free-throw line, offense on baseline
- Defenders pass the ball to offensive player and then it's two-on-one
- If the ball handler reaches the halfway line, the closest defender plays one-on-one for the remainder of the half

Two-on-Two trap

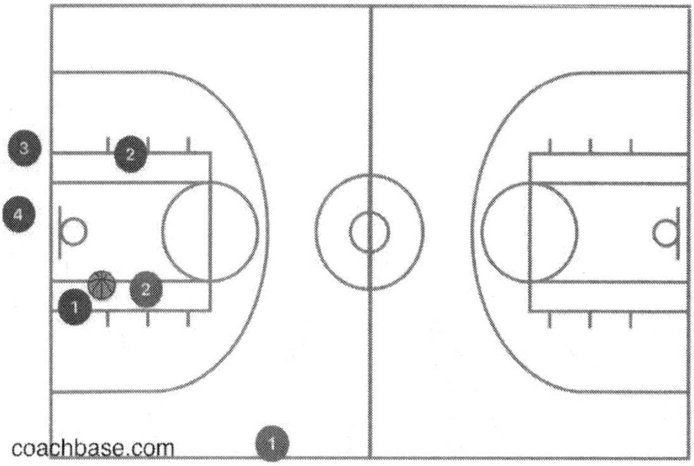

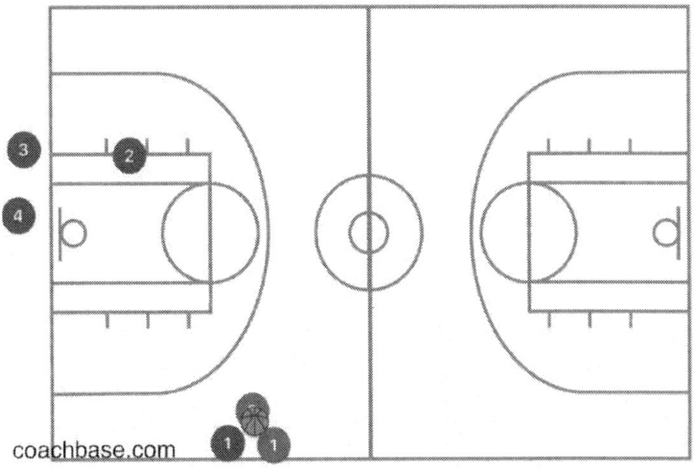
3
2
4
1
1
coachbase.com

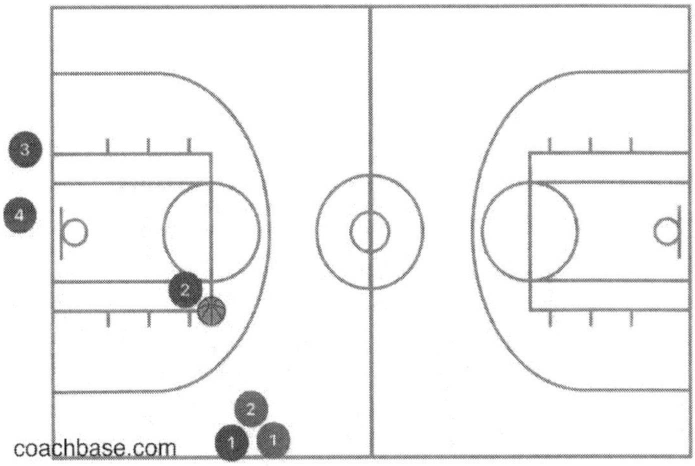
3
4
2
2
1
1
coachbase.com

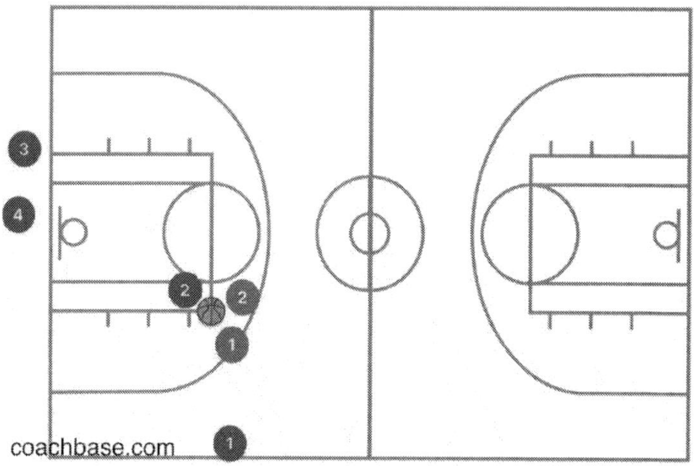
3
4
2
2
1
1
coachbase.com

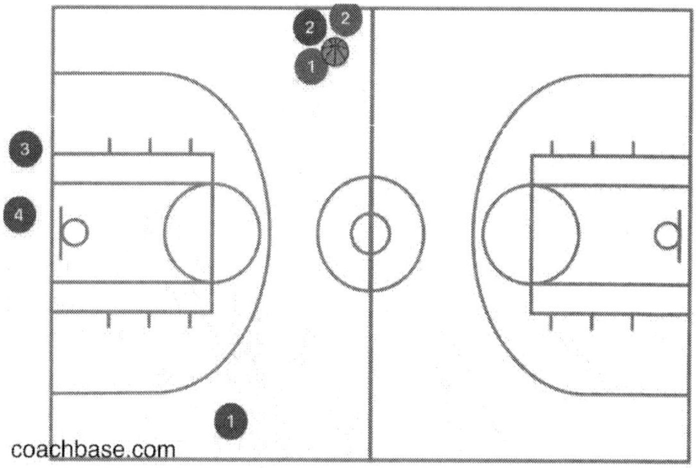
2
2
1
3
4
1
coachbase.com

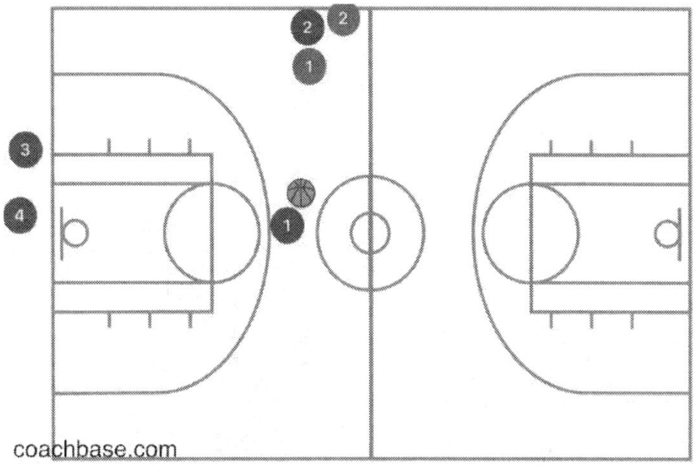
2
2
1
3
4
1
coachbase.com

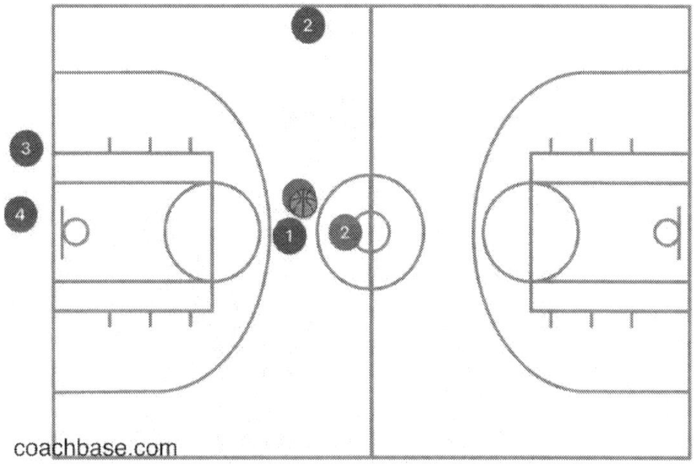
2
3
4
1
2
coachbase.com

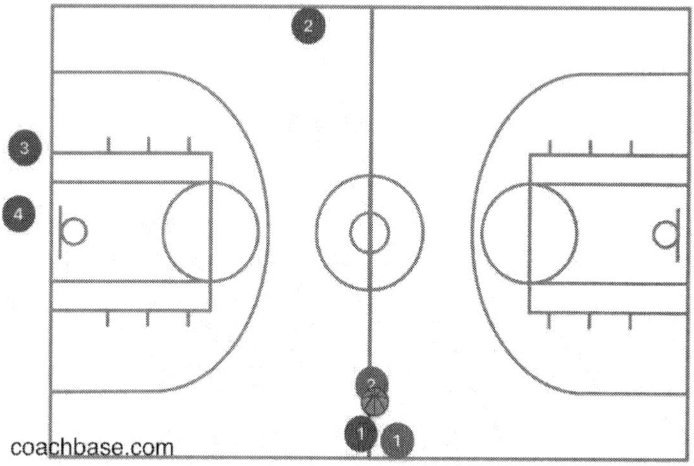

Purpose

The defense needs to learn to how to adjust when the ball handler passes the ball. This drill simulates that.

Instructions

- The ball handler tries to beat two defenders. Defenders must force the ball handler to pick up the ball
- The ball handler can only pass backward to the other offensive player
- Keep going until the other offensive player reaches the opposite baseline.
- If this is too hard, make the offense slow down

Two-on-One Slides

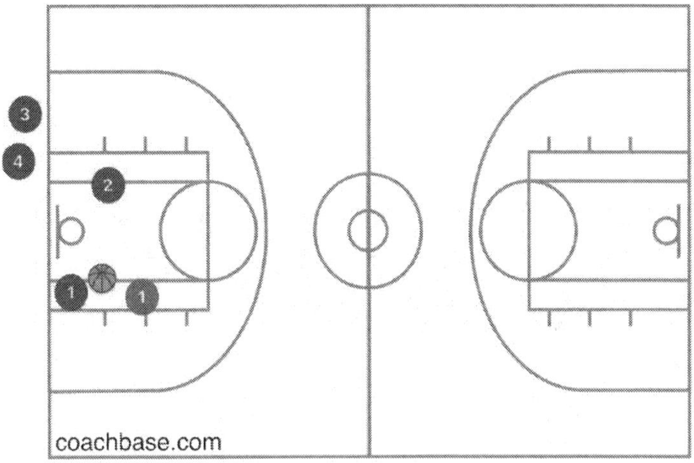

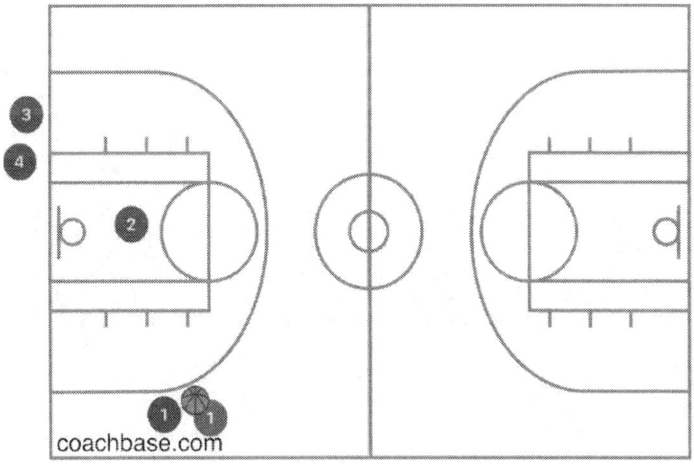

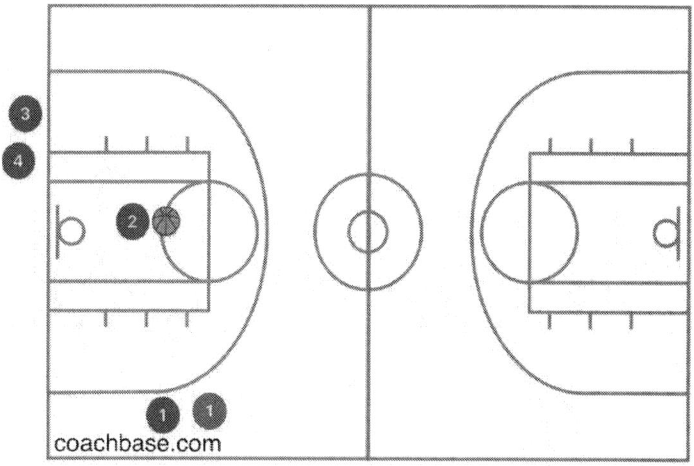
3
4
2
1
1
coachbase.com

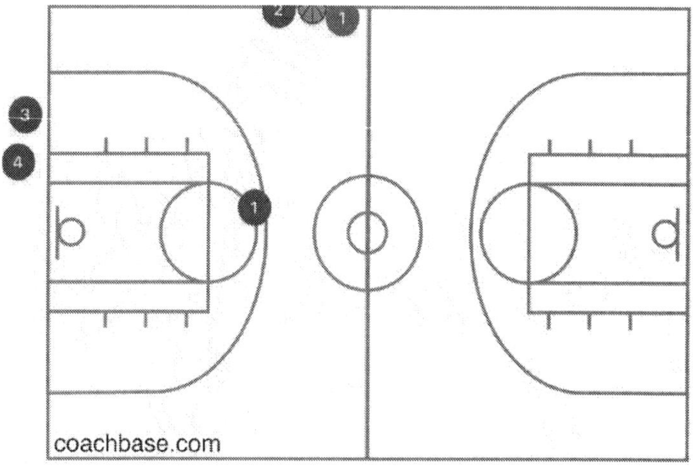
2
1
3
4
1
coachbase.com

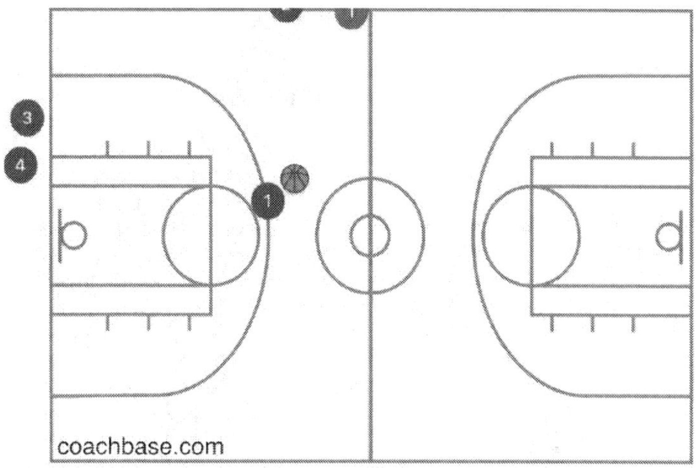
3
4
1
coachbase.com

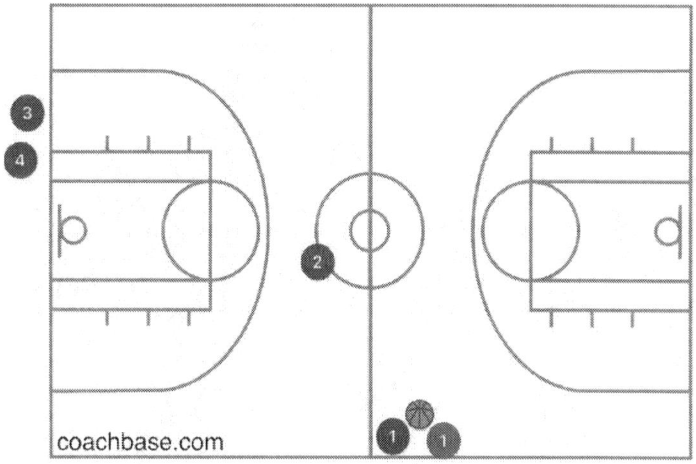
3
4
2
1
1
coachbase.com

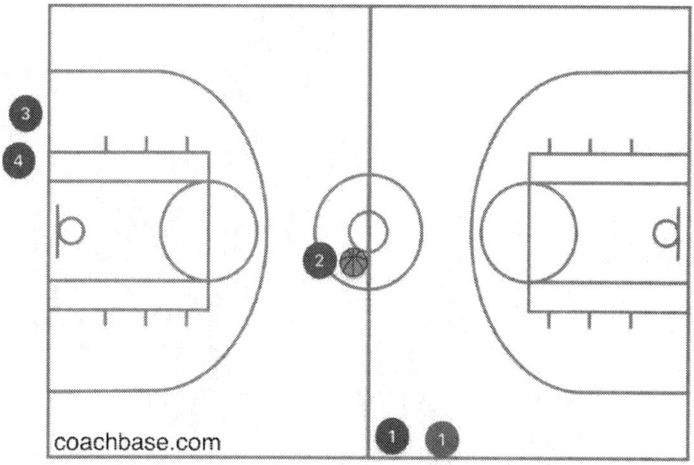
3
4
2
1
1
coachbase.com

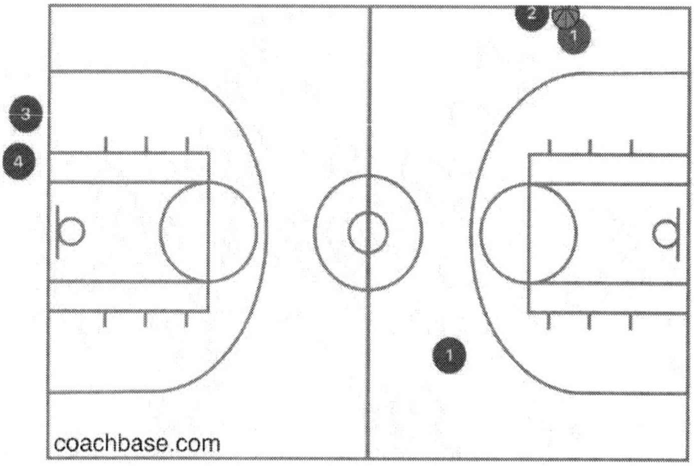
2
1
3
4
1
coachbase.com

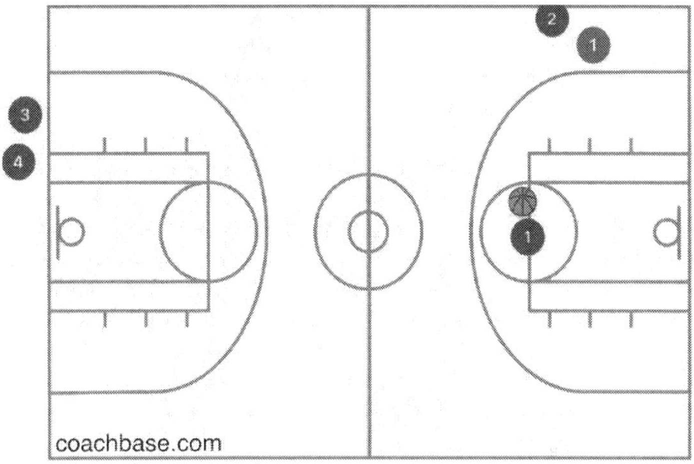

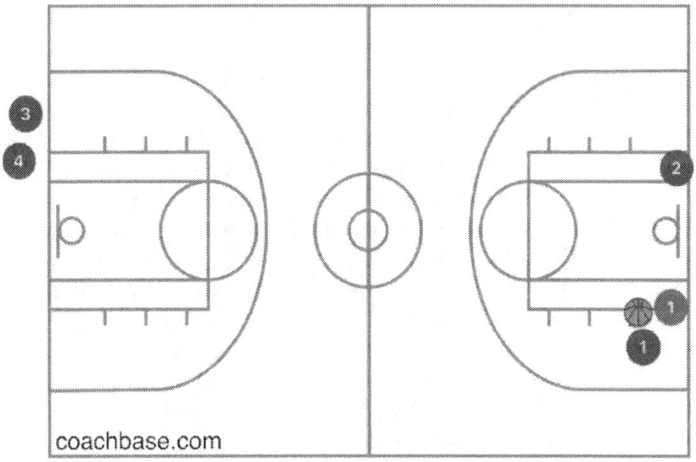

Purpose

This is a conditioning drill to get the defensive player moving in a defensive stance. Remember to stay low and imagine an unreachable ceiling.

Instructions

- Offensive players dribble upcourt
- Defensive player tries to force the ball handler to pick up the ball
- When offensive player reaches sideline or middle they should pass the ball to the other player
- Continue until baseline
- On the pass, the defensive player must turn hips and sprint to recover

Sprint Slides

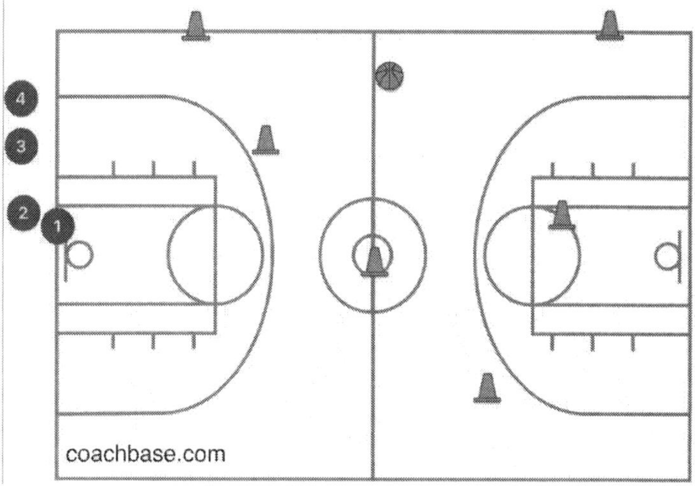

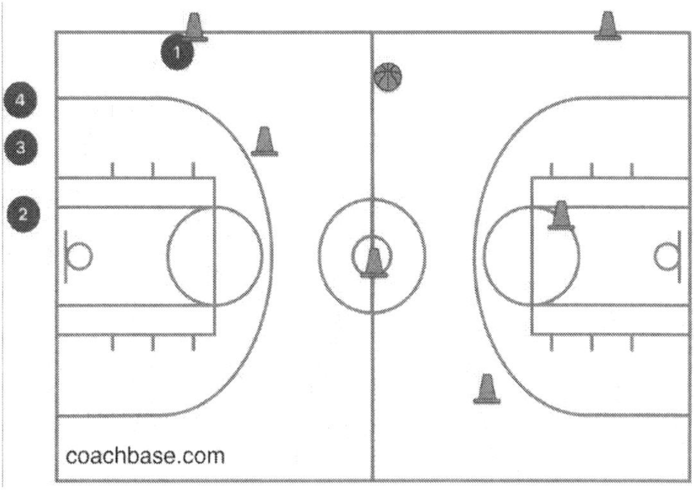
1
4
3
2
coachbase.com

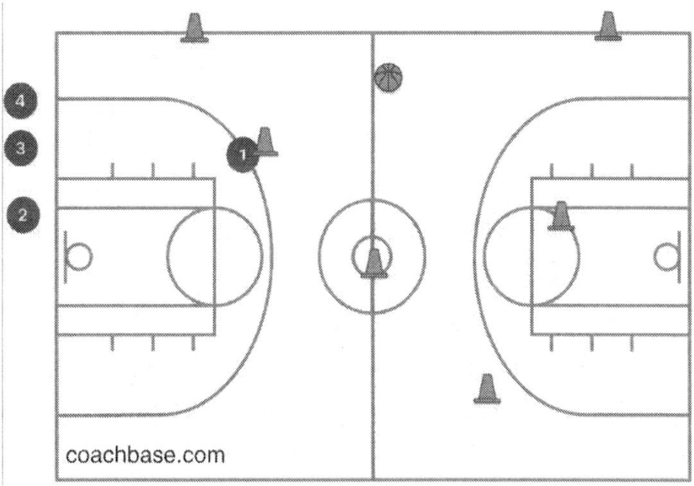
4
3
1
2
coachbase.com

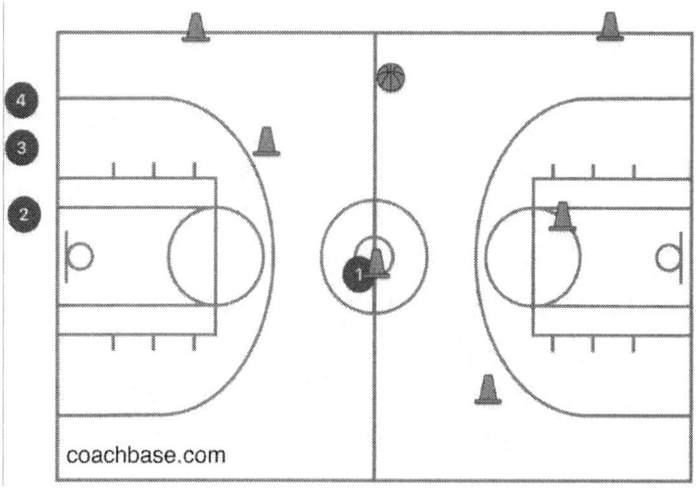
4
3
2
1
coachbase.com

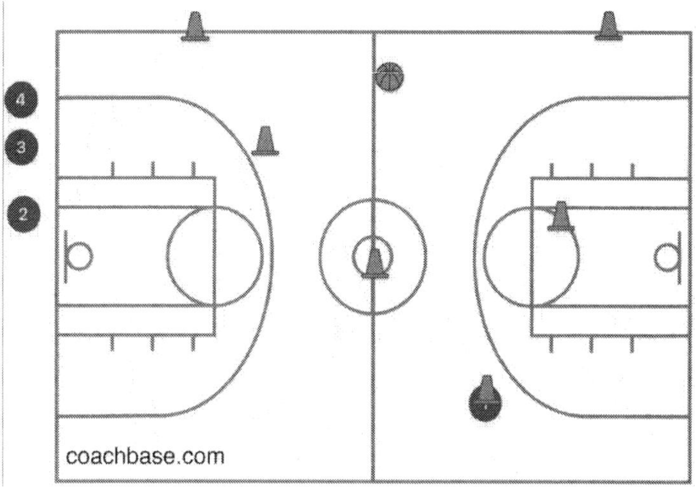
4
3
2
coachbase.com

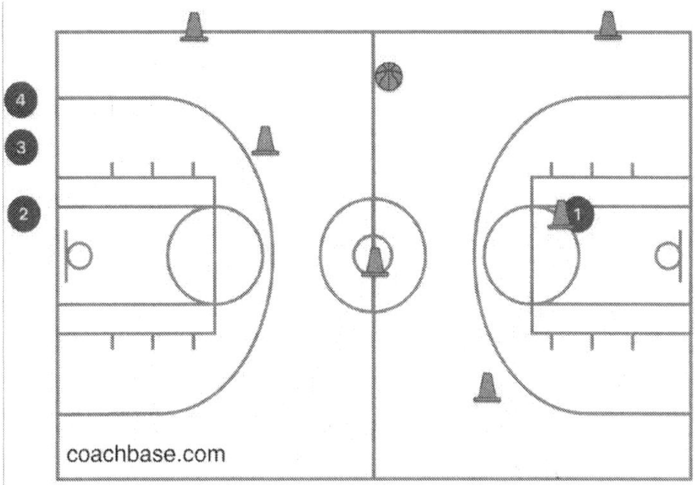

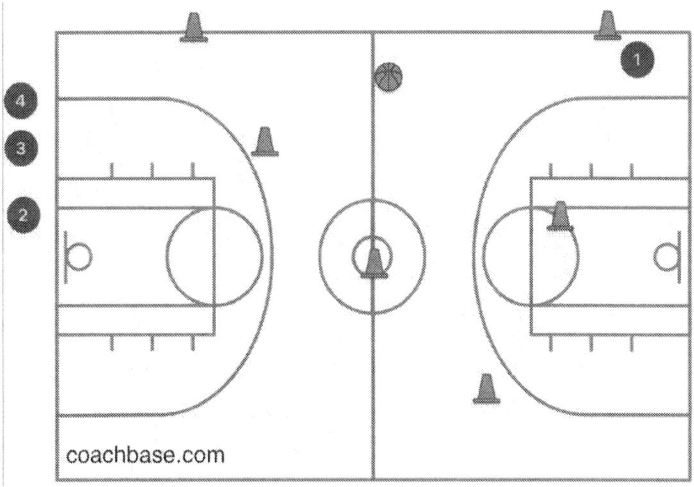

Purpose

This is a conditioning drill to work on defensive quickness.

Instructions

- Set up cones on the court
- Defensive slide from cone to cone then turn hips and sprint to the next one
- So defensive slide for one length, then sprint, and then slide

Mass Defensive Slides

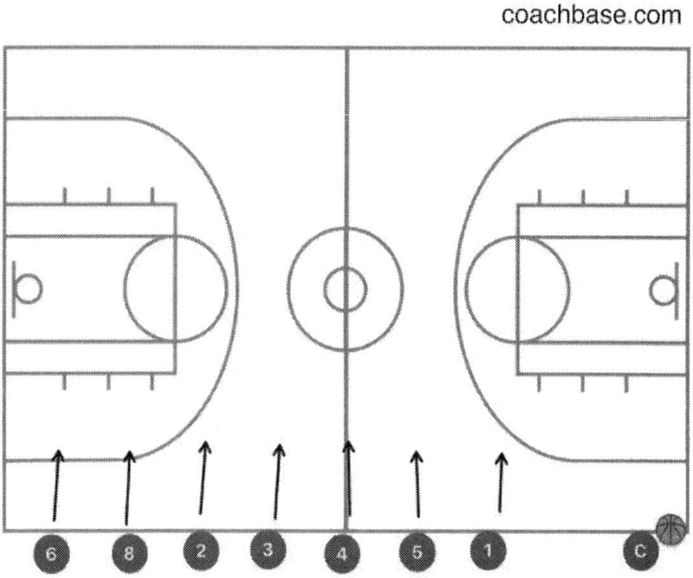

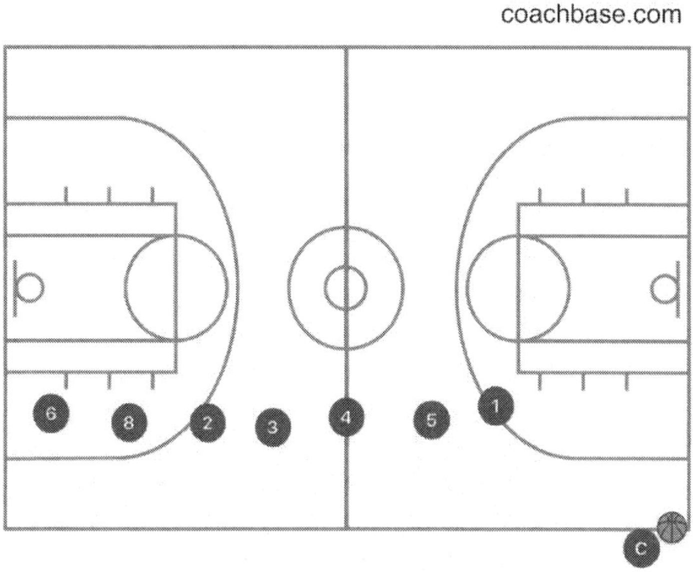
coachbase.com
6
8
2
3
4
5
1
C

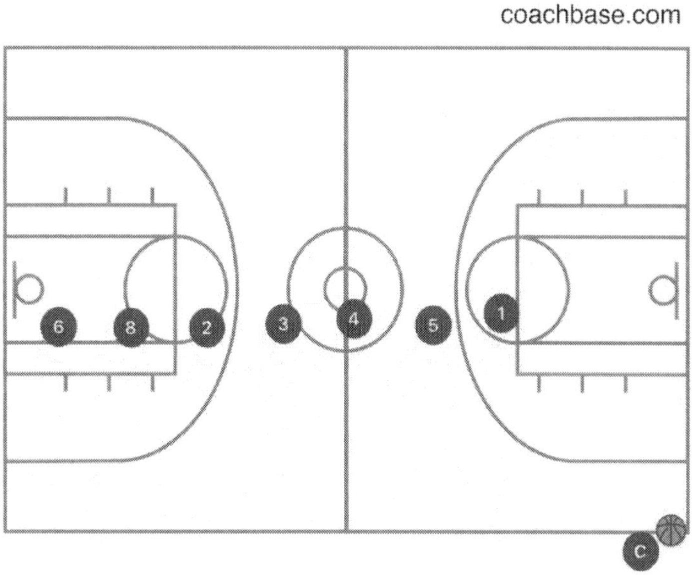
coachbase.com
6
8
2
3
4
5
1
C

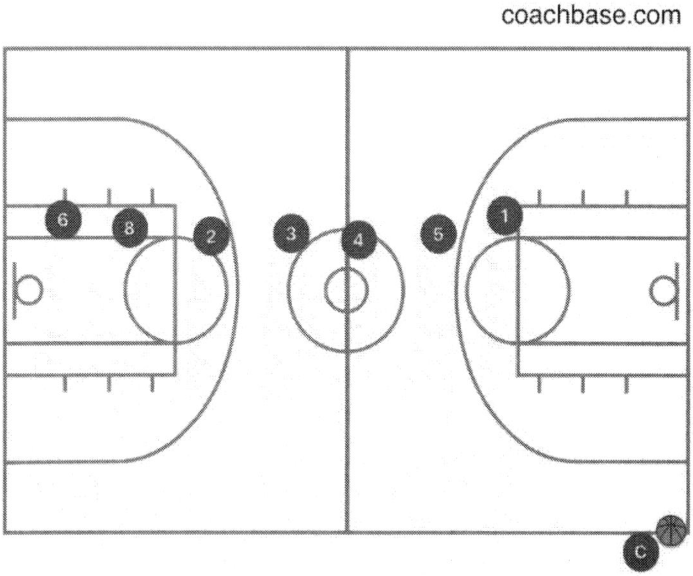
coachbase.com
6
8
2
3
4
5
1
C

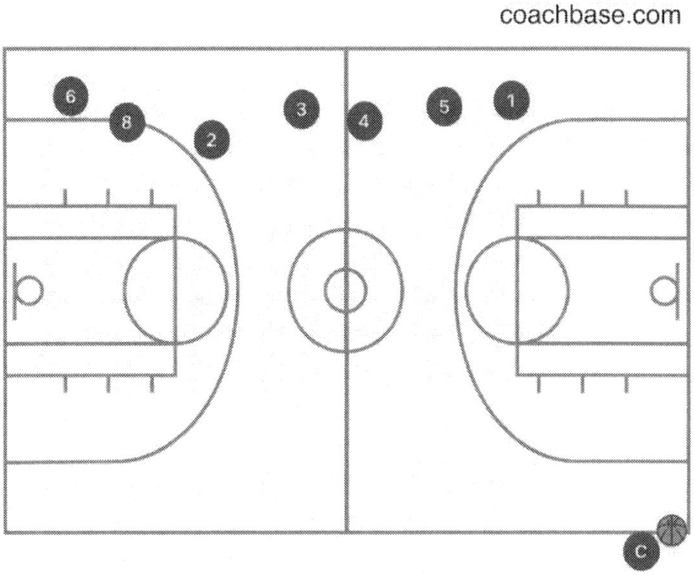
coachbase.com
6
8
2
3
4
5
1
C

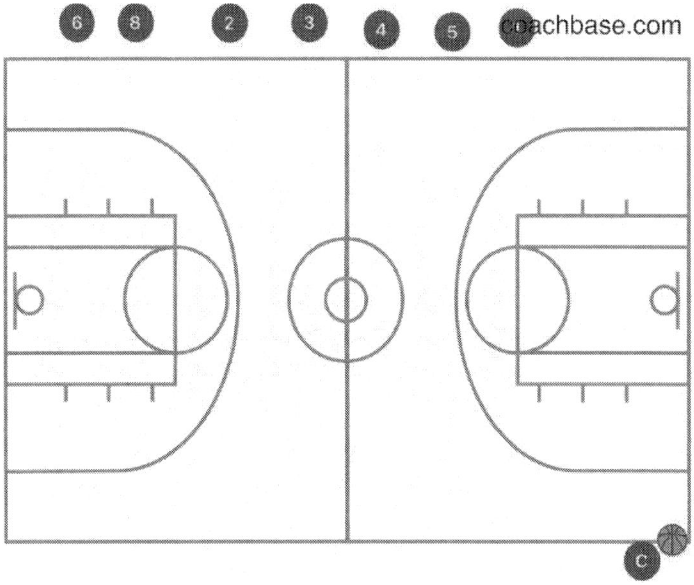
6
8
2
3
4
5
coachbase.com
C

Purpose

The oldest drill in the book – basic mass defensive slides to build team spirit.

Instructions

- Every player line up along the sideline. On the coach's call, everyone takes one defensive slide in
- Try to move in unity and have the team shout "BALL, BALL, BALL" after each step
- To make it harder, ask players to do foot fire (sprint in place) between each slide

9

Transition Defense

To implement this high-intensity defensive system, your players need to:

- Get comfortable in a defensive stance. Stay low – don't bob up and down. Imagine a ceiling they can't hit
- Attention to detail when trapping. Practice two-on-one trapping. You should never let someone split your defenders. The two defenders need to communicate and also have their legs toughing to prevent a split
- Toughness. Defense is 90% effort. These drills will be physically challenging, so stay focused and keep the intensity high
- When players get tired, they can foul with their arms. Move your feet and be aggressive with your lower body, not upper body

Tip Drill

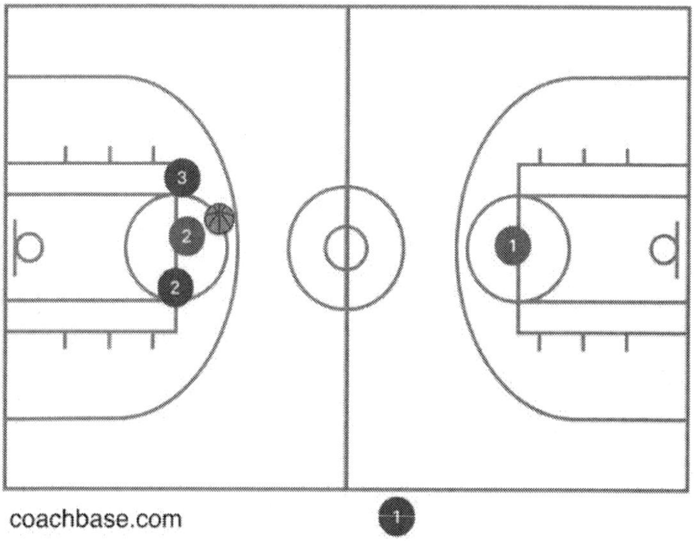

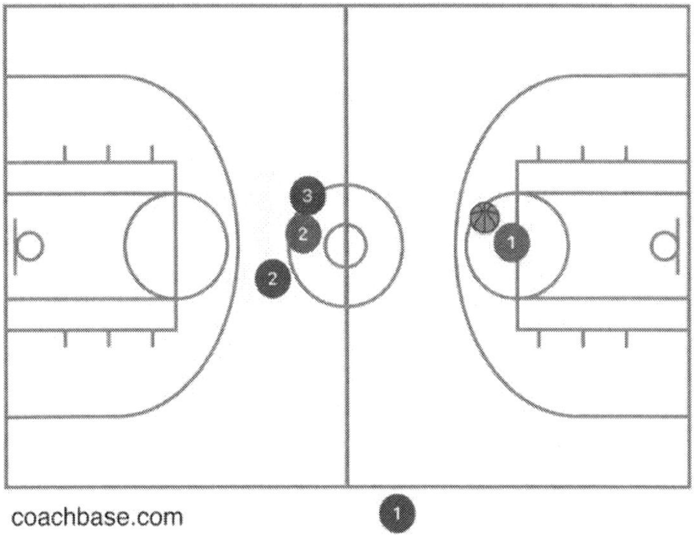
3
2
2
1
1
coachbase.com

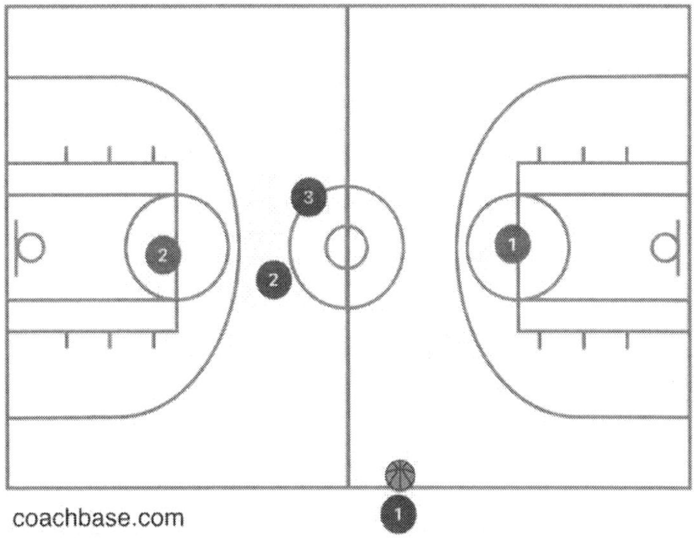
3
2
2
1
1
coachbase.com

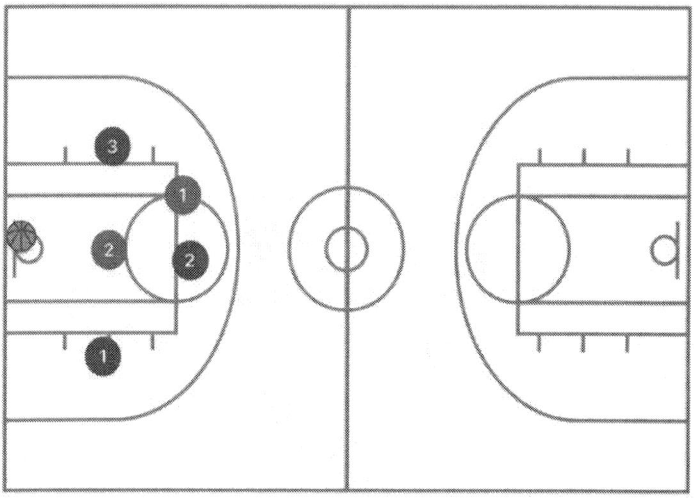

coachbase.com

Purpose

When your press gets beaten, a tip from behind will really deflate the offense. This drill simulates tipping the ball from behind and then into a three-on-two situation.

Instructions

- The ball handler starts inside the paint. He/she can only dribble with one hand
- The two defenders try to tip the ball from behind
- If the ball is tipped or the ball handler reaches halfway, one must pick up the ball and pass to the player on the sideline
- Play three-on-two

Mirror into One-on-One

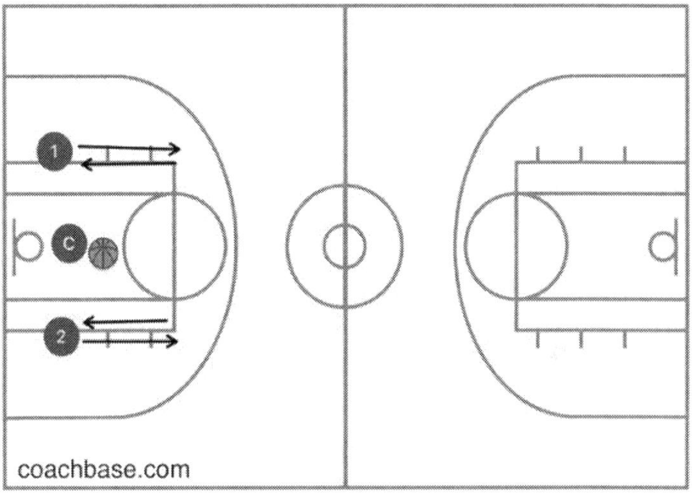

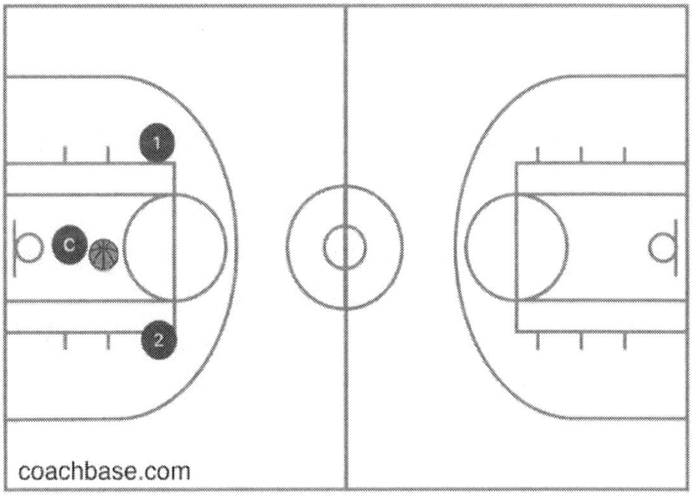

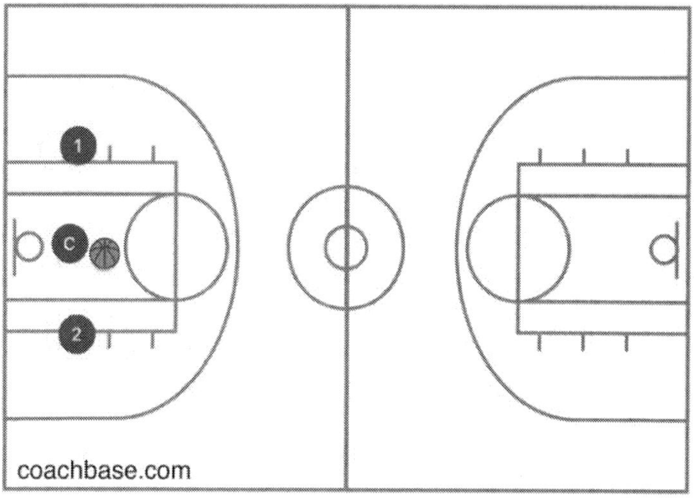
1
C
2
coachbase.com

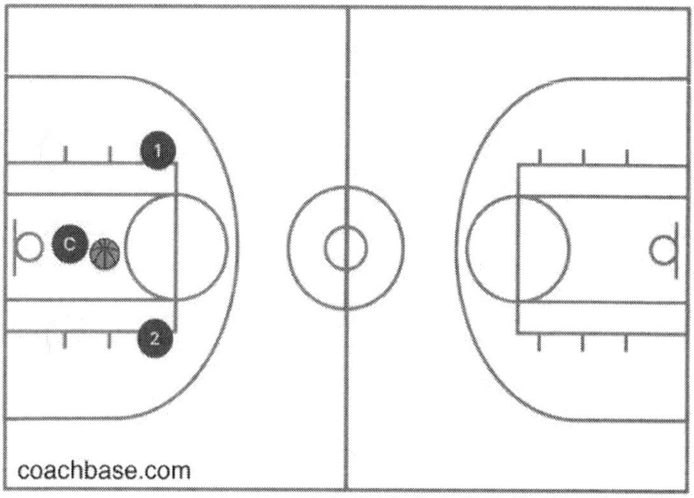
1
C
2
coachbase.com

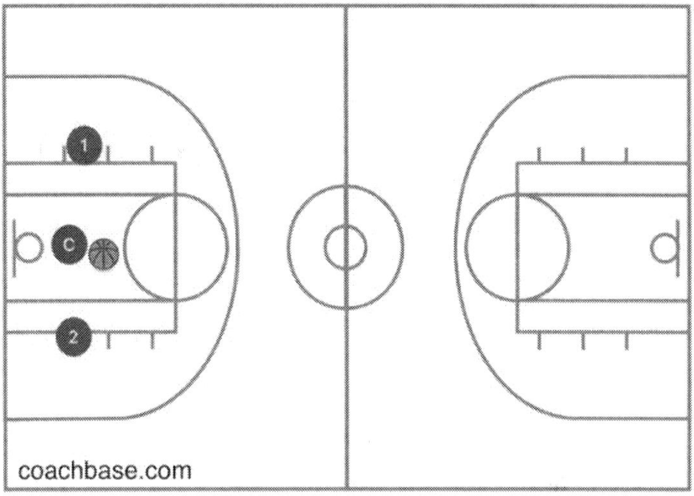

1
C
2
coachbase.com

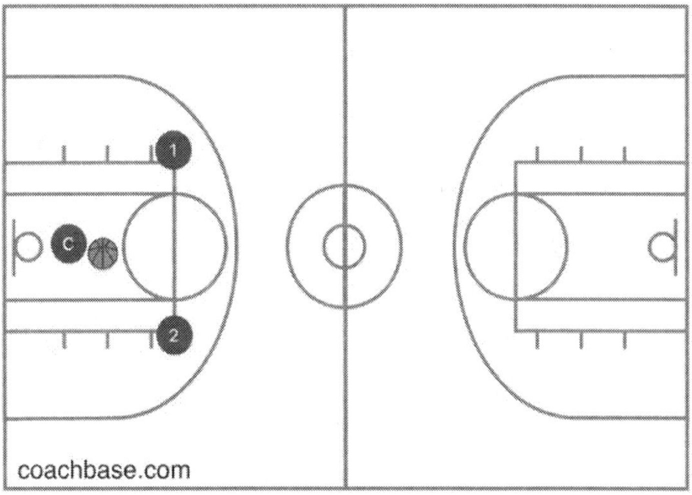

1
C
2
coachbase.com

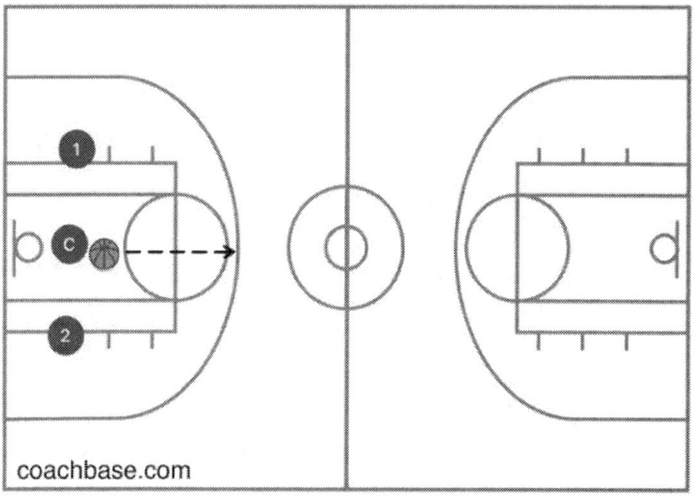
1
C
2
coachbase.com

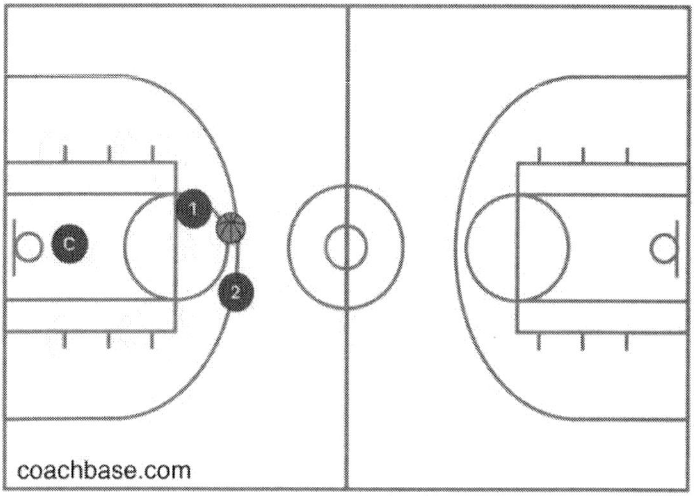
1
C
2
coachbase.com

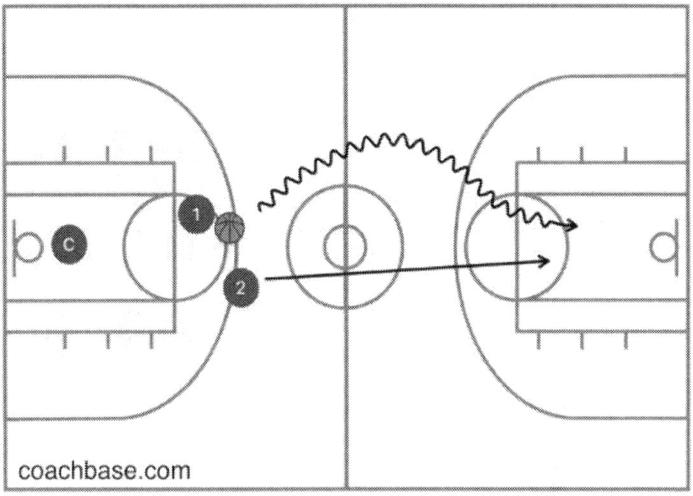
1
2
C
coachbase.com

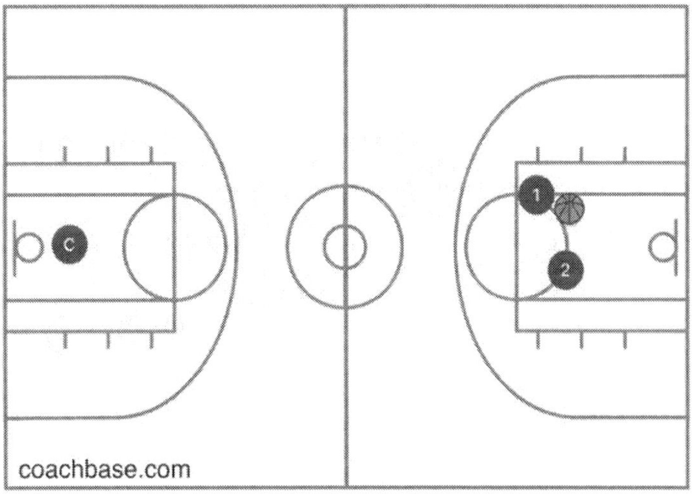
1
2
C
coachbase.com

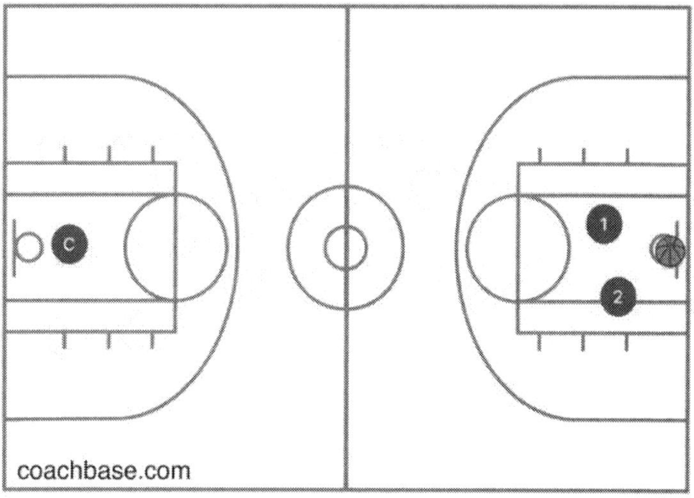

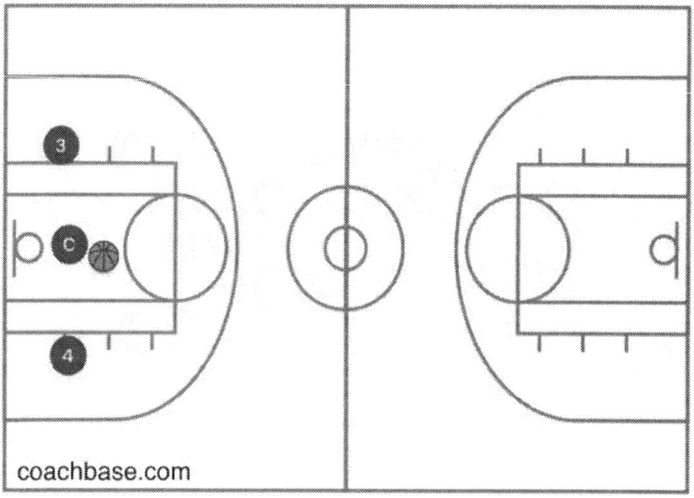

Purpose

This drill has two parts: mirror game and then into a one-on-one. Mirror defense is great for getting players into a defensive stance and moving quickly laterally. One-on-one is a great conditioning drill.

Instructions

- The coach holds the ball underneath the rim
- One player is defense, one is offense. The defense must 'mirror' the offense's lateral movements. The offense tries to not let defense mirror them and can only move laterally
- The coach will randomly throw the ball onto the court
- The two players must fight to get the ball. The person with the ball is offense
- Player full court one-on-one

Two-on-One Stunt

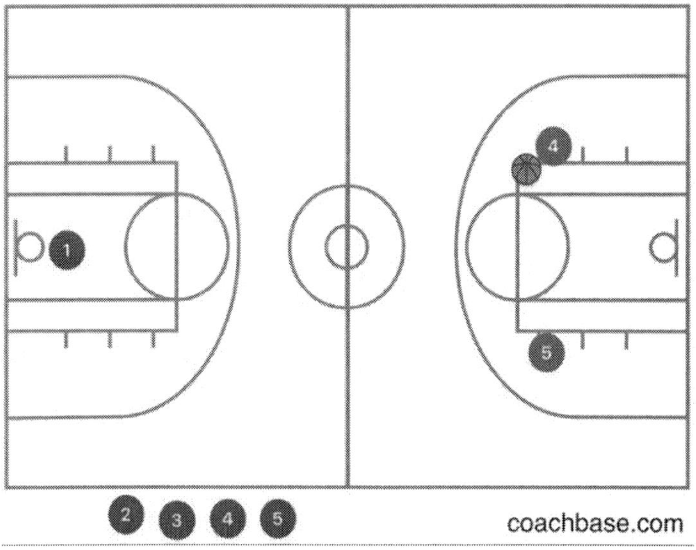
4
1
5
2
3
4
5
coachbase.com

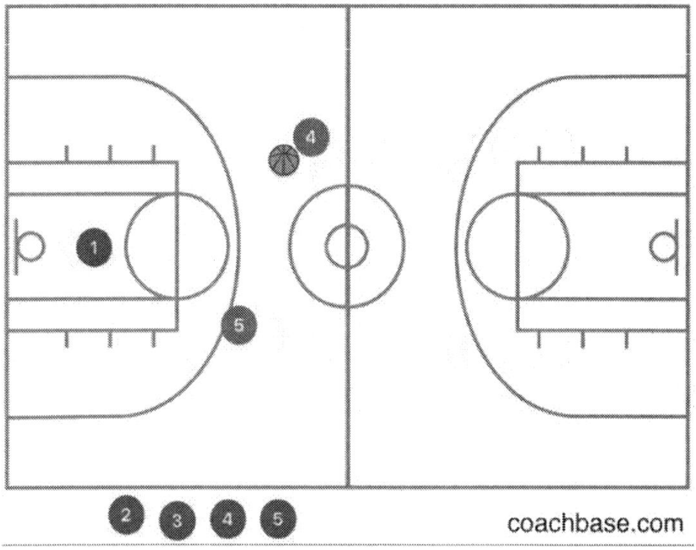
4
1
5
2
3
4
5
coachbase.com

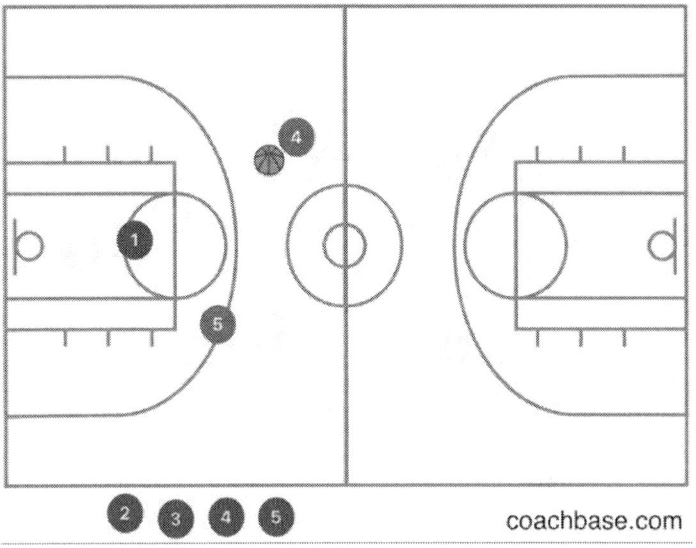
4
1
5
2
3
4
5
coachbase.com

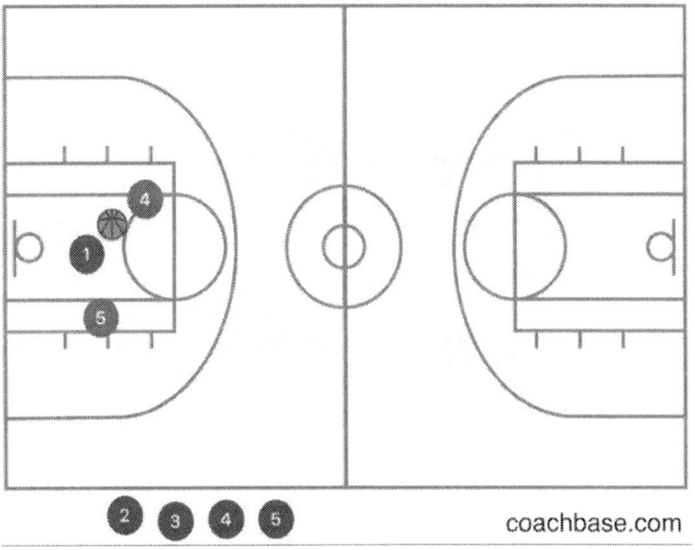
4
1
5
2
3
4
5
coachbase.com

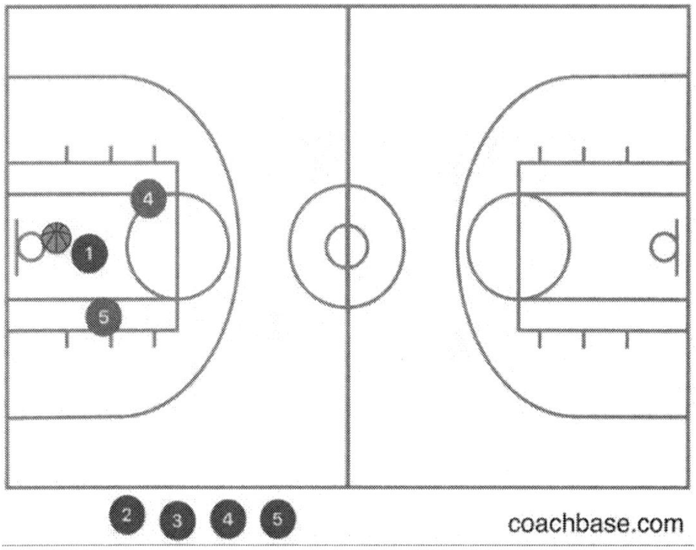
4
1
5
2
3
4
5
coachbase.com

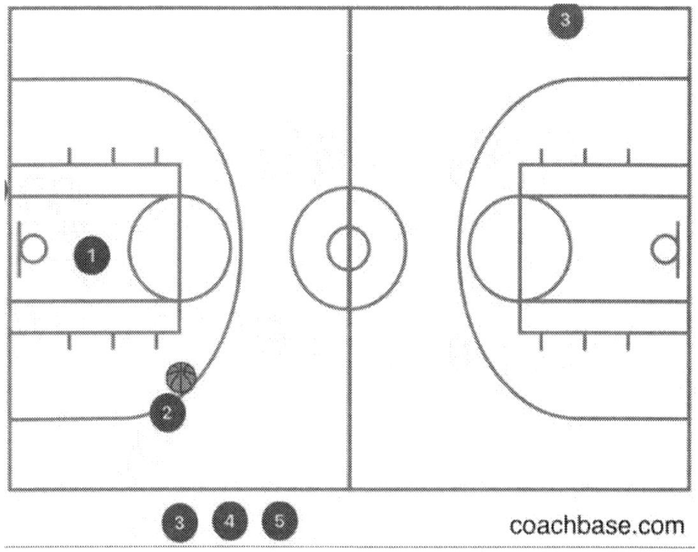
3
1
2
3
4
5
coachbase.com

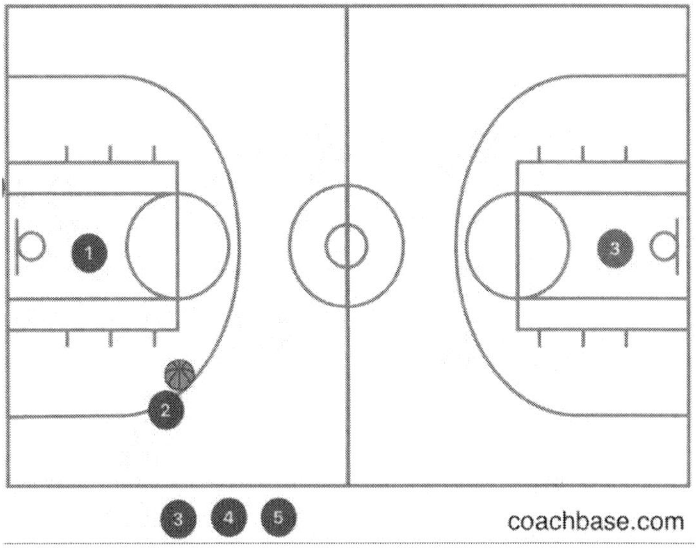
1
2
3
3
4
5
coachbase.com

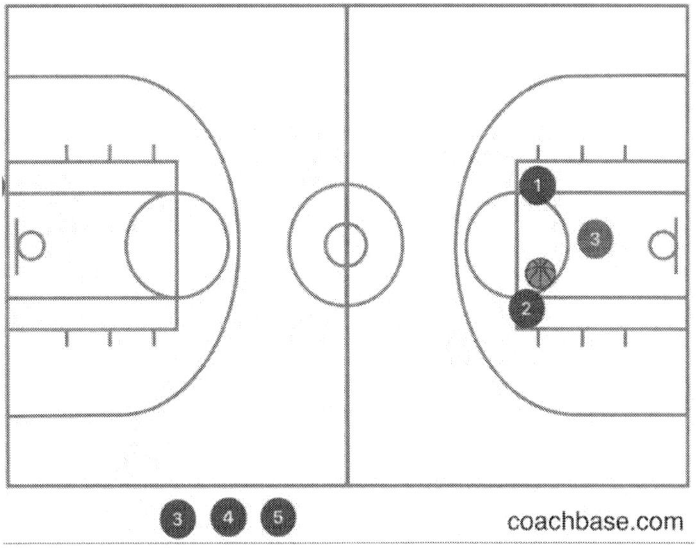
1
3
2
3
4
5
coachbase.com

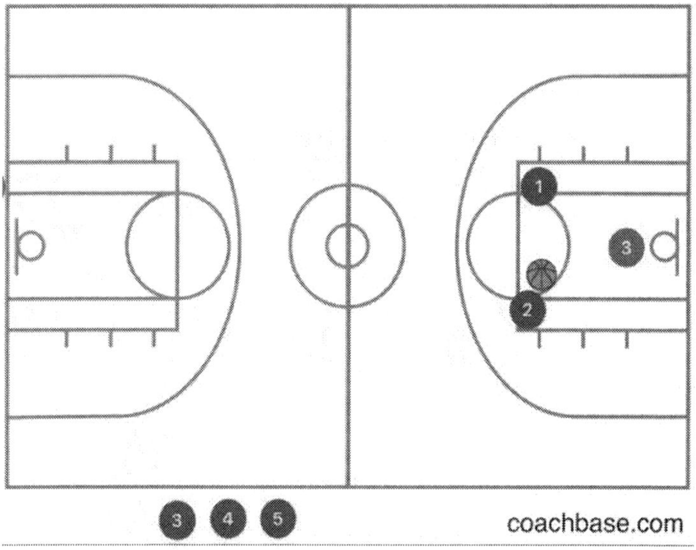
1
3
2
3
4
5
coachbase.com

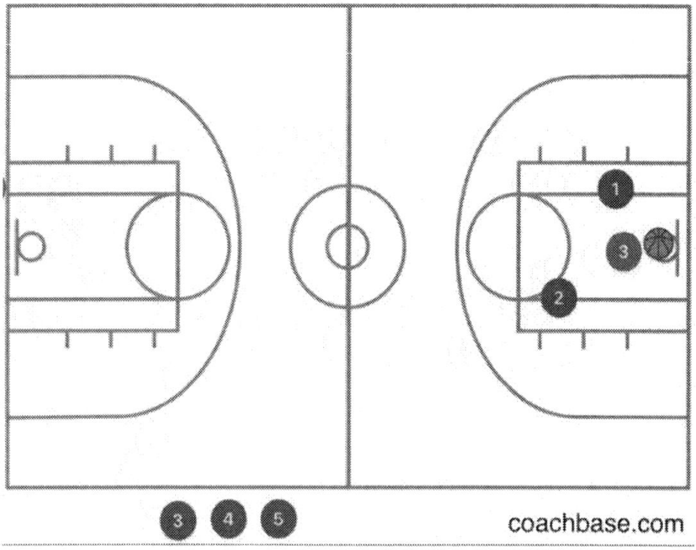
1
3
2
3
4
5
coachbase.com

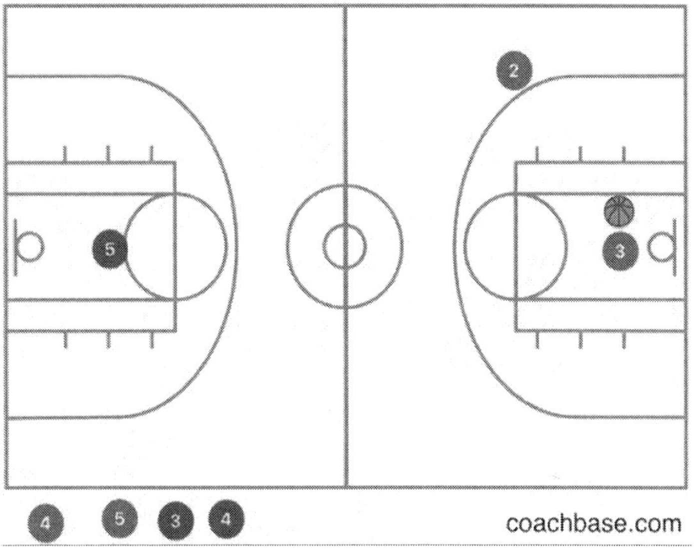
2
5
3
4
5
3
4
coachbase.com

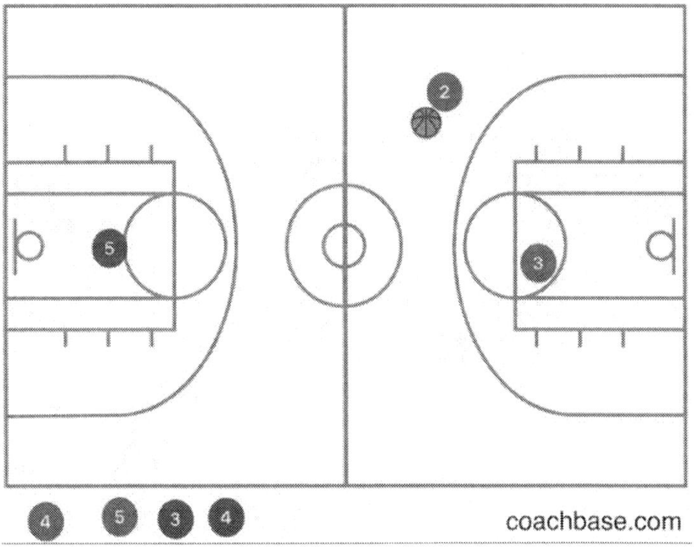
2
5
3
4
5
3
4
coachbase.com

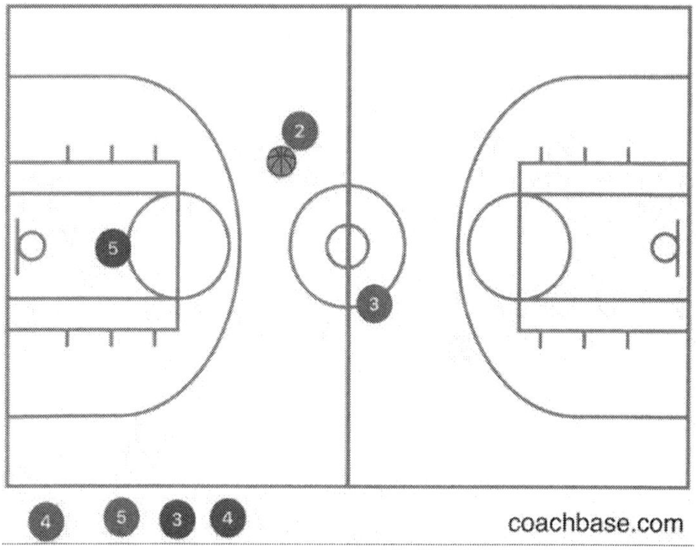

Purpose

One of the cardinal rules of the press is no layups. A lot of time you'll have a numbers disadvantage when the offense breaks the zone. This is when you want to stunt (pretend to commit by making a jab step).

Instructions

- Play two-on-one. The defender tries to prevent a layup
- Have two lines lining up along the sideline. Join in for two-on-one

One-on-Two into One-on-One

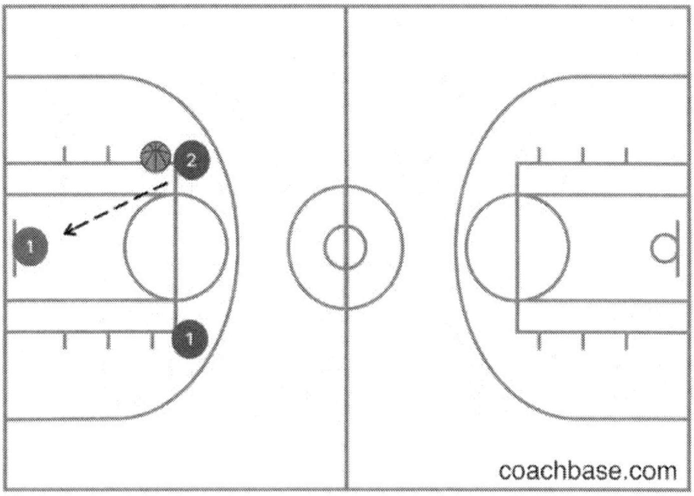

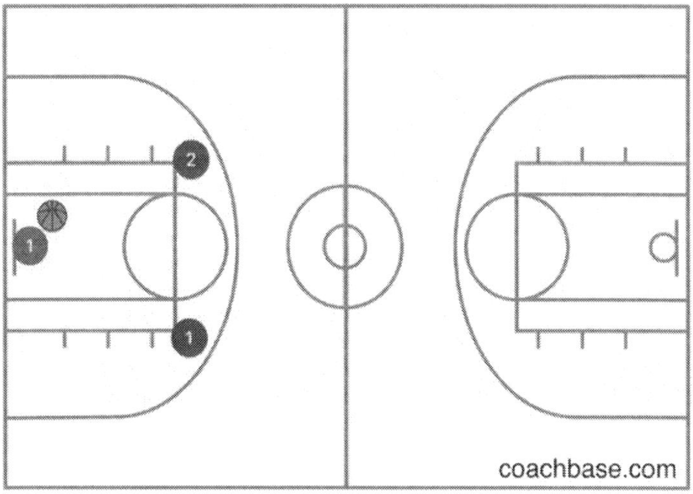

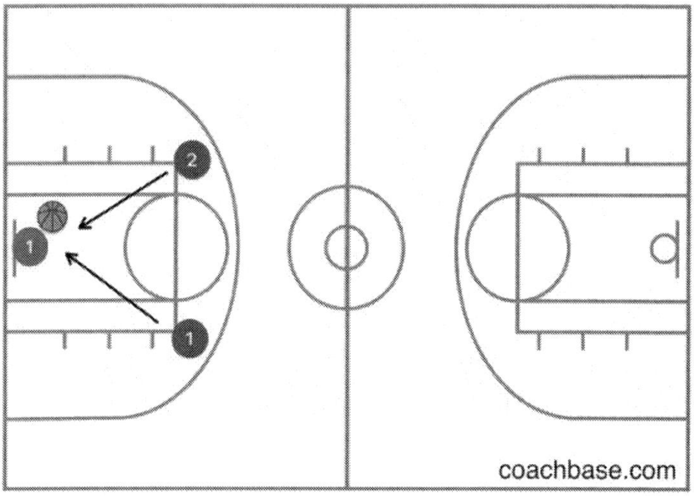
2
1
1
coachbase.com

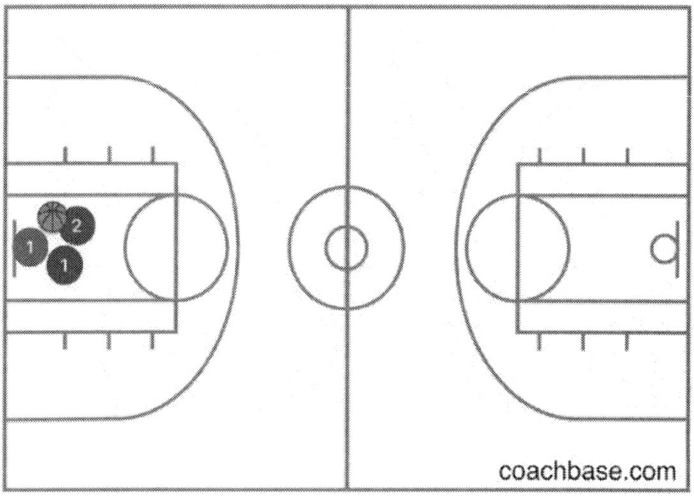
2
1
1
coachbase.com

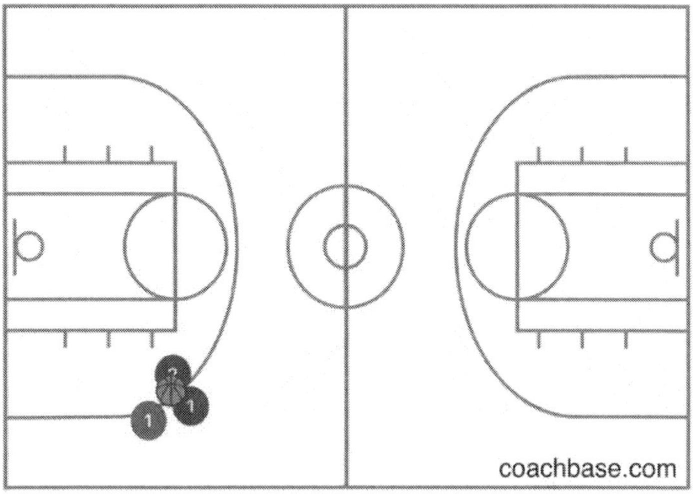
1
1
coachbase.com

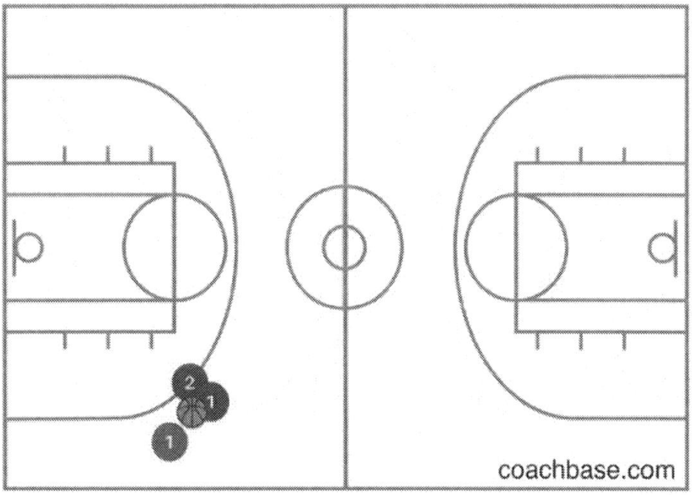
2
1
1
coachbase.com

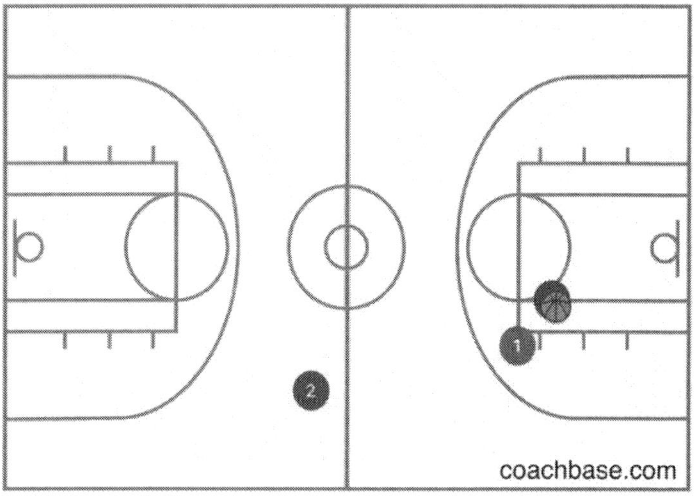

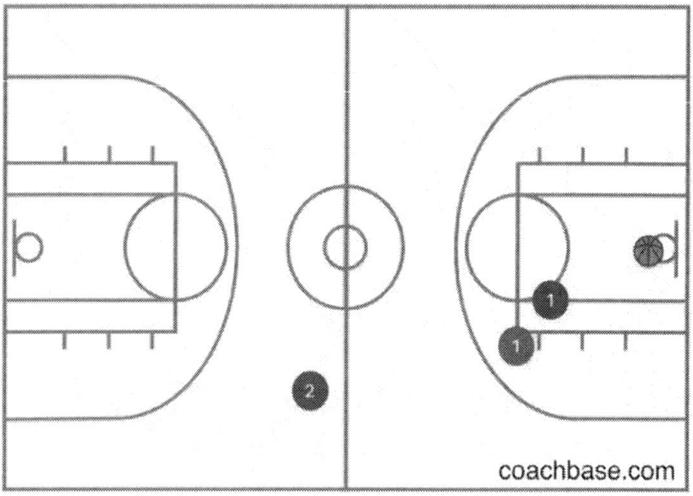

Purpose

In this press, it's important to trap the ball handler, especially in the coffin corner. Practice trapping and not letting the ball handler split the defense or beat the defenders down the sideline. Force the ball handler middle.

Instructions

- Two defenders at free-throw line, offense on baseline
- Defenders pass the ball to offensive player and then it's two-on-one
- If ball handler reaches halfway line, the closest defender plays one-on-one for the remainder of the half

Two-on-Two Trap

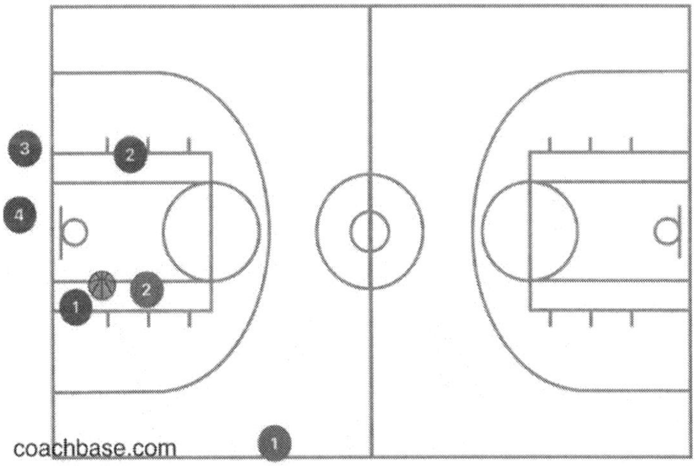

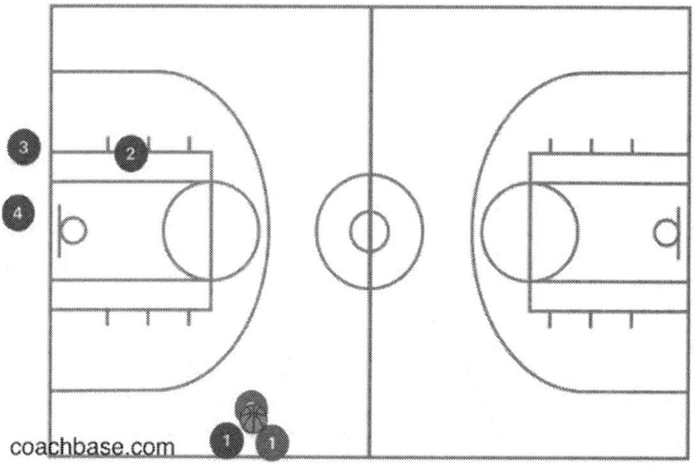
3
2
4
1
1
coachbase.com

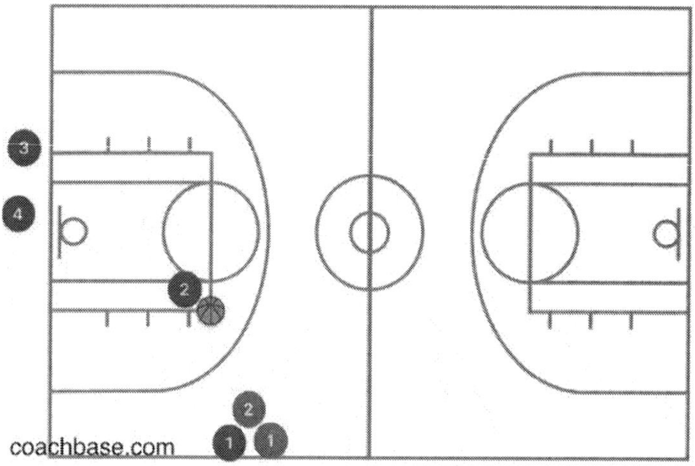
3
4
2
2
1
1
coachbase.com

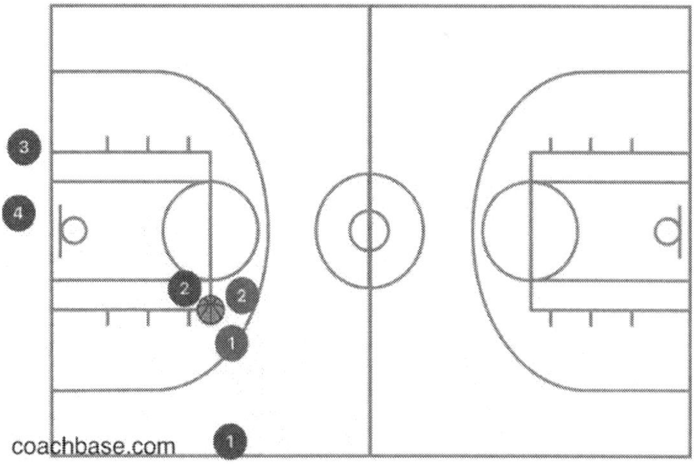
3
4
2
2
1
1
coachbase.com

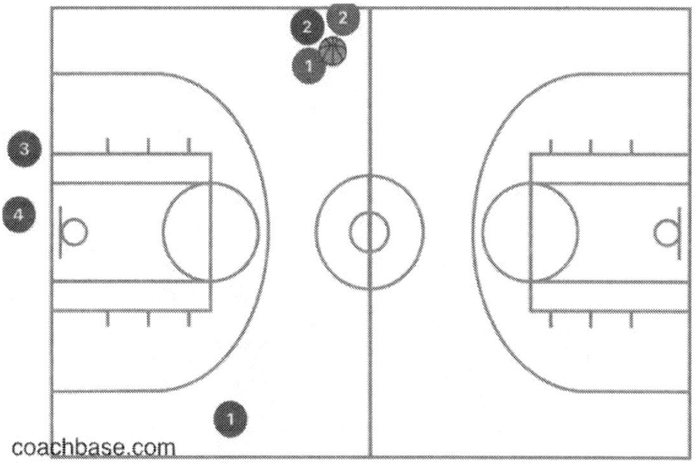
2
2
1
3
4
1
coachbase.com

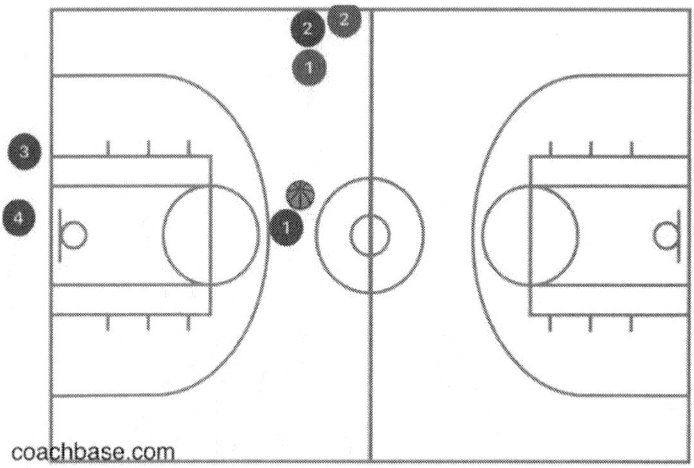
2
2
1
3
4
1
coachbase.com

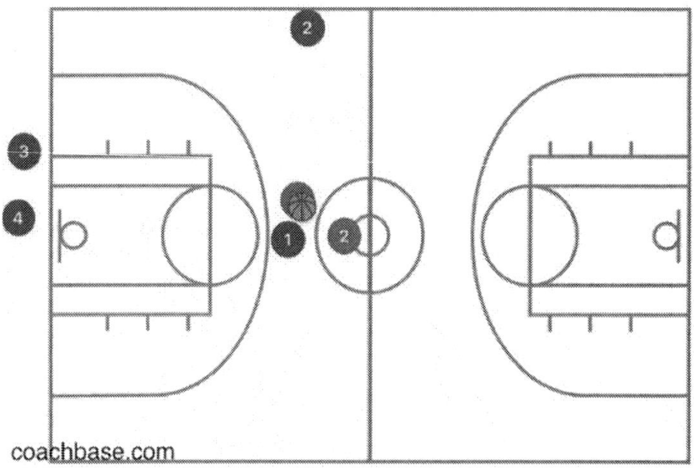
2
3
4
1
2
coachbase.com

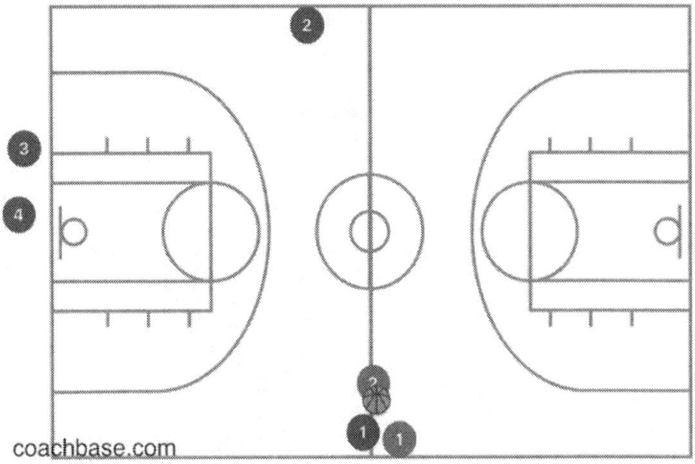

Purpose

The defense needs to learn to how to adjust when the ball handler passes the ball. This drill simulates that.

Instructions

- The ball handler tries to beat two defenders. Defenders must force the ball handler to pick up the ball
- The ball handler can only pass backward to the other offensive player
- Keep going until he/she gets to the other side
- If this is too hard, make the offense slow down

Two-on-One Slides

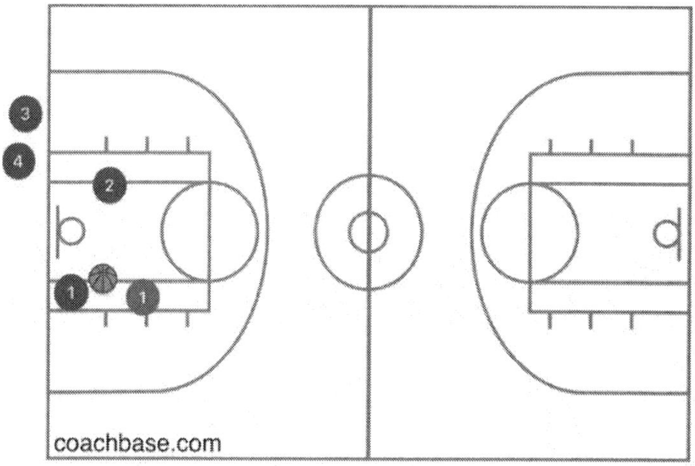

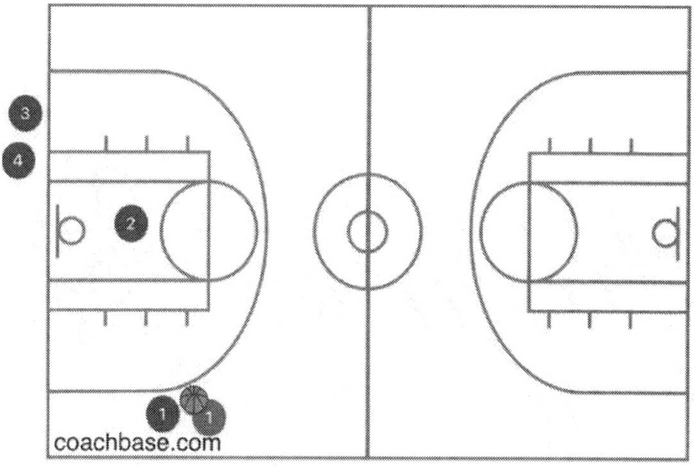

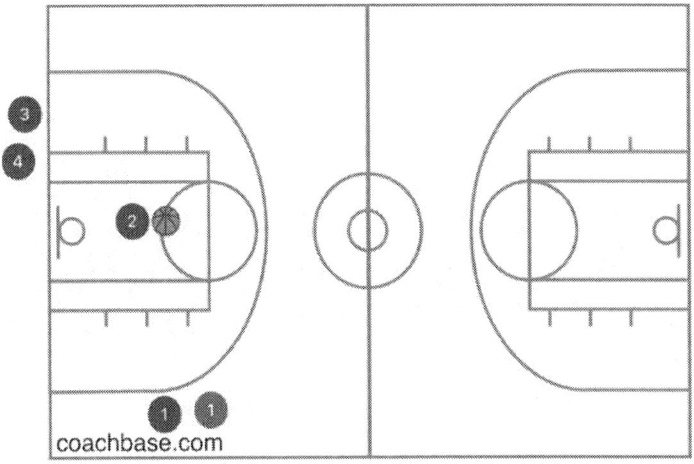
3
4
2
1
1
coachbase.com

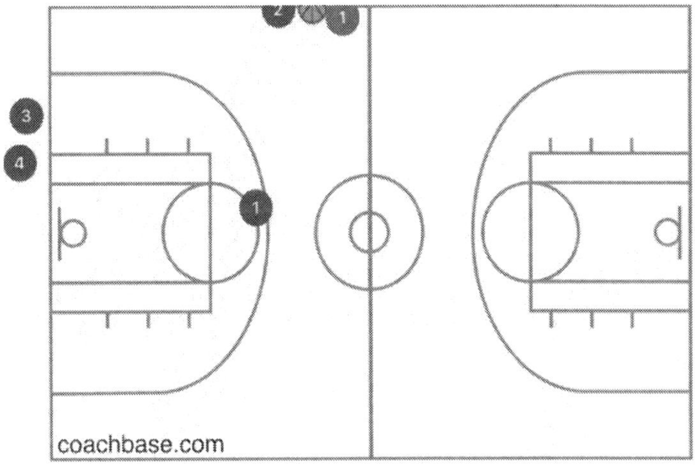
2
1
3
4
1
coachbase.com

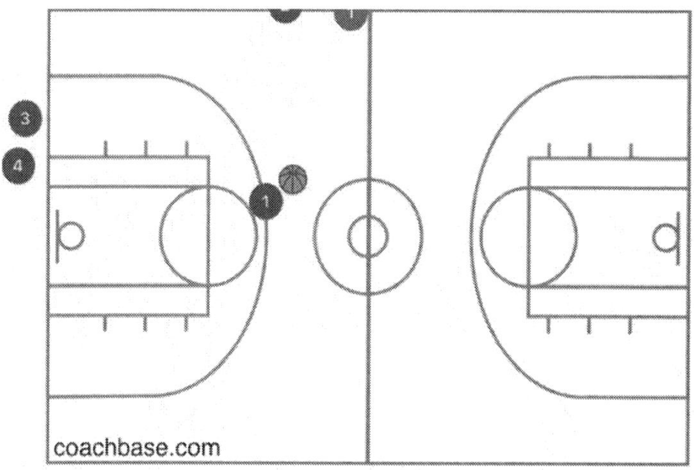
coachbase.com

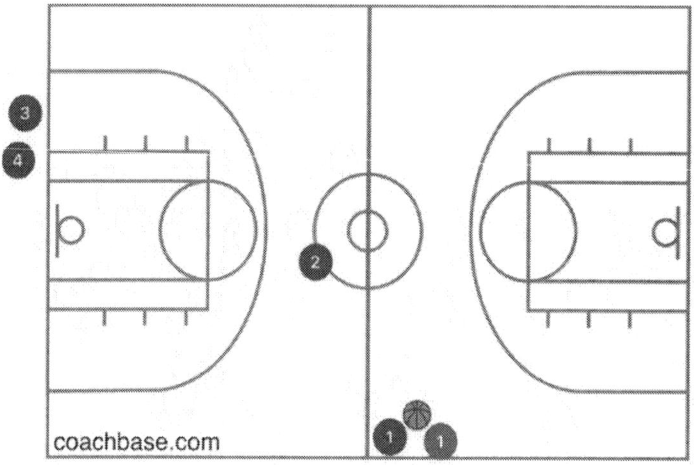
coachbase.com

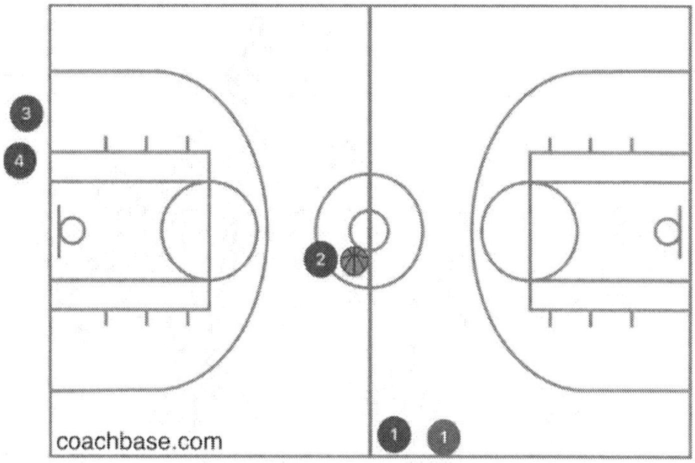
3
4
2
1
1
coachbase.com

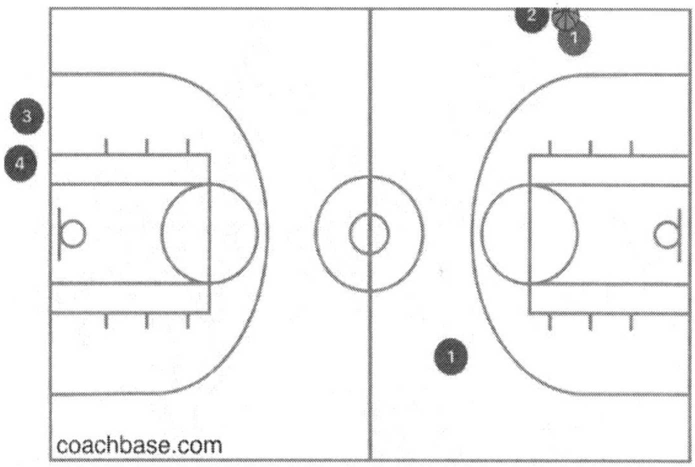
2
1
3
4
1
coachbase.com

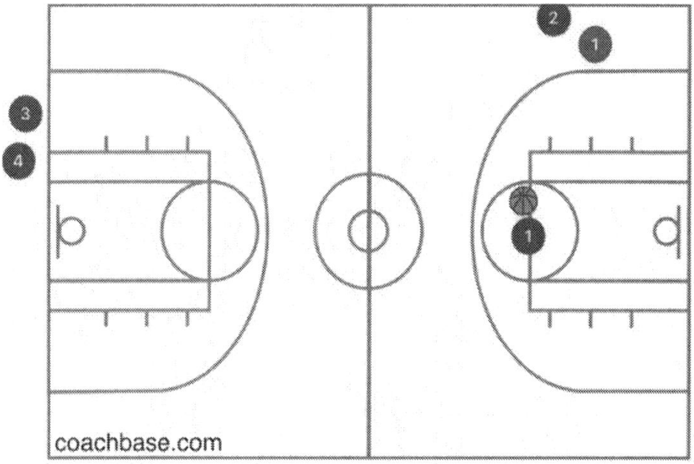

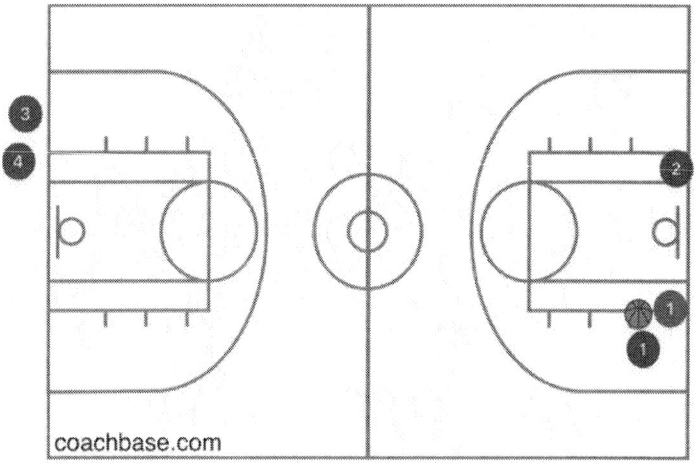

Purpose

This is a conditioning drill to get the defensive player moving in a defensive stance. Remember to stay low and imagine a ceiling that can't be reached.

Instructions

- The offensive players dribble upcourt
- The defensive player tries to force the ball handler to pick up the ball
- When offensive player reaches sideline or middle, pass the ball to the other player
- Continue until baseline
- On the pass, the defensive player must turn hips and sprint to recover

10

Conclusion

Thank you for reading to the end. I wrote it because I wish I had read this book when I first started coaching. It was so overwhelming to choose from so many defenses but once I understood the principles behind them it made a lot more sense to me.

I hope you take the principles in this book and adapt it to your own defensive system. You now have the knowledge to construct a full defensive system that suits your coaching style from the ground up. There will always be people who will disagree with you, just know that you've made a conscious decision about your principles. Your players will love you for it because you can explain to them the reasoning behind your choices and what you intend to achieve.

This is the third book in a series of books I've published. If you haven't read them already, please check out:

1. *Coaching From the Base Up* – a book about practice plan-

ning and drills.

2. *Complete Guide to Motion Offense* – a guide to building an offensive system.

With the knowledge from all three books, you'll have the blueprint you'll need for building a successful coaching program. Good luck with your season and thank you for being a coach.

Printed in Great Britain
by Amazon

20572167R00154